The
Bishop method
of clothing construction

Revised Edition

Edna Bryte Bishop

Originator and Developer of the Bishop Method

Marjorie Stotler Arch

Home Economics Consultant and Educator

Sketches by Dorothy L. Davids

Photographs by Stewart Love

Cover design by Larry and Helen Fritz

J. B. Lippincott Company   *Philadelphia • New York*

CONTENTS

Copyright © 1966, 1959
by J. B. Lippincott Company

Printed in the United States of America
50.7010.9

PREFACE

The Bishop Method of Clothing Construction, first presented in 1959, received widespread acceptance by homemakers, teachers, and students throughout the United States as well as certain areas of Canada, Europe, Free China, and Australia.

This revision reflects additions necessitated by fashion changes as well as certain modern techniques. The Bishop method is founded on a few revolutionary principles and techniques which are essential in the construction of the most elementary garment. It contemplates the maximum use of the sewing machine and the minimum amount of hand work. Sewing is made easier and the joy of accomplishment substituted for the old-fashioned, laborious, and time-consuming pinning and basting method.

The Bishop method embraces the following fundamental principles:
Grain perfection
Accuracy in preparing, cutting, and marking fabric
Cutting to fit
Perfection in stitching
Perfection in pressing

ABOUT THE

BISHOP METHOD

Mrs. Edna Bryte Bishop has devoted her life to one of the most important and interesting aspects of a family-centered homemaking program.

For more than thirty years, Mrs. Bishop shared her remarkable knowledge and perception of clothing selection and construction for the improvement of clothing programs in girls' trade high schools in Massachusetts and New Jersey.

Teachers of clothing in colleges, high schools, and adult classes throughout the country have been privileged to attend her many workshops. Here they have benefited greatly by the inspiration to improve standards of workmanship and production. From these workshops the terms "grain perfection," "cut to perfection," "stitch to perfection," and "press to perfection" have become familiar bywords in the clothing construction field.

Stressing the most efficient methods of construction, Mrs. Bishop emphasizes high standards, resulting in the joy of production and the wearing of well-selected and well-made garments.

Adherence to these principles will enable you to make quality-looking clothing and eliminate the "fireside touch" home sewing has so frequently represented in the past. Mastering the principles will make you grain-conscious.

Basic to the Bishop method is the perfect alignment of fabric grain from beginning to end in the construction of all garments. The importance of fabric grain is emphasized in the chapter entitled "Torn Projects." The chapters follow a definite sequence of learning, which guarantees professional-looking clothes and without exception stresses high standards resulting in the joy of production and the wearing of well-made garments.

The text, photographs, and sketches are not intended to replace a teacher's demonstration of the various sewing techniques, but they clarify each step and make the student independent of constant direction. For the person with limited experience in clothing construction, a review of the text with the supporting photographs and sketches will provide helpful information.

To assist the teachers who use this text, lists of new learnings have been prepared for each chapter and appear on pages 280-281. These are important learnings upon which additional learnings are based. As the concepts of the Bishop Method of Clothing Construction are studied, their interrelatedness becomes evident.

The authors wish to express their appreciation to the many homemakers and homemaking teachers who have submitted suggestions for improving this book. They wish to acknowledge especially Mr. and Mrs. Clifford Stotler, Ardythe Browning, Marie Forehan, Wanda Pope, Tami Sampson, Jane Shaner, Hilda Stotler, and Shirley Zalar for their continued encouragement and assistance.

This is the first revised edition of *The Bishop Method of Clothing Construction.* May it enrich your life, whether you sew to dress smartly, for personal pride, or as a creative hobby.

Edna Bryte Bishop
Marjorie Stotler Arch

For a number of years a leading merchandiser and a distinguished pattern company promoted the method which Mrs. Bishop originated and developed. Thousands of appreciative trade and homemaking teachers have successfully used publications made available through the generosity of these companies.

Few people have made a greater contribution to women who sew at home than Edna Bryte Bishop. From her earliest college days to the present time, her entire life has been spent on one goal: "How to teach more women to be better dressed at less cost."

The book on the Bishop Method of Clothing Construction, first published in 1959, has been of inestimable value to us. Prior to its publication, teachers attending workshops under Mrs. Bishop made their own notes.

This revision of the original edition does not mean that the first material is incorrect; rather, this revised edition includes the basic instruction of Bishop sewing, but also includes additional information related to the fashion changes and the new types of fabrics.

Use this book then, to your best advantage, remembering always that the method itself is based on two things: "grain line" and "cutting to fit." Recently one teacher on the Flint staff said, "Bishop method in Flint is not just learning to sew — it's a way of life." May you, too, derive as much pleasure and satisfaction from this method of clothing construction as it has brought to thousands of women in the Flint area.

Anna A. Kloss,
Senior Supervisor, Teacher-training
Division of Vocational Education,
Massachusetts Department of Education

Gertrude Harper, Director,
Bishop Method Division,
Mott Adult Education Program,
Flint Board of Education,
Flint, Michigan

Chapter 1

Sewing equipment and use of the sewing machine

This chapter covers the complete list of equipment used in the Bishop method of dressmaking and tailoring and some hints, when using the sewing machine, which will help raise the standard of your work. It is axiomatic that the most expert artist must have the right tools. A beginner may start out by purchasing only the most essential items from those listed. Although the list has been kept to a minimum, it includes all that is necessary to make high quality-looking clothes.

Almost as important as the right equipment is a convenient and efficient place to keep and to use it. All of your equipment should be kept together and close at hand. Just rearranging your pressing area alone may increase your sewing efficiency tremendously.

In the home, much time will be saved and shorter periods of time will be used to advantage if a working area can be planned in which all of the equipment can be left undisturbed between working periods. You need not put your equipment away when your sewing is interrupted, and you can always go back to utilize every moment available in a busy schedule.

SEWING EQUIPMENT

Matching thread

Mercerized thread is used for all sewing, including cotton fabrics. Exceptions are nylon or dacron fabrics, and wool jersey, in which cases a nylon thread called nymo or taslan is used for added strength and elasticity. This thread is also recommended for stitching all wash-and-wear fabrics to prevent puckering of seams.

If you cannot purchase a perfect match of thread, select a color slightly darker than the cloth with which it is to be used. The thread sews in lighter than it appears on the spool.

Basting thread

Contrasting mercerized thread is used for basting thread.

Rayon seam tape

Rayon seam tape is applied at some waistline seams of dresses and to some hems of dresses and skirts.

Zippers

Available for dress plackets are zippers of 10, 12, and 14 inches. Neckline zippers are available in any length, starting at 4 inches. When a center back neck opening is needed, frequently an 18-inch, 20-inch, 22-inch, or 24-inch zipper is used, which eliminates the side placket opening.

Since two-piece ensembles have become more prevalent in fashion, the lightweight separating zipper has been widely used (pp. 172-173). These are available in lengths from 10 to 22 inches.

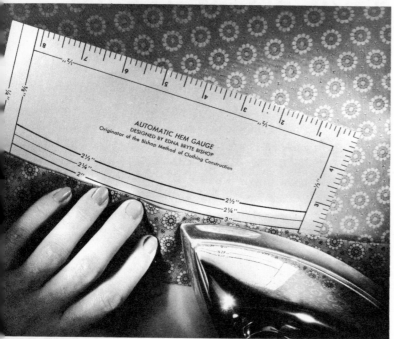

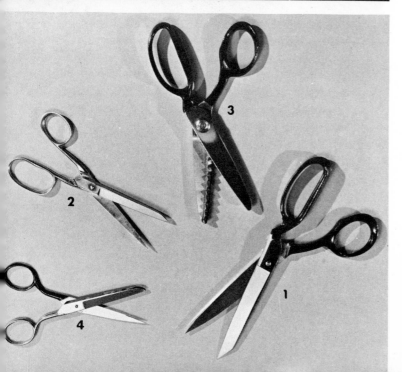

Dressmaker's tracing paper

A carbon-like paper available in many colors, dressmaker's tracing paper is the modern method for transferring pattern markings, such as darts, tucks, and buttonholes.

Tracing wheel

A tracing wheel is used with tracing paper to transfer pattern markings to fabric.

Transparent dressmaker's ruler

A transparent dressmaker's ruler is a real aid for marking straight lines, pattern alterations, widths of bias, etc.

Automatic hem gauge

An automatic hem gauge makes perfect hems and turned edges everywhere without measuring and pinning; just turn and press.

Scissors or shears

Cutting shears. Cutting shears differ from scissors in the handle and length of blades. Shears have one handle larger than the other and the blades vary from 5 to 12 inches, the most common being 7 to 8 inches. Buy bent-handled shears for cutting as shown in the photograph. With the straight-handled shears, the blades will not rest flat on the table when cutting, and you will not get as accurate a cutting line. If you are left-handed, left-handed cutting shears are available. (1)

Trimming or thread scissors. Trimming or thread scissors usually have round handles and are preferably 6 inches long. When construction begins on a garment, the scissors are used mostly to cut threads, to trim seams, and for light cutting. (2)

Pinking shears. Pinking shears are available in various sizes with beveled edges to finish seams that would ravel. Never cut out a garment with these shears. The proper time to use them will be shown with the garment construction. (Scalloping shears are now available, also, that make a scalloped cutting edge, compared to the zigzag edges made with pinking shears.) (3)

Ripping scissors. Ripping scissors are 5 or 6 inches long with dull points that will not cut. They hold both threads of machine stitching, and by pulling along line of stitching in one quick motion, stitches can be removed quickly and easily with no damage to fabric and no bits of thread left. (Other seam rippers are also available on the market.) (4)

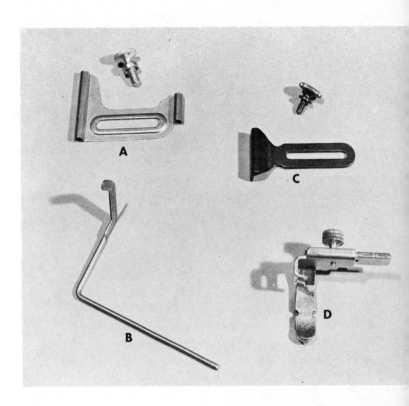

Seam guide

This attachment aids in making straight, even seams the exact width the pattern had indicated. It is adjustable for various widths of seams. Some of the styles available for various machines are shown in A, B, and C in the photo. Others are shown in the photographs on page 7. A new style is now available that has a magnet on the bottom to hold the seam guide on the machine.

Adjustable zipper foot

This attachment (D) helps to stitch close to the metal or nylon of a zipper, and can be adjusted to the right or left side of it.

Wrist pincushion

A small wrist pincushion with an elastic or plastic band is a very handy sewing tool that saves time. Pins can be obtained or returned quickly and easily. Your cushion will never disappear or get hidden among patterns and fabric just at the time you need it. Select a ready-made one (A) or make a pincushion yourself (B), and fill it with sawdust, coffee grounds, hair, or wool cut in strips.

Cut two pieces of wool on grain of fabric, 2¾ x 3½ inches each. Cut a piece of elastic 6 inches long. With small machine stitches, stitch a ¼-inch seam all around cushion, inserting elastic in center of long side. Trim corners, slash center back of cushion, turn right side out, fill as described, and insert a 1⅜ x 2⅜-inch piece of cardboard (C) to protect wrist from points of pins. Whip raw edges together by hand.

Pins

The glass-headed pins available in an assortment of colors are easily seen and used. Regular dressmaker's pins in sizes 15, 16, or 17 are also available, and are sharp and slender.

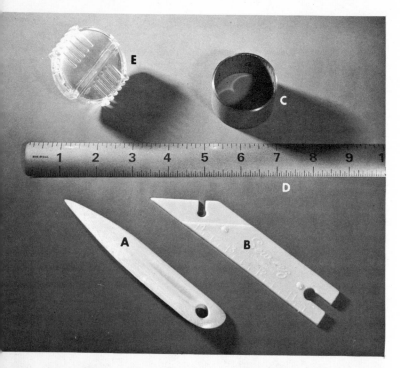

Tailor's clay chalk

Available in an assortment of colors, tailor's clay chalk has many uses. It can be used to identify the pieces of a garment, the wrong sides of fabric, and various pattern alterations. As shown on the left (top), it can be purchased in a plastic holder. A chalk pencil is also available on the market.

Gauge

For marking or measuring short distances, a pliable 6-inch gauge is convenient (left, bottom).

Point turner

A and B styles of point turners as shown in the photograph are available to use for turning points of collars, lapels, etc.

Roll-up yardstick

A yardstick is a necessary piece of sewing equipment for measuring and marking purposes. This one (C) of flexible metal will roll out and stay rigid and flat, and roll up again for easy storage (D).

Beeswax in holder

Beeswax is available in a plastic holder (E) with grooves through which you can slide thread on a needle. It is used to strengthen thread for sewing on buttons and for hand-picking zipper plackets.

Cutting board

A cutting board is marked with inches in each direction to provide for accurate placement of fabric on true grain in all directions. Fabric does not slide on this cardboard surface, either. The cutting board may be secured to a tabletop for a permanent cutting area. It is also useful for the person who has no permanent cutting area, because it folds easily for storage.

Press cloths

Cheesecloth. A good grade of cheesecloth is necessary because it holds excess moisture. A yard in grade 70 is a good buy. This is the cloth that holds extra moisture that is sometimes needed for pressing, even when a steam iron is being used.

Drill cloth. A drill cloth is used to protect fabric that cannot take moisture directly. Drill cloth should be washed before using to remove starch.

Steam-iron cloth. It is a nonwoven cloth, designed expressly for steam-iron use, and is used to prevent iron shine on some fabrics.

Steam-iron shoe. A shoe or cover to fit over the base of steam irons may be substituted for the above. It is available in various fabrics. (Photo: p. 140)

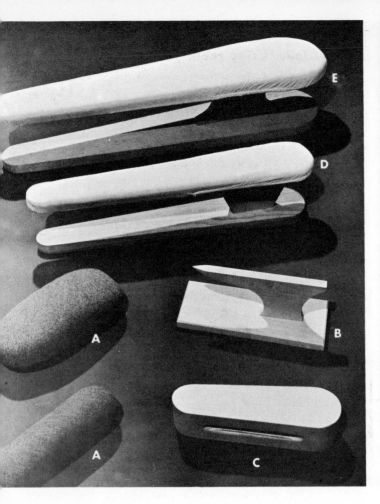

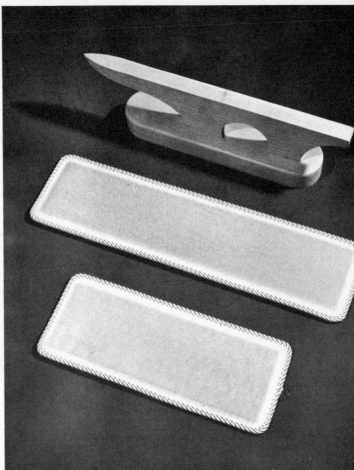

Pressing equipment

Pressing cushions. The roll and ham-shaped cushions are used in pressing curved or shaped areas of the garment to give further shape to shoulder line, bustline, hipline, etc. They can be made of finely sifted, thoroughly dried sawdust firmly packed into muslin and covered with wool. They are also commercially available (A).

Edge and point presser. An edge and point presser is used to press open the seams of stitched points. Examples are collar, revers, cuffs, and seams difficult to reach (B).

Pounding block. A pounding block is helpful to obtain sharp edges on heavy and resilient fabrics (C).

Sleeve board and press board. A sleeve board (D) and a press board (E) provide greater ease in pressing small areas than the laundry ironing board. Their use prevents stretching of fabric.

Press table. When space is available, a press table is very helpful for many uses. (Photo: p. 131)

Combination edge and point presser and block. A combination of B and C (shown above) is also available (top, photo at right).

Needle-board. A needle-board, available in two sizes (above, right), is excellent for pressing nap and pile fabrics. It prevents fabrics from flattening, matting, or marking.

Notions

Needles. For most hand sewing, sharps in sizes 7 to 10 are used. For very fine hand sewing use short needles which are known as betweens.

Tape measure. Select a tape measure 60 inches long made of firm fabric, such as linen or fiberglass. It should have metal tips and be numbered to read from either end.

Thimble. A thimble should be selected to fit the middle finger and is a must for hand sewing.

Buttonhole twist. Buttonhole twist is a stronger thread and has many uses.

Buttons. Buttons selected with taste can add a quality look to any garment. Develop the art of selecting the right button for the type of fabric, style of garment, proportion of figure, and number being used. Many times you may choose to vary the number shown on the commercial pattern. Often you can make your own interesting buttons, or other types of front closings as shown in Chapter 15 of this book.

USE OF MACHINE

How to thread, operate, adjust, and care for a sewing machine are expertly shown in manuals prepared by the companies that manufacture machines. However, there are a few techniques while using the machine, which are an integral part of the Bishop method, to be practiced when beginning to sew. One must use one's hands at the machine with ease and dexterity. A garment must be handled lightly and carefully. In developing sewing as the fine art it is today, the right feel about what is being done is important.

General work habits

Good working habits are as important as sewing skills. They should be developed along with skills.

Keeping everything relatively neat is helpful. It will save time. It will add to efficiency. As short bits of thread or little pieces of trimmed fabric accumulate, drop them into a wastebasket placed by the machine, or put them in a pile at the side of the machine head.

Where a wastebasket cannot be placed at every machine, a plastic or sandwich bag may be fastened on the machine for scraps of fabric, threads, or other odds and ends. The bag should be placed to the right of the machine head. (It is deliberately misplaced in the accompanying photograph to allow for the showing of other items in the same picture.)

Developing an organized mind is another valuable asset. The garment should be organized in units of work. Everything needed should be ready when work begins — thread, zipper, buttons, right snaps, and hooks and eyes.

Putting pins back in your pincushion as you remove them from your work saves clean-up time later and increases your efficiency.

Starting out

Selecting a needle. Be certain you have the correct size needle for the fabric on which you are working. See page 5 for hand sewing needles and your sewing machine manual for correct size machine needles.

Threading a needle. When threading a needle, cut the thread at an angle with sharp scissors. This makes a clean, sharp end which threads through the eye of the needle easily.

To sew by hand, thread the needle with the end of the thread that was cut from the spool. The same end that was cut from the spool and threaded through the needle should be knotted before beginning to sew.

Arranging the threads. Arrange the threads for stitching so that they will not tangle when starting to stitch. Bring up the bobbin thread, and place it away from you. Draw the upper thread between the toes of the presser foot, under it, and away from you. Both threads should be about 3 inches long.

Checking the stitch regulator. Form a habit of checking the stitch regulator, for it is changed frequently to the following stitch lengths:

1. *The regulation stitch* is the permanent stitch placed in a garment, 12 to 15 per inch. It varies with the type of fabric. A firm, fine fabric takes a shorter stitch than a thick, heavy fabric.

2. *The baste-stitch* is an elongated machine stitch, 6 to 8 per inch. It is usually the longest stitch the machine will make. In matching thread, it is used to facilitate gathering and to create ease. In contrasting thread, it is used for basting at the machine, and for marking buttonholes and center fronts.

3. *A shorter stitch,* 18 to 20 per inch, is used for reinforcement on comparatively limited areas, such as points on collars, underarm curves that will be clipped, gusset points, and for stitching on buttonhole strips.

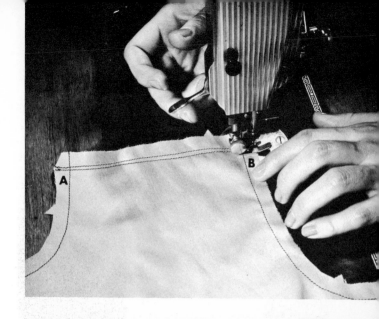

Hand turning of wheel. Place your fabric under the presser foot and just under the point of the needle. Turn the wheel by hand, and lower the needle at the exact point where you want the stitching to begin. Lower presser foot.

Lockstitching the threads. Lockstitch or knot threads at the beginning and end of permanent stitching to secure them in fabric. This eliminates the time and nuisance of tying threads, and the time and motion in using a reverse stitch. Place the needle in fabric on stitching line; lower presser foot. Hold fabric firm with left hand. Release pressure on presser foot slightly with right hand (the height of one thread is the amount to release it). Stitch several times in one spot. Holding the fabric with the left hand and releasing pressure with the right hand prevents the feed dog from feeding through the fabric, and keeps it in one place. Note the completed lockstitching at A, and that being made at B in the accompanying photograph.

Using the seam guide or alternate

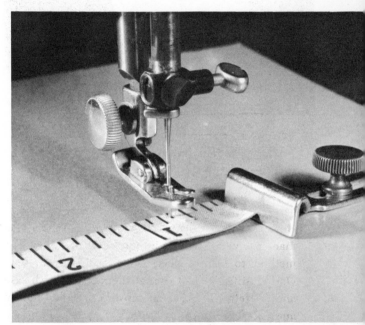

The metal seam guide is fastened securely at the desired distance from the needle for stitching.

If the machine does not have a guide line etched on the throat plate to aid in setting the guide correctly, use a tape measure.

A seam guide helps to keep the stitching line at a uniform distance from the fabric edge. In stitching, keep your eyes at the edge of the guide to direct the fabric correctly. The left hand is kept near the guide to manage fabric.

A new seam guide is now available which is particularly helpful for stitching slippery fabric with ease and perfection (see the photograph, page 6). Ridges on the gauge help to hold the fabric in position for stitching, and to feed it evenly toward the presser foot.

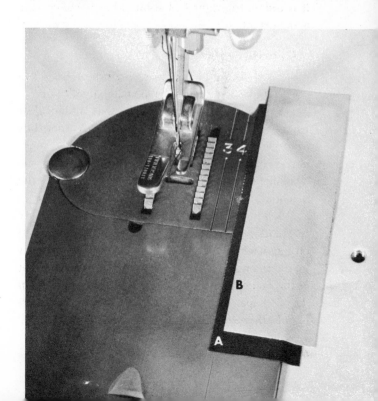

If a seam guide is not available, two strips of cloth tape can be placed on the machine. Place one color (A) a few threads less than ⅝ inch from the needle for staystitching (see page 64), and a second color exactly on the seamline ⅝ inch (B). The strips are also useful to help set the guide.

If you use cloth tape for staystitching and seam allowance, you don't have to remove it for darts, zippers, etc.

Stitching curves. When stitching around a curve, the only part of the seam that can be right up to the guide or the cloth tape is the area exactly opposite the needle (A). This is true for either an outside curve, as shown, or for an inside curve. Sometimes it is easier to stitch around some curves — and in some fabrics — if the seam allowance is trimmed down to ¼ inch before stitching. Always release the presser foot the height of one thread with your right hand as you stitch, so you can roll fabric up to the guide with your left hand.

Controlling fabric

In sewing, place the bulk of the fabric to the left of the presser foot. The bulk of the fabric should be up on the machine, folded or adjusted if necessary, so that the weight will not drag on the stitching or stretch the cut edges. Your hands should not pull, push, or clutch the fabric. When stopping in the middle of a line of stitching, turn the wheel to bring the needle down in the fabric.

If some fabrics (heavy or slippery ones, for example) seem to push ahead on the top layer, keep your right hand at the take-up lever and release its pressure as you sew (see top photograph, page 7). Your left hand will continue to place the fabric along the seam guide. This same procedure is suggested for stitching curves.

When sewing on pile fabrics, keep the two layers of fabric separated with the right hand in front of the guide, so that the pile will not lock together. This assures stitching with perfection. The left hand is still kept near the guide to control the fabric during stitching.

Reinforcing corners

To reinforce corners that will be trimmed before turning right side out, use about 20 stitches per inch for about ½ inch on either side of corner point. Always have the needle in the fabric when you lift the presser foot to turn fabric before stitching in the second direction.

Using pins

If you feel that you need a few pins in a seam of some fabrics, place them back from the line of stitching. Sewing over pins is not recommended. By placing the pins back from the line of stitching you will not have to remove them until the entire line of stitching has been completed.

Making several clips at once

To increase your sewing efficiency, very often you will find it to be workable not to pick up the scissors until you have several clips to make. In this photograph, many edges of a blouse have been staystitched before any clipping was necessary. Running from one piece to the other saves thread.

Ending a line of stitching

When finishing a line of stitching, the wheel should be turned by hand to have the take-up lever at its highest point. This prevents the thread from pulling from the needle when starting again to sew.

If it is difficult to stop the machine exactly at the end of a line of stitching, stop back a short distance, and make the last stitches by turning the wheel by hand.

If one more stitch would take the stitching too far, but there is still a short distance to do, change the length of the stitch to a shorter one.

Clean-cut threads as you proceed.

Before cutting threads, pull the fabric to the back (or to the side) of the machine leaving both threads between the toes of the presser foot. Cut the threads using trimming scissors, which are always used at the machine. Do not use a thread cutter at the machine. Leave 3 inches in length — ready to begin again.

Chapter **2**

Torn projects

Whether or not a beginner continues to develop the art of sewing after her first few projects is very often determined by the simplicity of the beginning projects and by the speed and success with which she completes them. Interest and enthusiasm must be developed, and sewing should be fun.

Torn projects are designed to meet these needs. The beginner does not yet need to learn to use a pattern. Fundamental principles of sewing, of working with the grain of fabric, and of using a machine are taught. We must never attempt to teach or to expect too much too soon for a first project, such as a skirt or apron with long threads to gather along an edge. Also, two pieces in a garment are enough for a beginner to handle.

With this in mind, we present ten torn projects in this chapter, and the skirt on page 59, that could belong here. There is no special sequence to the order in which these projects are presented. Other ideas may be substituted and some projects presented may be omitted — as long as the objectives to be accomplished with torn projects are recognized.

In planning sewing units, the teacher may select one or many torn projects to meet the needs, the age, and time limit of her group. Everyone should make the same first project. This assignment should be presented as a means of learning several basic principles and should be referred to as a torn project. The fact that it is a blouse or apron is secondary.

A beginner should select a fabric that is firmly woven and does not ravel easily. Cotton broadcloth, gingham, and percale are wise choices. Avoid very thin or slippery fabric such as voile. Stiff, glazed, or hard finished fabrics with a stabilizing finish would never be a suitable choice for a beginner, because the grain cannot be straightened (see p. 42).

Before you begin any of the torn projects in this chapter, refer to the pages in this text for:

1. Tearing fabric to grain perfection (p. 40).
2. Pulling threads and cutting fabric to grain perfection, if it will not tear (p. 40).
3. Straightening fabric to grain perfection (p. 43).
4. Restoring line of fabric to torn edges (p. 46).
5. Hints on use of sewing machine (pp. 6-9).

Yardage Chart

Torn Project	Amount of Fabric Needed
1. Apron with four pockets	1 yd. fabric
2. The poncho	⅓ to ½ yd. 54″ to 60″ fabric (see p. 14), or 1 yd. 39″ fabric
3. A blouse for young ladies	½ yd. fabric
4. A bag for hair rollers — or for odds and ends	½ yd. fabric
5. The simplest of all aprons	¾ yd. fabric
6. A triangular head scarf	½ yd. fabric will make two of them
7. A daytime or an evening purse	⅓ yd. fabric, depending on width, will probably make two of them
8. A softly pleated apron	⅔ yd. fabric
9. A softly pleated skirt	1½ to 2½ yd. fabric (see p. 29)
10. An overvest or barbecue apron	1¼ yd. fabric

Apron with four pockets

Before you begin this project, read the last paragraph on page 10. There is a reference to that paragraph with each of the torn projects in this chapter.

If edges of fabric were not torn on grain when purchased, tear or pull threads and cut. Straighten fabric to grain perfection. Measure and tear apron pieces as shown in diagram. Fold each piece in half to press again to grain perfection and to restore line to torn edges.

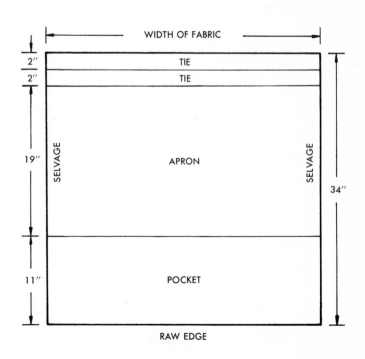

Torn projects

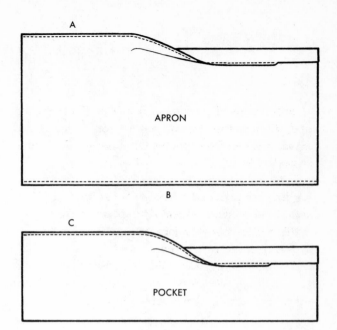

Staystitch A, B, and C edges ¼ inch from edge. Use the seam guide at the machine, a permanent stitch, and matching thread. Staystitching on a crosswise edge always indicates there is further construction ahead.

Then, using the hem gauge, block a 2-inch hem in the top of the apron (A) and top of the pocket (C). Next, turn under the raw edges of hems on the ¼-inch staystitching and press.

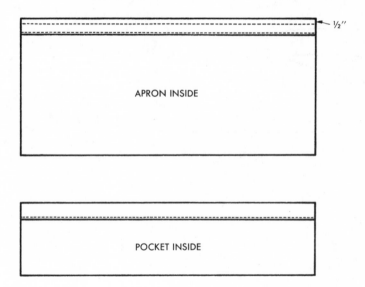

Stitch a machine hem in apron and pocket near folded edge of hem. Place seam guide ½ inch from needle and stitch ½-inch heading in top of apron.

Place right side of pocket to wrong side of seam. Using seam guide, stitch a ¼-inch seam. Understitch lower edge of apron. Turn seam toward apron and catch in understitching. Turn pocket to right side of apron and press in place.

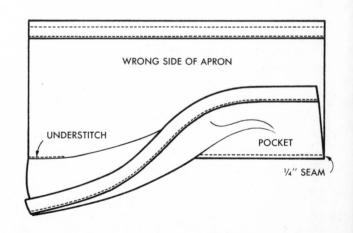

Stitch ends of pockets at A and B. Turn corner, and stitch across top of pocket for ¼ inch, turn again, and reinforce pocket stitching to lower edge of pocket hem.

Fold and press pocket in quarters to mark a stitching line for pockets. Stitch on press lines at C, D, and E and reinforce stitching as directed above.

Right sides together, join two sections for tie at A in ¼-inch seam; press open.

Right sides together, fold tie in half and stitch a ¼-inch seam (B). Press open seam on a wooden dowel (see p. 162). Turn right side out.

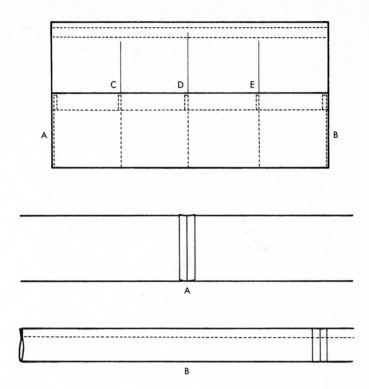

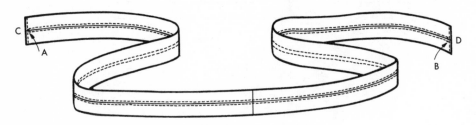

Place seam in center of tie and press tie flat. Beginning a distance from an edge, topstitch on two sides of seamline; cross over at A and B. Finally, stitch selvages closed at C and D.

With a crosswise grain for an apron tie, the seam should be in the center. On an edge, the seam neither wears well nor ties well. This topstitching gives it added strength and is a good experience for a beginner.

Feed tie through apron with a large safety pin. Have ends of tie extending equally at each side of apron. Stitch tie in place at center front as shown at A.

Final-press apron on lengthwise grain as shown in photograph on page 62. Pull up on ties to gather apron.

One feature about this apron is that it opens out flat for ease in laundering.

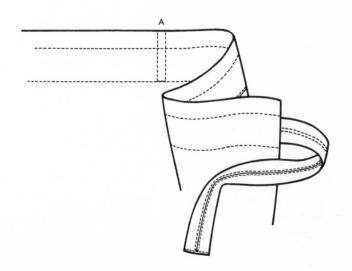

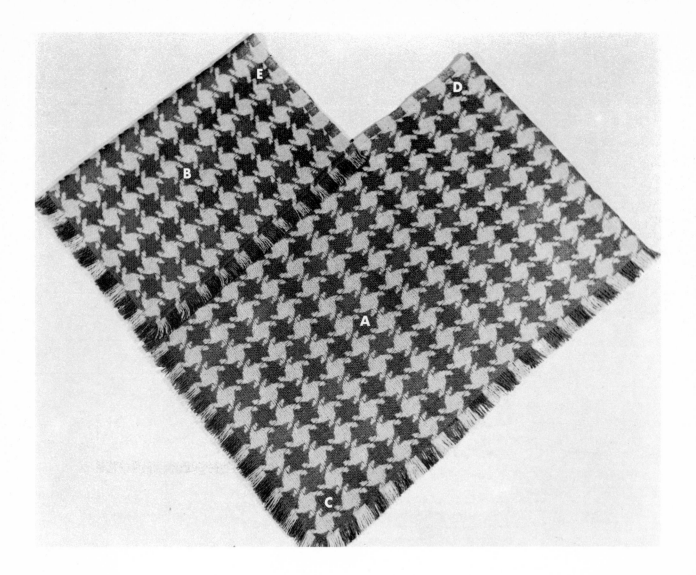

The poncho

The poncho can be made from striped, plaid, or plain fabric — also in two colors, red at A for example, and navy at B to wear over a white sheath dress.

It can be worn as shown, and if the dress has a belt, the points at C in the front and back can be placed under it. Another way to wear the poncho is to unfold it and place D and E straight across the neckline in front and back.

You may wish to try the size given on the chart from scraps of fabric to determine if it needs to be larger or smaller for the proportions of your figure.

Use loosely woven fabric of a coarse weave that will make attractive fringe. Two large towels can be used to make a poncho for a beach coat.

Before you begin this project, read the paragraph on page 10.

Tear or pull threads and cut the two needed pieces in the size shown. If fabric is 60 inches wide when purchased, you would need only 13 inches. Press each piece to absolute grain perfection.

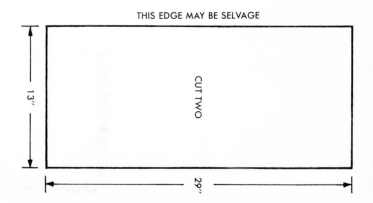

THIS EDGE MAY BE SELVAGE

CUT TWO

13"

29"

Pull out one or two threads ¾ inch from edge as shown at A and B; then machine stitch in open area. Next, pull out all threads up to machine stitching to make fringe ¾ inch wide as shown at C. If D edge is not selvage, make fringe at this edge, also.

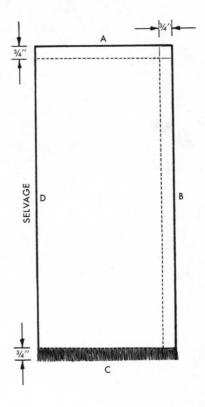

Overlap short end at A for 1¼ inches and stitch with two rows of stitching ¼ inch apart. Repeat at B and B.

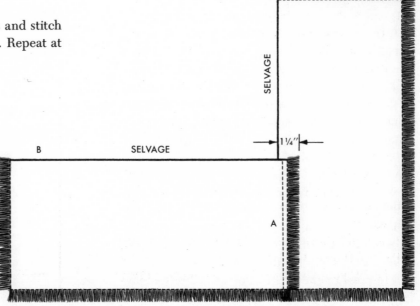

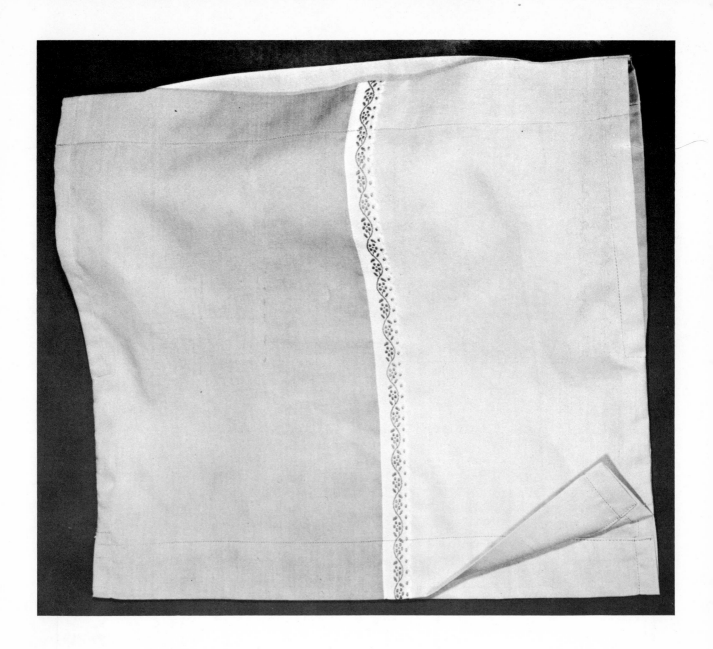

A blouse for young ladies

This blouse was made in two colors in the front by creating a seam just off center, and stitching a braid trim over it. That was not done in the sketches to follow, but a trim was sewn to one side of the front. You will have many ideas of your own.

To try the blouse for size, from scraps tear two strips the size given in the sketch shown here. You may wish to pin the strips together to try on and determine if the blouse needs to be torn larger or smaller, or longer or wider.

Before you begin this project, read the paragraph on page 10. Measure and tear two pieces for the blouse as shown in the diagram. Fold each piece in half to press to grain perfection and to restore line to torn edges.

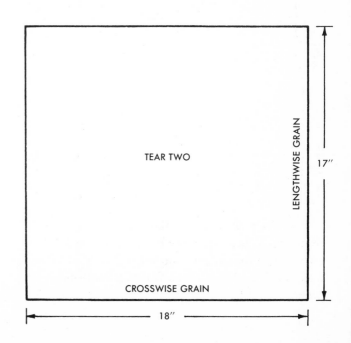

TEAR TWO

LENGTHWISE GRAIN

17″

CROSSWISE GRAIN

18″

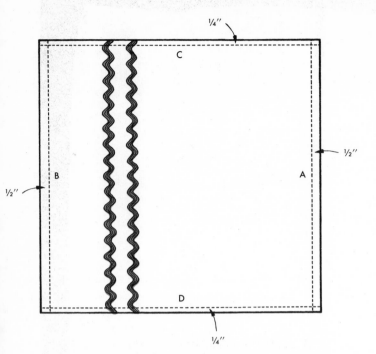

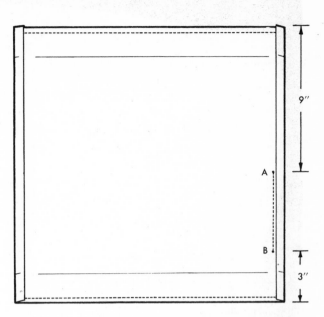

Staystitch A and B edges (lengthwise grain) ½ inch from edge, and C and D edges (crosswise grain) ¼ inch from edge. Use the seam guide at the machine, a permanent stitch, and matching thread. Sew on any trim at this time.

Open up turned hems. Begin 9 inches from upper edge at A and sew a ⅝-inch seam to 3 inches from lower edge at B. Leave side edges turned in ½ inch up to staystitching when sewing ⅝-inch seam. Press open seam; continue to press back ⅝ inch at top and bottom openings.

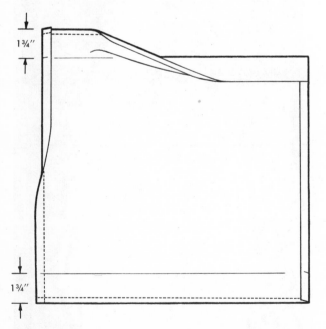

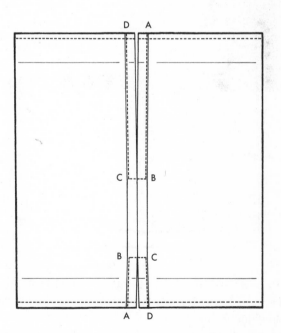

Press back the sides on the staystitching ½ inch from edge. Then, using the hem gauge, block a 1¾-inch hem in the top and bottom of the blouse. Next, turn under the hems on the ¼-inch staystitching and press.

Stitch openings near the fold from A to B to C to D.

Torn projects

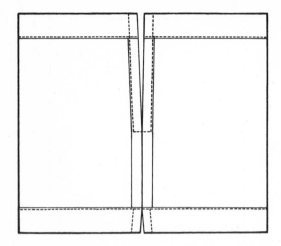

Press to restore hemlines at top and bottom of blouse. Stitch hems near folded edge of hem.

Final-press blouse on lengthwise grain (see p. 62). If desired, a drawstring may be used in the bottom of the blouse.

A useful bag for hair rollers — or for odds and ends

The learnings for this bag are identical to the previous blouse except that the torn pieces vary in size. A large, round, plastic, bleach bottle was cut off

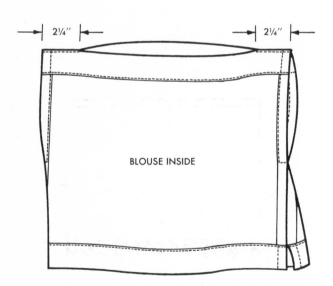

BLOUSE INSIDE

2¼″ 2¼″

On wrong side of blouse, bring together front and back, and stitch a fine tuck for 2¼ inches to make shoulder seams.

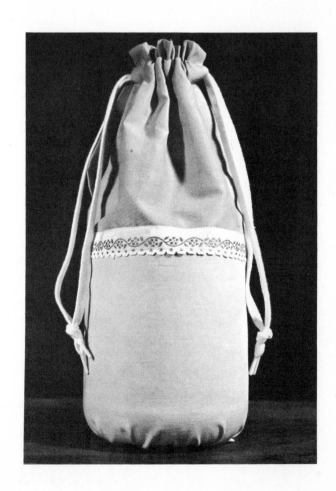

half-way up with sharp scissors, and was inserted in the finished bag to provide the firm circle up to the braid.

You may want to try your torn pieces for size before stitching them, because the plastic bottles may vary in size.

Before you begin this project, read the paragraph on page 10.

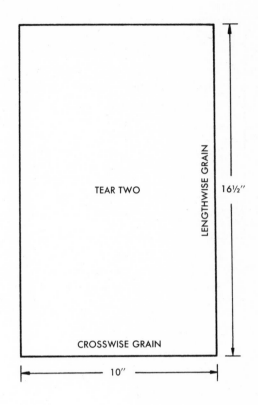

Measure and tear two pieces for the bag as shown in the diagram. Fold each piece in half to press to grain perfection and to restore line to torn edges.

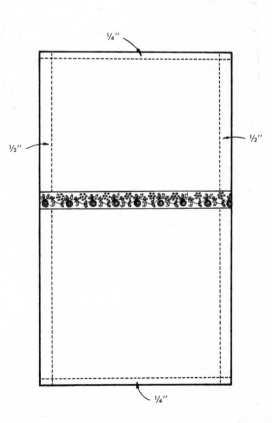

Staystitch sides ½ inch from edge, and top and bottom ¼ inch from edge. Use the seam guide, a permanent stitch, and matching thread. Sew on any desired trim at this time.

Press back the sides on the staystitching ½ inch from the edge. Then, using the hem gauge, press a 1¾-inch hem in the top and a 1-inch hem in the bottom. Turn under raw edges at A and B on the ¼-inch staystitching and press.

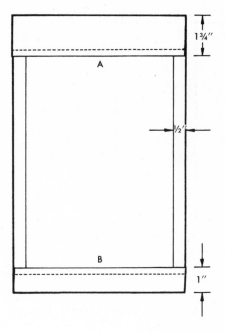

Open up turned hems. Beginning 7 inches from upper edge at A, sew a ⅝-inch seam to 2 inches from lower edge at B. Leave side edges turned in ½ inch up to staystitching when sewing ⅝-inch seam. Press open seam. Continue to press back ⅝ inch at top and bottom openings.

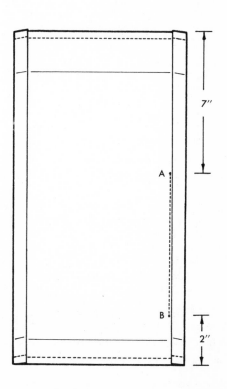

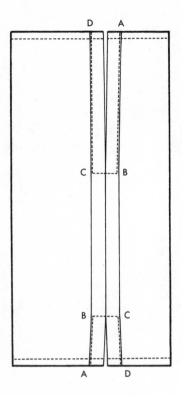

Stitch openings near the fold from A to B to C to D.

Insert two shoestrings or other ties. Feed one through from each opening and tie in knot. Insert plastic bottle. Feed heavy cord through two openings at bottom of bag. Pull up to fit under bottle and tie in strong knot; cut off ends.

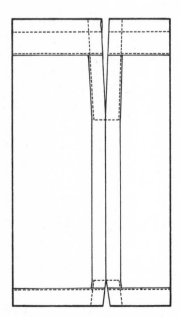

Press to restore hemlines at top and bottom of bag. Stitch hems near folded edge of hem. Place seam guide ½ inch from needle and stitch a ½-inch heading in top of bag. Final-press bag.

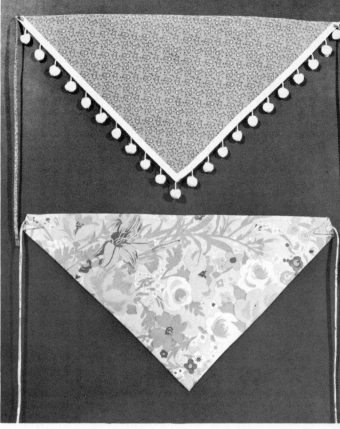

The simplest of all aprons

Compared to the apron that has the pockets and is made from two pieces of fabric, and to the pleated one that builds for a pleated skirt, this apron is more simple to make. It has fewer learnings. It could be made in one lesson, and would be a good learning to precede the skirt on page 59. It is also popular because of its ease in laundering and folding.

Before you begin this project, read the paragraph on page 10.

This apron finishes 18 inches long, so you could tear the strip 22½ inches long which will include the 2½-inch hem at the bottom and the 2-inch hem and heading at the top precisely like the learnings on page 12. Use the fabric at purchased widths and leave the selvages at the sides. Tear two strips 2 inches wide for the tie strings.

Fold each piece in half to press to grain perfection and to restore line to torn edges.

The hem is stitched precisely like the apron on page 12, and the top of the apron and tie strings are completed like the learnings on page 13.

Final-press apron on lengthwise grain as shown in photograph on page 62. Pull up on ties to gather apron, and place fullness as desired to flatter the figure. The apron flattens out for ease in laundering.

A triangular head scarf

This scarf could be made to wear with the skirt on page 29, the overvest on page 32 or any other project you will be undertaking. The second one in the photograph is worn with the shift on page 89. Many designers make matching purses to accompany scarves. (For purses, see page 24.)

Before you begin this project, read the paragraph on page 10.

Tear or pull threads and cut a perfect square. If you are a little short of fabric, it could be 16 or 17 inches square; or, if you are making a scarf for a small child, perhaps, even a 10-inch square would make one the right size. Try it from a scrap of fabric.

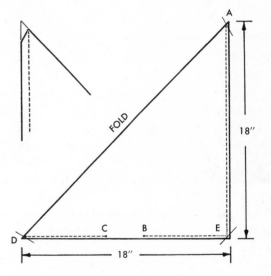

Fold the square to form two triangles. Press to grain perfection and to restore line to torn edges. Using the seam guide, stitch a ¼-inch seam and leave an opening in the middle of one side to turn it. Fasten your threads securely at A, B, C, and D (see p. 7), and use small stitches at corner E (see p. 8). Trim corners at A, D, and E (see p. 152).

In lightweight fabrics, cut the fold apart, and make a seam there, also, for greater support on this bias edge.

This was done on both scarves in the photograph, because two colors were being used in the one with the ball fringe. Then, too, there was not enough fabric for the print, and there was not enough to cut a square.

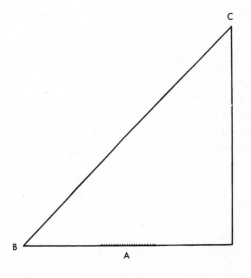

Turn scarf right side out. Whipstitch edge with hand stitches at A. Smooth edges with fingers, and press flat with iron.

Sew on a 16-inch strip of grosgrain ribbon at B and C, or make a strip of bias (p. 259) from matching scarf fabric. Bias was used on both scarves in the photograph.

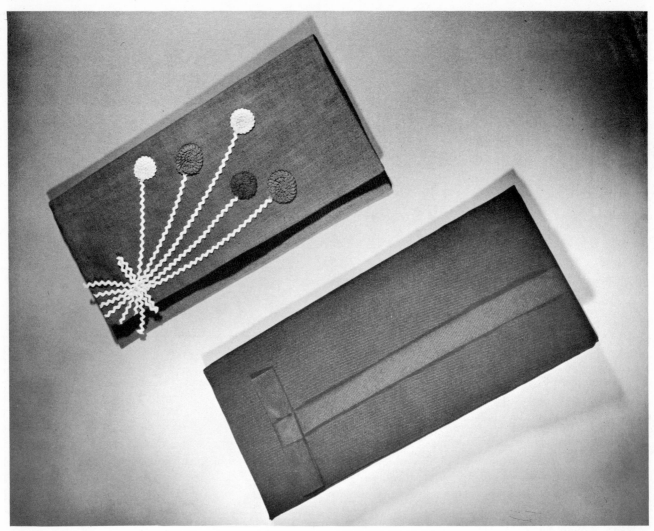

A daytime or an evening purse

There are many interesting fabrics you could use for this purse and many ways you could add a quality-looking trim. Because of the zipper, this would not be a good choice for a first torn project. It would be better to make it as your second or third project.

Before you begin this project, read the last paragraph on page 10.

Tear or pull threads and cut two pieces of fabric the sizes shown in the sketch. If edges were torn, press to restore line to torn edges.

If fabric is soft, lightweight, or crushable, cut a piece of flannelette the same size as two pieces and stitch ¼ inch from the edge on underside. Another suggestion is to cut two pieces of press-on underlining ¾ inch smaller all around than two pieces, and press on underside ¾ inch from edges (see p. 150).

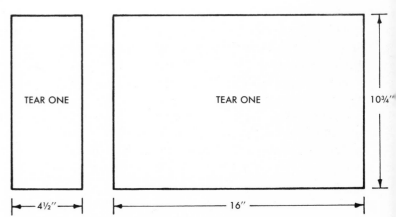

TEAR ONE   TEAR ONE   10¾″

4½″   16″

Join two pieces in a ⅝-inch seam. Baste-stitch at A for length of zipper plus ⅞ inch extra at top. A 7-inch skirt zipper is desirable to use. At end of baste-stitching, change to permanent stitch and lock-stitch threads at B. Continue to sew remainder of seam with permanent stitching. Press open seam. Cut first baste-stitch at lockstitching.

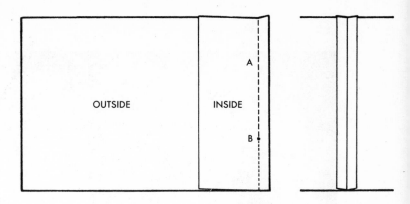

Apply zipper in the machine-basted area of seam as shown on page 67.

If you are going to use a trim that would be sewn in the seams, it should be applied now. The narrow rickrack on the first purse in the photograph was sewn on when the purse was completed. The bias trim on the second purse was sewn in the seam, as this sketch illustrates.

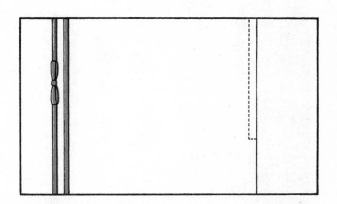

Stitch across the upper edge of placket at A about ½ inch from edge. Remove baste-stitching. Open zipper. Fold fabric in half, right sides together, and stitch ⅝-inch seam. Use short stitches at corners B, C, D, and E (see p. 8). Trim seam to ¼ inch and trim away seam at corners (see p. 152).

Turn purse to right side through open zipper. Smooth edges with fingers and press flat. Fold purse in half. The zipper will be inside the lower half.

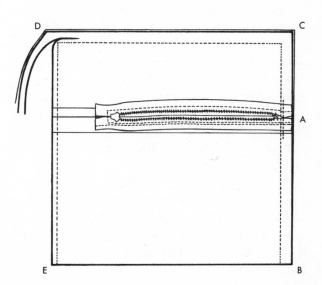

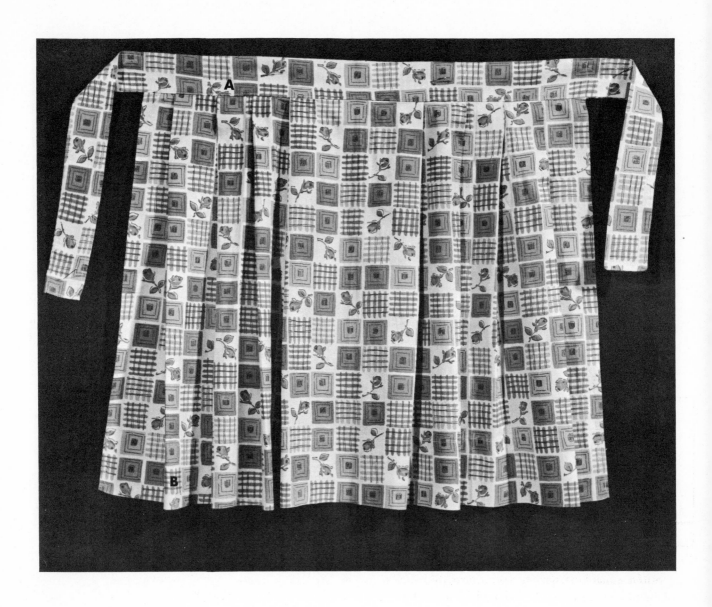

A softly pleated apron

This apron is simple to make, yet incorporates the basic learnings required of torn projects. In addition, it builds for the softly pleated skirt that could follow as a next project (see page 29).

It is interesting to note that this apron was made from fabric that was printed off grain. When you look across the top and bottom of the apron in the photograph above, this shows up at A and B.

Before you begin this project, read the paragraph on page 10.

If edges of fabric were not torn on grain when purchased, tear or pull threads and cut apron to desired size from sketch. If your fabric is wider than 36 inches, see paragraph on page 27. Fold piece in half to press to grain perfection and to restore line to torn edges.

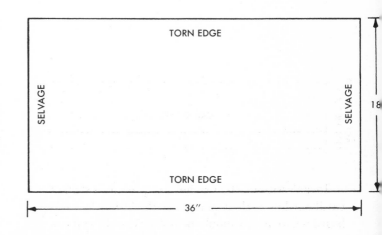

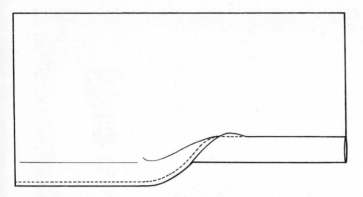

Staystitch lower edge ¼ inch from edge. Use the seam guide at the machine, a permanent stitch and matching thread. Then, using the hem gauge, block a 2½-inch hem. Next, turn under the raw edges of the hem on ¼-inch staystitching and press.

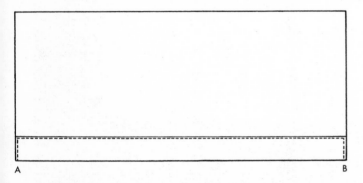

Stitch a machine hem in apron near folded edge of hem, beginning at A and ending at B. Fasten threads at A and B.

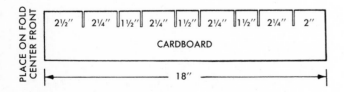

(In a classroom, the teacher can prepare a strip of cardboard as a pleat pattern with slashes in cardboard where pleats should be made. The student can then place the cardboard over the upper edge of apron fabric and make a ¼-inch snip with scissors

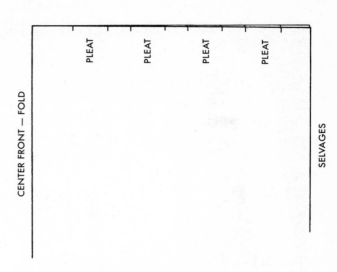

for pleats. If the fabric is purchased wider than 36 inches, another cardboard may be made with the number and depth of pleats adjusted; or the fabric may be torn to be 36 inches wide.)

This apron finishes 18 inches in width.

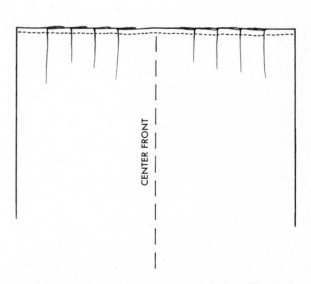

Fold pleats in place, working out from center to ends, and stitch at machine ¼ inch from edge.

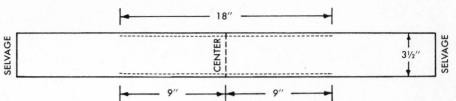

To make the band and ties as one, tear a crosswise strip width of fabric 3½ inches deep. Fold strip in half at center line as in sketch to press to grain perfection and to restore line to torn edges. Measure out from center of strip for 9 inches in both directions. Staystitch both edges ¼ inch from edge.

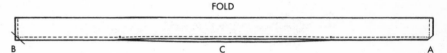

Fold in half, right sides together, and stitch a ¼-inch seam. Using small stitches at A and B, leave an opening for 18 inches where it was staystitched at C. Fasten threads securely at beginning and ending of stitching. Trim off corners at A and B near stitching line. Press open seam on a yardstick or wooden dowel (p. 162). Turn band and apron ties to right side.

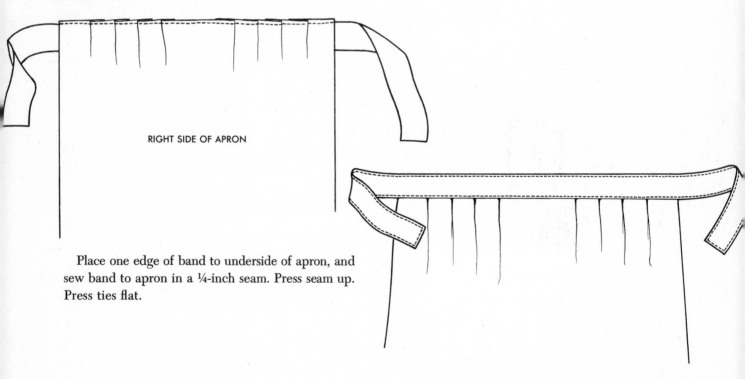

Place one edge of band to underside of apron, and sew band to apron in a ¼-inch seam. Press seam up. Press ties flat.

On topside of band, turn under raw edge on ¼-inch staystitching line. Close this opening with topstitching near the edge. Continue to stitch all around the band and ties for added strength.

Final-press band and ties. Final-press apron on lengthwise grain as shown on page 62. Press pleats in place for one inch down from band.

A softly pleated skirt

This skirt has many desirable features. It enables the beginner to make a skirt without using a pattern. There are no seams to sew, no plackets to make, and the skirt can be adjusted easily to a changing waistline. It is a popular style with all age groups.

The skirt shown on page 58 in Chapter 6 could be included here with torn projects.

Before you begin this project, read the paragraph on page 10.

This skirt was made from a lengthwise strip, 55 inches long. It was pleated to finish 29 inches across the top. With the 5-inch overlap at the front, this skirt would fit a 24-inch waistline. Depending upon the size of the waistline, and the desired depth of pleats, purchase 1½ yards (54 inches) to 2½ yards (90 inches) of fabric. With a plaid, it is interesting to follow one of the darker plaid lines for the top of the pleats. Press fabric to grain perfection.

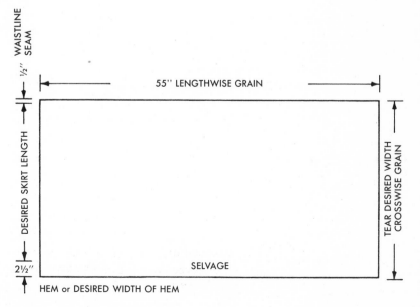

Staystitch crosswise edge, A, ¼ inch from edge. Turn in on the ¼-inch staystitching and stitch ¼-inch hem at machine.

Use hem gauge to turn up hem desired amount and press. One of lengthwise edges will be selvage. Use it at B for the hem, so that no edge finish will be required. Finish with hand stitch shown on page 62.

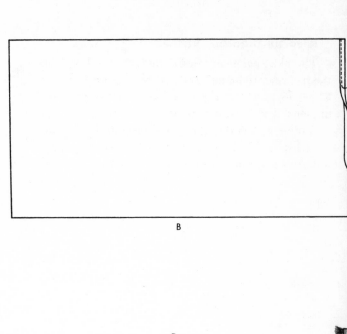

B

If you desire to use fringe at C edge, place right side of fringe to right side of skirt and stitch in place. Leave approximately 1½ inches of extra fringe at top of skirt, D, so that fringe can be included in edge of waistband.

Then, stitch on a 3-inch strip of fabric through same line of stitching to turn back and press as a facing. Extend ½ inch at B, so this raw edge can be turned in and stitched in place by hand at lower edge of skirt. (Use selvage at A which will not require finishing.) You can tear this strip of fabric from remaining strip when skirt is torn desired length.

If you do not wish to use fringe at the front edge, turn back edge for 1½ inches and press. Clean-finish raw edge (p. 34) and fasten this self-facing with hand stitches at lower edge. You may even prefer to sew on one or more rows of braid or bandings near the front edge instead of using the fringe in the facing seam.

Self-fringe can be used at the bottom of this skirt instead of a hem.

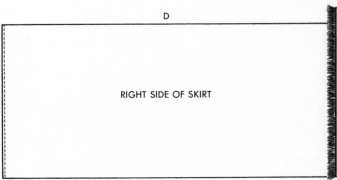

D

RIGHT SIDE OF SKIRT

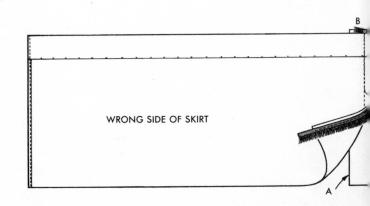

B

WRONG SIDE OF SKIRT

A

Beginning 5 inches from front edge A, fold and pin pleats in place at B. End pleats 5 inches from edge at C. Skirt must pleat across entire top edge to size of waistline plus 5 inches extra. Stitch pleats in place ½ inch from top edge.

You may find it easier to pleat fabric first, and then tear away excess at D to correct size. Then hem this edge now as directed earlier on page 30.

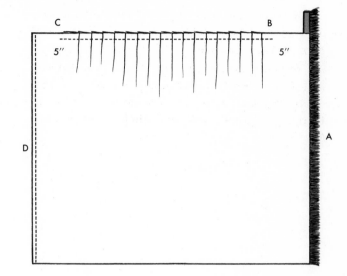

Tear strip desired length for waistband and apply exactly as explained on pages 68 to 70.

Make two buttonholes in waistband about 3½ inches apart. Overlap skirt for 5 inches and sew buttons in proper position.

Buttonholes at A and B and buttons at C and D are optional. If they are made, reinforce with a small strip of fabric underneath. Reinforce single layer of fabric at C and D for buttons with small square of pellon on underside.

Final-press skirt on lengthwise grain as shown on page 62. Press pleats in place for one inch down from band.

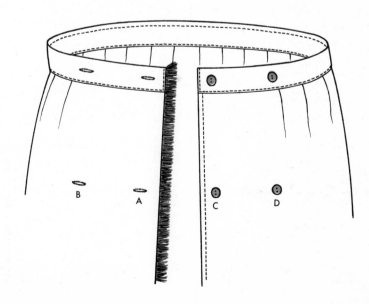

An overvest or barbecue apron

This photograph shows our last torn project as an overall barbecue apron. Many fashion magazines feature this apron, in a shorter version, sometimes with interesting pockets, worn over a sheath dress as an overvest. Instead of the ties, a tailored belt can be worn over both dress and vest. The overvest lends itself to many different images. It may have a low V neckline in front. It may be fringed — either fringing the fabric itself or sewing on purchased fringe at the lower edge. It may be made of brocade or embroidered material. It may be bold in color for a needed change to a basic dress.

Many men like this with large pockets (p. 13) in a gaily printed sailcloth or denim fabric for a barbecue or "fix-all at home" apron.

Before you begin this project, read the paragraph on page 10.

Straighten fabric to grain perfection. Measure, then tear or pull threads and cut two apron pieces as illustrated in the diagram at the left unless you wish to change length for an overvest.

Cut the square neckline for front and back as shown in the diagrams below. It will be finished with a fitted facing to follow.

However, you may prefer to round out the corners for a scooped neckline as shown in the photograph.

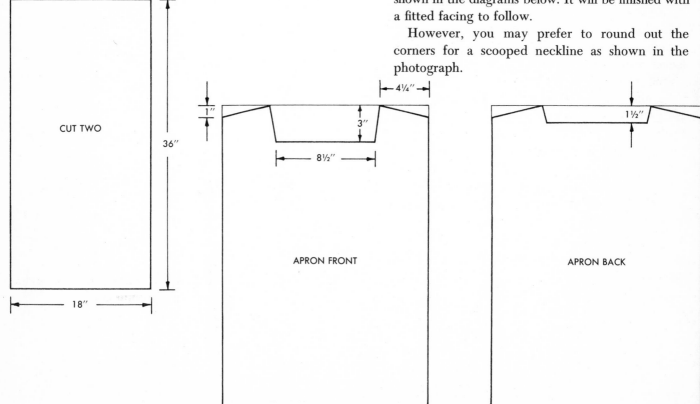

CUT TWO

36″

18″

4¼″

1″

3″

8½″

APRON FRONT

1½″

APRON BACK

On same true grain line, cut front and back facings 3 inches deep and 2 inches wide.

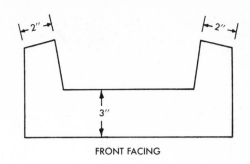

FRONT FACING

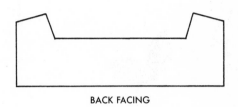

BACK FACING

At A, B, and C, staystitch neckline and shoulders ¼ inch from edge and in direction of arrows.

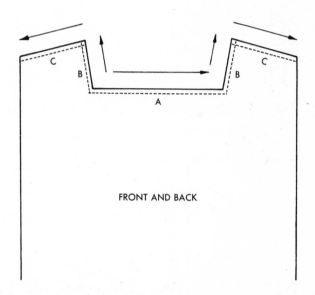

FRONT AND BACK

Right sides together, join front to back at shoulders in a ½-inch seam. Next, 1¼ inches from edge at A, with machine needle in fabric, lift presser foot, and turn fabric so that seam can slope to ¼ inch at outer edge of shoulder line. Clip up to stitching at A and pink seams with pinking shears. Press open.

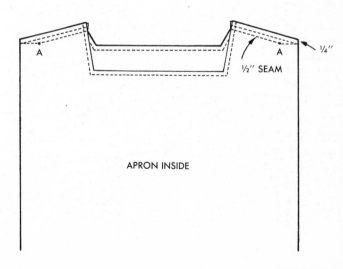

APRON INSIDE

Torn projects

Staystitch all edges of front and back facings ¼ inch from edge in direction of arrows.

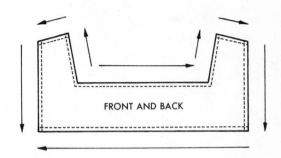

FRONT AND BACK

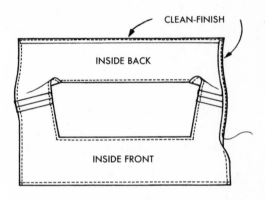

CLEAN-FINISH

INSIDE BACK

INSIDE FRONT

Right sides together, join front facing to back facing at shoulders with a ½-inch seam. Press open.

Clean-finish outer edges of facing. To clean-finish, turn under on ¼-inch staystitching line, and stitch near folded edge.

Right sides together, and with garment side up, stitch on facing with a ¼-inch seam. Use small stitches in all four corners as shown at A and B for reinforcing; clip up to stitching in corners. Understitch facing. (Understitching is a row of machine stitching along the edge of the facing. It catches the seam to the facing.) Turn facing to inside of garment. Press.

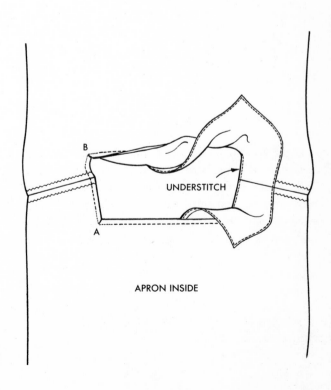

B

UNDERSTITCH

A

APRON INSIDE

The facing can be topstitched in all four corners as shown in the sketch and in the photograph which follows. The topstitching will add a trim feature and will hold facing securely in place.

The hem is then staystitched, turned up 1½ inches, pressed, and machine stitched exactly as you learned with the softly pleated apron (page 27).

Then, using the hem gauge, turn back the sides 1¼ inches. Press. Unless fabric is difficult to turn, staystitching will not be required on the lengthwise grain to turn under these raw edges ¼ inch. Machine stitch side hems in place.

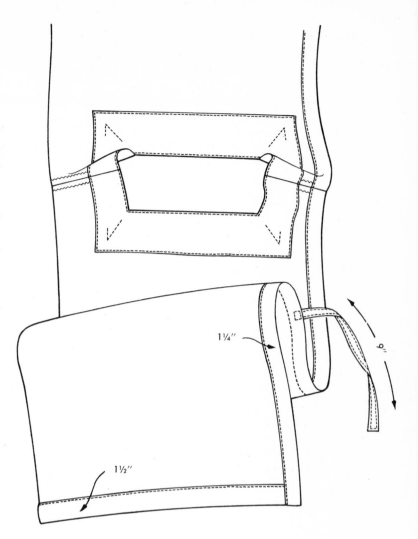

Ties, each 9 inches long, are sewn on at the waistline, approximately 16 inches down from the shoulders. On the plaid apron (photograph at right) the ties were made from purchased bias binding, laid double, and stitched all around to conceal raw edges. This also gives added strength. On the first photograph of the apron, they were made of grosgrain ribbon.

The pocket is made from a 6-inch square folded into a triangle, right sides together. Then, it is sewn with a ¼-inch seam. An opening is left to turn it right side out (see p. 23). Finally, it is held with some fullness of line to topstitch in place to the apron.

The pocket in the first photograph is a circle, stitched double the same way, with an opening to turn right side out (see p. 23). The circle was then stitched to the apron and an area left free to be the pocket opening. The leaves of the "apple pocket" are a single layer of fabric stitched to the apron with a zigzag machine stitch.

Final-press apron on lengthwise grain (see p. 62).

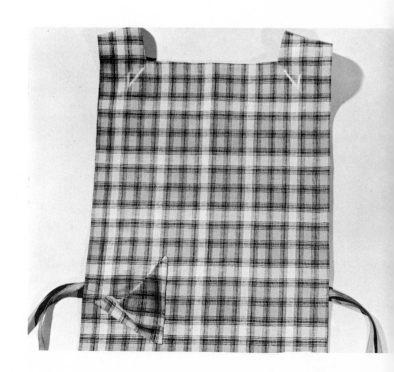

Chapter 3

Buying patterns correctly

When you make simple projects like those you learned in the preceding chapter, you can use various sizes of torn strips of fabric. However, when you make a garment such as a dress, you need a guide called a pattern that has shaped pieces of tissue paper the right size and shape for each piece of fabric you will cut.

It is best to use good commercial patterns. There are several companies that adapt current fashions into designs for home sewing. These companies prepare the large pattern catalogues that are found in pattern departments in stores. From these, you can choose a design you like.

Now, you must learn how to choose the best type of pattern and the correct size for your own personal needs.

Determining your figure type

Determining your figure type precedes the selection of a correct pattern size. If ten girls or women who wore about the same size dress stood before you, there would probably be no two exactly alike. There would be differences in height and in body contour. Because of the varying shapes of girls and women, pattern companies have classified patterns into nine figure types. If you determine the best type for your figure, the cut and the fit will be more correct for you, and the designs will be more appropriate for you.

Check your height, and compare your general proportions with the following list and the silhouettes on the next page. If you have doubts about which figure type you really are, it would be worthwhile for you to pretest one or more types. To pretest, cut the pattern out of an old sheet or on an inexpensive piece of cotton fabric. Sew it together as discussed on page 92, Chapter 8. (In a classroom, your teacher may have various figure types made up ahead of time for you to try on. You can then choose the figure type that most nearly fits you.)

Girls'. These patterns are designed for a growing, immature figure. It has less need for dart fitting than the other types and does not require an underarm bust dart. The patterns are short from shoulder to waistline. They are designed for the smallest of the nine figure types.

Chubby or Chub-deb. The Chubby or Chub-deb figure is still a Girls' figure but is fuller or rounder. These patterns are designed to be fashionable within this age group. The back waist is a little longer than the Girls', because of body roundness.

Sub-teen or Pre-teen. These patterns are designed for a figure that is still growing, but beginning to develop with more bust than the Girls', but less than the Teen. The patterns are designed to give a grown-up appearance.

Teen. Teen patterns are designed for a figure more developed and taller than the Sub-teen or Pre-teen, but not so tall as the Junior figure.

Junior. Junior patterns are designed for a slender figure that has a high, firm bust. This figure is not as tall as the Misses'. Because of this, the waistline looks more defined. This type gives the impression of being an average figure with a slightly short waist.

Junior petites. These patterns are designed for a well-developed figure which is very diminutive in size. This is a size, not an age group. The figure is short, shapely, thin, with smaller waist in proportion to bust and hips than the other types.

Misses'. This is the most popular pattern. It is designed for a fully-developed, well-proportioned figure that is taller than any of the other types.

Women's. Women's patterns are proportionately larger throughout than the Misses' patterns and are made in larger sizes. Their design provides comfort and a slenderizing style.

Half sizes. Half-sizes patterns are designed for the mature figure that is shorter than the Misses' or Women's. The shoulders are narrow, waist length is shorter, and bust, waist, and hips are larger. The general impression is of a stocky figure.

GIRLS'

CHUBBY
OR CHUB-DEB

SUB-TEEN
OR PRE-TEEN

TEEN

JUNIOR

JUNIOR PETITES

MISSES'

WOMEN'S

HALF SIZES

Determining your correct size

The pattern size that is purchased is determined by measurements only. It will have no dependable relationship to the size purchased in ready-made clothes, or to the age of the person buying it.

To begin with, ready-to-wear clothing is not uniform or standardized in size. Each manufacturer sets his own sizing. However, patterns are standardized, and all pattern companies use the same standard body measurements that are given in the chart near the end of this chapter. These have been established by a National Bureau of Standards. The only change you will find with patterns is a certain design ease that changes with fashion.

Bust measurement. The upper part of the body is the most difficult to fit. The bust measurement is the most important, therefore, in determining the correct size pattern to buy for a blouse, dress, suit, or coat. If the waist and hip measurements vary from the size pattern chosen, those alterations are easily made. When taking measurements, wear the undergarments you expect to wear with the garment you plan to make. Remember that properly fitted foundation garments are the framework for any apparel. The bust measurement is taken over

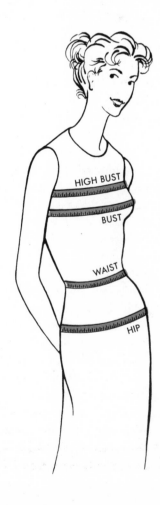

the fullest part of the bust, with the tape measure held firmly, but not tightly. If the bust measures 34 inches, then the size pattern should be 14, as in the pattern companies' size charts given here.

However, when an individual has a medium or large size bust, it is advisable to take a high bust measurement also. This is done by placing the tape firmly under the arms, then straight across the back and bringing it over the bust in front. This measurement is sometimes called a high chest measurement. If there is several inches' difference in the two bust measurements, then the pattern may be purchased a size smaller than the full bust and cut to fit the figure at that part, if necessary. This is important because the most difficult places to fit a garment are through the chest, and at the neckline, shoulder, and armholes. The smaller pattern more closely approaches the correct size. See page 39 about ease given in patterns. Should you find it necessary to add on for a larger bust, see Chapter 8.

If you measure between two sizes, it is worthwhile to experiment once and pretest both sizes. (In a classroom your teacher may have basic patterns in various sizes for you to try on.) Determine which size will make the smarter-fitting dress with fewer needed alterations for the chest, neckline, shoulder, and armholes.

Other alterations will be made easily for the person whose waist and hips are larger. If you find your measurements fall in between two sizes, and if you have a small bone structure, you will generally select the smaller size. You will choose the larger size if your bone structure is very large, or if you are very firm-fleshed or muscular.

Ease need not be considered when buying a pattern for a coat, suit, or jacket, because adequate ease is given by the pattern companies.

Waist and hip measurements. Waist and hip measurements must be known when purchasing a pattern for a skirt, shorts, or slacks and in determining if any cutting-to-fit is necessary for the pattern size purchased by bust measurement for a dress, suit, or coat. The waist measurement is taken over the proper foundation for the garment and with the tape measure held firmly at the smallest part of the figure.

Hips are measured over the proper foundation and with the tape held firmly over the fullest part of the figure. This may be 6 to 12 inches below the waistline.

If you find a set of measurements in the chart below that exactly matches yours, you are fortunate. Most people have some variations. You will learn how to take care of those in Chapter 8.

Measurement Chart

GIRLS'

Size	7	8	10	12	14
Chest	25½	26	28	30	32
Waist	22½	23	24	25	26
Hip	27	28	30	32½	35
Back waist length	11	11½	12¼	13	13¾

CHUBBY OR CHUB-DEB

Size	8½c	10½c	12½c	14½c
Chest	30	31½	33	34½
Waist	28	29	30	31
Hip	33	34½	36	37½
Back waist length	12	12¾	13½	14¼

SUB-TEEN OR PRE-TEEN

Size	8s	10s	12s	14s
Bust	28	29	31	33
Waist	23	24	25	26
Hip	31	32	34	36
Back waist length	13½	13¾	14	14¼

TEEN

Size	10	12	14	16
Bust	30	32	34	36
Waist	24	25	26	28
Hip	32	34	36	38
Back waist length	14¾	15	15¼	15½

JUNIOR

Size	9	11	13	15
Bust	30½	31½	33	35
Waist	23½	24½	25½	27
Hip	32½	33½	35	37
Back waist length	15	15¼	15½	15¾

JUNIOR PETITES

Size	3JP	5JP	7JP	9JP	11JP	13JP
Bust	31	31½	32	32½	33	33½
Waist	22½	23	23½	24	24½	25
Hip	32½	33	33½	34	34½	35
Back waist length	14	14¼	14½	14¾	15	15¼

MISSES'

Size	10	12	14	16	18	20
Bust	31	32	34	36	38	40
Waist	24	25	26	28	30	32
Hip	33	34	36	38	40	42
Back waist length	15¾	16	16¼	16½	16¾	17

WOMEN'S

Size	40	42	44	46	48
Bust	42	44	46	48	50
Waist	34	36	38½	41	43½
Hip	44	46	48	50	52
Back waist length	17⅛	17¼	17⅜	17½	17⅝

HALF SIZES

Size	12½	14½	16½	18½	20½	22½	24½
Bust	33	35	37	39	41	43	45
Waist	27	29	31	33	35	37½	40
Hip	37	39	41	43	45	47	49
Back waist length	15¼	15½	15¾	16	16¼	16½	16¾

Variations in patterns

Before deciding if any cutting-to-fit is necessary at the bust, waist, and hip, when the individual measurements vary from the pattern size purchased, the following information is useful:

Bustline. At the bustline, in addition to the seam allowance, commercial patterns allow a tolerance of 2 to 4 inches beyond that of the bust measurement, depending upon style and company. That is why the person with a slightly larger measurement than the pattern still does not need to add extra in cutting.

Hipline. At the hipline, commercial patterns allow 1½ to 2½ inches extra tolerance besides the seam allowance. This extra tolerance is needed on a straight skirt, and if the individual's measurement is larger than the pattern, extra should be allowed in the cutting. However, in a fuller-styled skirt — because of the style of the skirt and because of the extra tolerance given — extra in the cutting may not be necessary.

Waistline. No extra tolerance is given on the pattern that could be used for increasing the waistline. The amount that is given (½ to 1 inch) must be used for ease of garment on the figure (p. 69; p. 146).

Chapter 4

Preparing fabrics for cutting

An understanding of fabric grain line determines your success in making clothes.

Fabric is made by weaving two or more sets of yarns at right angles to each other. One set of yarns, the warp, parallel to the selvages, is lengthwise of the fabric. The other set, the filling or woof yarns, that runs between the selvages, is crosswise of the fabric. The direction of the yarns is termed the grain. There is lengthwise and crosswise grain. When the lengthwise and crosswise yarns are at right angles to each other, as you can see in this sketch, the grain is true.

True grain is your all-important key to success in clothing construction. In the Bishop method, all of the cutting, the stitching, the pressing, and the fitting is based on making apparel that is grain perfect. A finished garment that is grain perfect keeps its shape because grain always seeks its true position. It will hang and wear well, and it can fit perfectly. True grain, then, is a law of quality clothing construction, and there is only one exception as explained on page 42.

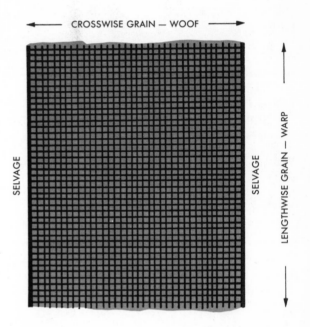

CROSSWISE GRAIN — WOOF

SELVAGE

SELVAGE

LENGTHWISE GRAIN — WARP

Determining grain perfection

The majority of fabrics can be torn at both ends when purchased. If your piece of fabric has not been torn, but was cut freehand from the bolt, test it to see if it can be torn. About an inch down from the cut edge, clip into the first selvage with your scissors, tear with a quick, firm pull to the second selvage, and then cut through it.

Sheer, ribbed, loosely woven, or embroidered fabrics cannot be torn. To get these grain perfect at both ends, pull out the first thread that goes all the way across the fabric. Pull one, or even two threads, very gently with the right hand, slipping the fabric back on the thread with the left hand to prevent breaking it. Try to pull it across the entire width of the fabric, but if it breaks, cut where it has been pulled, pick up the end of the broken thread, and continue pulling and cutting along the puckered thread line. See left photograph, next page.

On some fabrics with heavy or rough threads, nap surfaces, etc. it may not be possible to either tear or pull a thread. Instead, the crosswise threads may be raveled until one thread comes off the entire width to be straightened (A). After raveling, cut off the ends of the lengthwise threads (right photo).

The line may be made by a crosswise thread that is a prominent woven line, rib, or yarn. You can easily see to cut along that one thread (B), and it is not necessary to pull it or ravel the fabric first.

Very seldom will you purchase a woven fabric that will not tear or for which a crosswise thread to cut on grain cannot be found.

For knits, see page 246.

To determine whether a fabric will lay grain perfect for cutting, it must be torn or cut on the crosswise grain from selvage to selvage at both ends. This you have just learned.

Fabric occasionally gets pulled from its true grain position and is called an off-grain fabric. Sometimes this happens in the factory in some of the finishing processes. Other times the winding of the cloth on the bolt causes the grain to deviate from its true position. This is shown in one of the sketches.

It is easy to determine if the fabric is off grain by laying it down and trying to align it precisely with the marks on the cutting board (p. 4), the corner of a table, or a T square (p. 44).

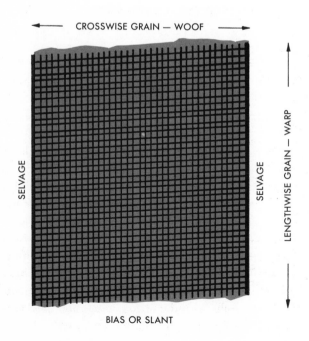

CROSSWISE GRAIN — WOOF

SELVAGE

SELVAGE

LENGTHWISE GRAIN — WARP

BIAS OR SLANT

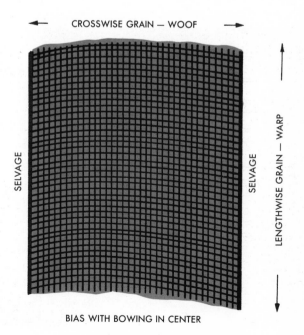

CROSSWISE GRAIN — WOOF

SELVAGE

SELVAGE

LENGTHWISE GRAIN — WARP

BIAS WITH BOWING IN CENTER

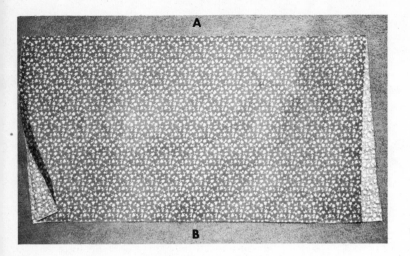

This photograph shows a fabric that is off grain on the bias or slant. The lengthwise fold is at A, and the two selvages are at B.

Ways of making off-grain fabrics grain perfect are discussed on the following pages. Fibers and fabrics with a softer finish are easily rectified.

Nowadays, however, durable resin or stabilizing finishes may be applied to some fabrics, usually cottons, to give them such features as crease resistance, wash and wear properties, shrinkage control, water repellency, resistance to soil, and durable pleat retention. These resins also are used to give such appearance finishes as embossing, glazing, or polishing, especially to cottons. Any of these give the fabrics a harder finish. If these stabilizing finishes are applied to a fabric that is off grain, the crosswise grain cannot be straightened, since it is not free to take its natural position at right angles to the lengthwise grain. The off-grain condition, then, is permanent. Fabrics with this type of a stabilizing finish, for which the grain cannot be straightened, are not suitable choices for beginners' projects. Nevertheless, it may be possible to partially straighten the off-grain condition by using the techniques on pages 43-44. However, if it will not straighten, use the lengthwise grain for cutting as described in Chapter 5, and disregard the crosswise grain.

Analyzing fabric

The following chart summarizes some of the problems encountered with various fabrics. Techniques of correcting these problems are discussed on the pages following this chart.

Silk
Rayon
Man-made fibers (besides rayon) and their blends: arnel, dacron, orlon, vicara, nylon, and so forth.

1. It does not need to be preshrunk, and is ready to cut when purchased.
2. If it lies off grain, it can be straightened by pressing as shown on the next page, unless it has a permanent stabilized finish.

Cotton

Linen

1. Crosswise edges of linen cannot be torn. Pull threads and cut as shown on previous page.
2. Quality cottons are almost totally preshrunk when purchased. Be certain to check label or bolt for manufacturer's information.
3. If cotton and linen are not labeled preshrunk, follow the method on page 44 for shrinking them.
4. If cotton and linen are labeled preshrunk, but are off grain, they can often be straightened by pressing as shown on the next page. The only exception will be cotton that may have a permanent stabilized finish.
5. If cotton and linen are labeled preshrunk, but are off grain, sometimes they can be straightened more by going through the shrinking process, if pressing did not help to attain grain perfection. This all depends on the amount of the stabilizing finish in the fabric.
6. See page 45 for handling cotton corduroy.

Wool	1. If not labeled preshrunk, follow the method on pages 45 and 46 for woolen fabrics.
	2. If preshrunk, but off grain, follow the method on pages 45 and 46 for woolen fabrics.
	3. A third reason why woolen fabric may need to go through the shrinking process (even though it is labeled preshrunk, and is on straight of grain) is of the utmost importance in home sewing. Some woolens have a finish on them that disappears in pressing with wet steam, and it should be removed from the entire piece before cutting out.

To determine if a fabric has a finish, press a corner with a dampened cheese-cloth. If the pressed corner looks dull compared to the rest of the fabric, or if it looks softer than the harsh finish of the fabric, the shrinking process for woolens should be applied to remove the finish completely.

Almost every piece of wool will need to be processed before it is cut out for a garment.

Combination of fibers	Many fabrics are woven from a combination of fibers, such as 40% cotton and 60% rayon, or 20% wool and 80% orlon. When fibers are combined, and when the fabric is not labeled preshrunk, it must be preshrunk by one of the methods on pages 44 to 46 for the fiber in it that will shrink. This is necessary even if the fabric contains only 20% of that shrinkable fiber, such as 20% wool and 80% orlon.

Straightening fabric by pressing

If a fabric is preshrunk, but lies off grain on a bias or slant, or with bowing in the center, shown on pages 41 and 42, it can sometimes be straightened by pressing. However, if it is not preshrunk, it can be straightened at the same time you are shrinking it as shown on page 44.

Fold the fabric in half, right side in. Pin or baste-stitch it so the two selvages are together, and the two halves of each torn end are together. If you use pins, place them parallel with the selvage edges and close to the edge. Analyze the fabric to see if the grain forms true right angles. If there are diagonal wrinkles and puckers, the fabric is off grain.

Sponge pressing area for moisture on the bottom area; the steam iron will provide moisture on the top area. Keep selvages to the right on the pressing area; use iron firmly on lengthwise grain. Sometimes, you may use the iron on the crosswise grain, but that will depend on the amount of the off-grain condition, and the firmness of the fabric weave.

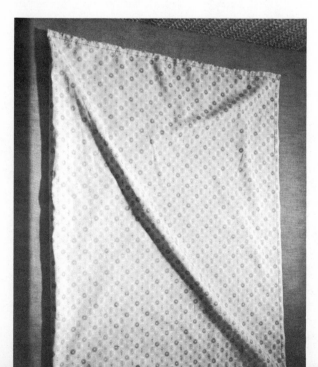

Do not press on center fold of fabric as this is often difficult to press out later. Press to within ½ inch of it. It is much easier to straighten the grain on shorter lengths. Therefore, tear or cut the fabric in skirt lengths, or in lengths on which major pattern pieces will fit. This technique does not require more fabric in cutting.

This photograph shows the fabric shown in the photographs on the previous page after it has been straightened. When the grain is off with either a slant or with a bowing in the center, it must be straightened, if at all possible.

Straightening and/or shrinking cotton and linen fabrics

Both ends must be torn or cut on the thread as described on pages 40-41.

Fold right sides together. Thus, the pieces of the garment will be easier to mark after cutting, and they will be in position for sewing without unnecessary handling.

Pin or baste-stitch together the selvages and the crosswise edges. If pins are used, they should be close to the edges, parallel with them, and about 6 inches apart.

Fold the fabric loosely in tablecloth or accordion-pleat folds about 8 inches apart. Immerse it in warm

water until it is completely wet. The pleat folds help you to look into the layers and check on the wetness.

Carefully lift the fabric from the water and push out excess water. Do not wring fabric, but you may wrap it in a Turkish towel to remove more moisture, if necessary.

As in the photograph above, lay fabric out flat on a sheet or a piece of plastic to dry. Smooth and pull gently with your hands to achieve grain perfection. Keep smoothing occasionally during drying period to insure this. With some fabric, it may also be necessary to place weights around the edges to insure grain perfection. Never drape fabric over a clothesline, a clothes rack, or a shower rod to dry.

After the fabric is thoroughly dry (and only then), press with a steam iron, or with a regular iron and dampened cheesecloth placed under fabric. Use the iron on up and down grain to retain grain perfection. The T square illustrates that fabric is now grain perfect. The importance of this grain perfection is one of the fundamental principles of the Bishop method.

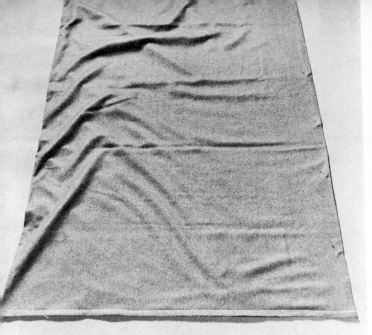

Cotton corduroy must be handled differently, since the pile on it crushes easily when wet. Follow all the procedures above for preparing ends of fabric, but after it has been soaked in warm water, gently press out some moisture with the palms of your hands. Do not wring. Place the corduroy at once in an automatic dryer. The blowing air helps to raise up the pile. Usually, no pressing is needed.

However, if you are going to dry-clean the garment made from corduroy, this special preparation is not needed, and fabric may be cut as purchased.

Straightening, shrinking, and/or removing possible finish from woolen fabrics

At the same time that you will be learning about shrinking woolen fabrics, you will be learning about straightening them, and removing a possible finish.

One to three aims will be accomplished at the same time, depending upon the piece of fabric. This technique is called "processing" the woolen fabric before it is cut.

Both ends must be torn or cut on the thread as described on pages 40-41.

Woolen fabric is purchased with right sides folded together, and is left that way to process and cut.

Baste-stitch crosswise ends together. Depending upon the need, pin or baste-stitch selvages together.

Make special processing cloths to hold moisture for processing wool. Woolen fabrics vary from 54 to 60 inches in width, and the processing cloths should be several inches wider (30 to 36 inches) than the fabric when it is folded in half. They should be as long as the yardage of wool. Processing cloths can also be made by laying several pieces side by side to meet. Old sheets or cotton draperies torn the correct

size are satisfactory. Any absorbent cotton fabric can be purchased and kept for this purpose. Wet the cloths completely and then wring them out, leaving enough moisture for the woolen fabric to feel thoroughly damp. The moisture relaxes the wool fiber so that it can straighten and shrink. A heavy fabric requires more moisture than a lightweight one.

Place wet cloths on fabric.

Lay fabric in deep folds to center of yardage; then, starting at other end, repeat to center to meet first half. As you fold, press down on fabric to help push the moisture into it.

It should then be covered with another wet cloth to prevent the outside from drying too quickly.

Place all of it in a plastic bag or wrap it in a piece of plastic to distribute the moisture evenly through

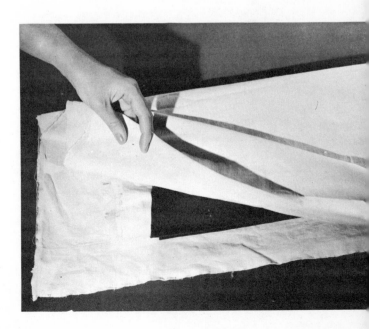

the fabric, and to prevent it from drying out before it is unfolded. This procedure is especially helpful in warm weather.

After 2 to 6 hours, when all moisture will have been absorbed by wool, take it out.

Unfold fabric; it will be thoroughly damp. Lay it out on a flat surface. Smooth it with the hands to achieve grain perfection.

Allow to dry flat, and never hang. It may be necessary to turn fabric over in order to dry and shrink evenly.

Pressing will be unnecessary for most fabrics, but if needed, use a steam iron, or a regular iron with dampened cheesecloth on top of the fabric. Press on up and down grain to retain grain perfection.

You can see in the photograph that the grain of the fabric forms true right angles, just as it does in the photograph with the T square on page 44.

To work with knitted fabrics, see page 246.

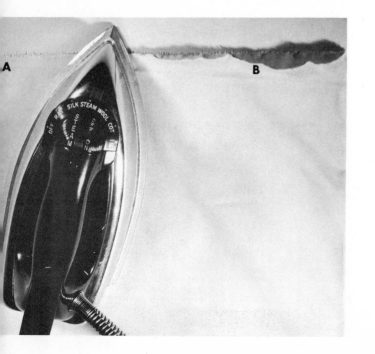

Pressing to restore grain on torn edges

Any edges of fabric that have been torn when purchased, or any edges that have been torn to make a garment such as an apron and its ties, should always be pressed with a steam iron, even if the fabric lies grain perfect.

The pressing is needed to restore the smooth grain (A) to these rippled, disturbed, puckered torn edges (B). It is done to both lengthwise and crosswise edges, if fabric is torn in both directions (see Torn Projects, Chapter 2). The pieces of fabric are folded in half for pressing to further assure grain perfection.

Chapter 5

Cutting and marking

Learning to do each step of clothing construction correctly is important in making quality-looking garments, but cutting to perfection is the foundation for all good sewing. There is no question that you cut much of the good construction and real perfection into your garment. If you do not cut on grain, how can you sew on grain? And if you do not cut to perfection, how can you sew to perfection? Cutting properly takes a long time compared to the speed of sewing techniques, but it is time well spent.

Factors to recognize about fabric before cutting

Nap fabrics. These fabrics have a definite surface texture, and must be laid out and cut in one direction to avoid shading, and to get the full benefit of the color. If you make a mistake and cut your pieces in both directions, the garment will appear to have been cut from two different shades of the same color. As the yardage chart on the pattern envelope indicates, it takes more fabric to cut a garment in one direction.

Short nap. Those fabrics with a short nap are cut so that the nap goes up toward the top of the garment. When you rub the palm of your hand in the direction of the nap, the nap feels smooth. Contrast this to the resistance you feel when you run your hand the wrong way, as on an animal's fur, for instance. Examples of short-nap fabrics are corduroy, velveteen, and suede cloth. When the nap runs up on these fabrics, the color is darker and richer. An exception to the typical short-nap fabric is broadcloth, which is cut with the nap going down. It is characteristic of this fabric to look lighter and shinier than other short-nap fabrics.

Long nap. Long-nap fabrics are cut with the nap going down. Examples are fleece and camel's hair coating. Long-nap fabrics wear better with nap going down, and they never look roughed up from sitting or moving.

After you have decided which way a nap fabric should go, mark which end is to be the top.

When the right sides of nap fabrics are placed together, one side of the nap or pile will push against the other, especially while being cut. Therefore, for perfection in cutting these fabrics, place the smooth or wrong sides of the fabric together.

Some fabrics such as satins and iridescents reflect light differently when held in opposite directions. These should be cut in one direction, just as nap fabrics are cut.

One-way design. If a print is designed to go in one direction, then every piece of the garment must be cut accordingly, keeping the design always in the same direction.

Sometimes the direction of a design will not be as easy to detect as it is in the one in the photograph. Therefore, the print should be analyzed closely for one-way design. As is indicated in the yardage chart on the pattern envelope, more fabric is required when cutting a garment in one direction.

Off-grain design. If the design on a fabric is stamped off grain in its manufacture, the completed garment can never appear to be grain perfect. A large, regularly spaced design printed in this way will be more conspicuously off grain than a small, irregularly spaced design.

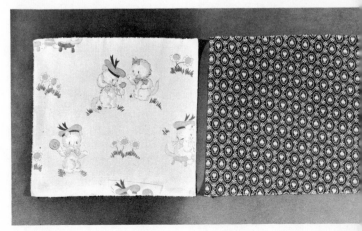

Sometimes it is possible to use a fabric with a small print even if it is printed off grain. This photograph shows how such a design would appear in a gathered or pleated skirt, apron, or curtain. The off-grain aspect is even less obvious when cut up with pattern pieces, and is no real problem in use.

However, regular spacing of design, when stamped off grain, emphasizes the fabric's off-grain aspect. Such a piece of fabric would not be suitable for use. When shopping, check for this off-grain aspect on the crosswise grain and avoid buying such fabric. (See lower photograph.)

In photographing all three of these off-grain design fabrics, either a selvage or torn edge was included in order to emphasize that the design is off grain.

Following the print design instead of the grain of the fabric with off-grain, resin-finished prints is a common practice. (See p. 42 on resin finishes.) This is the best choice in a bad situation, after all. In any event, the consequences of using a fabric off grain need to be considered carefully.

Design fabrics. Most plaids and stripes, and some prints, require matching or planned placement. In a plaid or check, if the distance from one complete design to another is ¼ inch or less, it is never necessary to match the pieces. However, a straight-of-grain seam should be avoided, if possible, because it may bring together two light or two dark lines in a seam. (See pp. 251 to 253 for more on plaids and stripes.)

Selvage. Rarely is it necessary to cut off selvage before cutting out a garment. Use it wherever possible as a seam finish. If it appears to be tight or

drawn in some fabrics, clip three or four selvage yarns on the diagonal every five or six inches. Interesting selvage is often used as a trimming detail on the right side of the garment.

Features to be analyzed in your pattern before cutting

Before starting to cut out the garment, spend some time getting to know your pattern. Thoroughly study your pattern envelope. It gives information that helps you decide on the style features within the garment, and to know what notions to buy. It also suggests a suitable fabric, which is most important and so often most ignored.

Take the tissue from the envelope, pick out the needed pieces for your chosen view of the garment, and return the extras to the envelope. If the tissue is wrinkled, press with a warm, dry iron. Moisture or steam will shrink and pucker the tissue pattern. It will no longer then be the true size.

All patterns have an extra margin beyond the actual cutting line of the pattern itself. This is a safety margin to insure that you will always get a perfect size pattern. After patterns are printed on large sheets, they are piled up many-ply deep and then cut with a knife around each pattern piece. If patterns were trimmed along the actual cutting line, you could not be as certain of true accuracy, because of a natural shifting of the thin paper.

It is not necessary to cut off this margin before cutting out firm fabrics such as cottons, linens, and underlinings. When you cut the garment along the actual cutting line, the margin will drop away. However, if you are cutting slippery fabrics or very thick ones such as wool, it will be easier to cut out the garment along the edge of the tissue rather than through it.

There are two kinds of pattern markings. One kind helps you to lay out the pattern and cut it. There are markings to show the direction of the grain, and to tell you which pieces should be placed on a fold of the fabric. There are also directions for cutting more than one piece of fabric, lines for making alterations, and cutting lines for your shears to follow.

The second kind of pattern markings helps you to put the pieces together correctly, and to do actual construction on the garment. There are numbered notches to match with corresponding notches on the various pattern pieces. There are seamlines, darts to sew, pleat or tuck lines, and other details such as pocket and buttonhole locations.

The next step is to learn how to work with these pattern markings.

Seam allowance. Inside the cutting line, there is a broken line printed all around the pattern pieces. This is the seam allowance line that shows you where to sew the pieces of the garment together. It is now a standard ⅝ inch on all patterns, unless a design or construction detail calls for a different width of stitching. In such a case, the pattern will be marked, so study it carefully for any such variances.

When making the garment, it is essential to follow precisely the seam allowance. Yet, it is never marked on the fabric from the pattern. The technique for making a perfect width seam is shown on page 7.

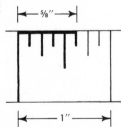

Placing on fold. Some pattern pieces are marked to be cut on the fold of the fabric, which will make them twice the size of the tissue. This fold should be lengthwise (parallel to the selvages) unless otherwise

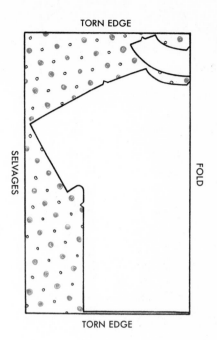

stated, and on the straight of grain. A facing is cut on the same grain as the part of the garment to which it will be sewn.

There are a few exceptions when a crosswise fold (at right angles to the selvage) is acceptable. Two of these exceptions are shown in the illustration below. They are the collar and yoke for a shirt or shirtwaist dress.

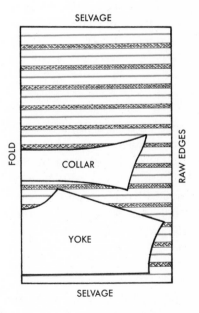

Straight of grain. If a pattern piece is not to be placed on a straight fold of the fabric, then it must be measured from a line given on the tissue for straight of grain, and cut single or double. It can be

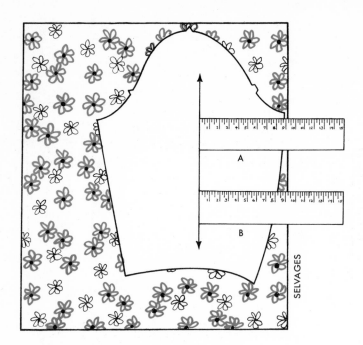

measured to either edge of the fabric, but must be an identical amount of distance from either end of the line. (That is, A and B must be the same distance from the edge of the fabric.) The pattern pieces are almost always laid on the lengthwise grain of fabric.

It is imperative to follow the grain line in cutting, because the entire style, hang, fit, and proper construction can be spoiled if the grain line is ignored.

Construction markings. Study your pattern pieces for the construction markings that will be needed on the underside of the fabric to make the details on your garment. These will be transferred, after cutting, with a tracing paper or in another suitable manner.

A dart is stitched to a point. Mark a line across at the point known as the termination point, to make sure that the darts will be stitched the same length. For a beginner, it is also helpful to mark a line through the center of the dart, known as the pickup line.

A tuck may narrow down but does not end in a point. Mark with a termination point the same as a dart. For a beginner, it is also helpful to mark a line through the center of the tuck, known as the pickup line.

When a garment is underlined, and the darts and tucks are stitched through both layers, they are marked on the underlining alone.

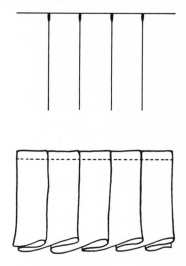

If a tuck or unpressed pleat is to be folded in place, but not stitched down, it can be marked with a ⅛-inch snip of the scissors. However, with deeper pleats, instead of snipping, you may prefer to mark with tracing paper and then run a line of hand basting down several inches from the top edge. Pleats can then be folded in the correct direction, according to pattern instructions, from right side of fabric. The baste-stitching also serves as a check that pleats are folded on true grain, when the baste-stitching will be brought to meet, along with the cut edges at the top of the skirt (see p. 145).

Then, stitch across the top when tucks or pleats are folded in place.

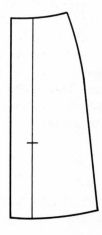

Pressed pleats are marked all the way down the skirt. Make a termination point where the stitching ends and the pleat opening begins.

50

Markings for center fronts and buttonholes will be placed on interfacings or underlinings that will be cut and stitched to the underside of fabric.

Markings for pockets, tabs, and other trimming details will be placed on the underside of the fabric. They can be made to show on the top side of the fabric with a basting stitch in a contrasting color of thread.

Use two short, crossed lines to indicate any circle markings on a pattern.

Notches. They are triangular markings at the edge of tissue to help put the garment together correctly. They should be cut out, away from the tissue. Double and triple notches are cut straight across, as one. Their width identifies their difference. Extra notches are very helpful at:

1. Top of the sleeve cap where joined to the shoulder seam.

2. Underarm of two-piece sleeve where joined to garment side seam.

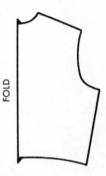

3. Front or back of garment when placed on fold to join precisely to skirt below and collar or facing above.

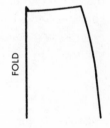

4. Front or back of skirt when placed on fold to join to blouse or skirt band.

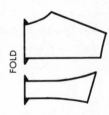

5. Collars, facings, and yokes cut on fold to join precisely to the garment.

Some experienced seamstresses use a ⅛-inch snip of the scissors at these areas, but for a beginner, the extra notches are more readily seen and used. Using notches is safer than cutting into the fabric.

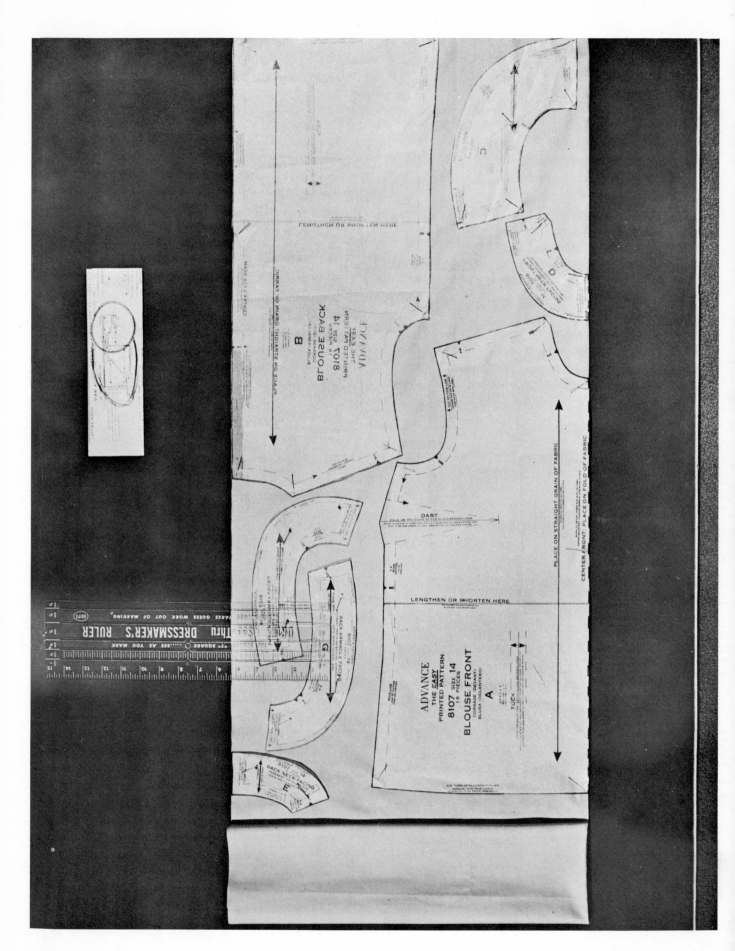

Cutting to fit. If the pattern you buy fits you perfectly, you are an exception, and are very fortunate. Since proportions vary from figure to figure, the pattern may not fit exactly.

It is always wise for a beginner to start with a style of blouse, skirt, robe, or dress pattern that does not require much fitting. In any case, you may still have to make a few changes in your cutting. For example, you can't make a blouse or skirt long enough when you are sewing it, if there isn't enough fabric there after it has been cut.

Once you learn how your figure differs from the pattern measurements, and how a pattern needs to be changed to fit you, you can make these changes in all your patterns.

When you become more experienced, you may want to make a basic pattern which solves all your fitting problems, as described in Chapter 8. However, for the present time, you could settle for checking your skirt length, bodice length, bust, waist, and hip measurements against the pattern measurements, and see if any changes are necessary before cutting. If so, refer to Chapter 8 for these changes.

Never pin the tissue pattern together to try it on. This is not recommended in the Bishop method as a technique for checking the pattern for fit.

Cutting with perfection

Keep the fabric double whenever possible. Fold the right sides together. Thus, the pieces of the garment will be easier to mark after cutting, and they are placed in position for sewing without unnecessary handling. Before placing any of the pattern on knits and wash and wear fabrics, etc., you may want to check if the center crease will press out. Use a steam iron on the crosswise grain; even try using white vinegar on a little brush on the crease and press again. If the crease will not press out, refold your fabric and try to cut the garment sections to avoid this crease mark.

A cutting board (shown on p. 4) is excellent for placing fabric on true grain and for holding it in place before cutting. Never use a slippery surface such as formica or a wooden tabletop. And never use a bed for cutting, or even to place a cutting board on, because a bed does not give firm enough support for accuracy.

Never allow ends of fabric to hang off a table. The fabric should be folded on the true grain until it is unfolded for use. Even though it is recommended that you tear or pull threads and cut your fabric in shorter lengths for cutting, you will still want to make a trial layout to be certain there is ample yardage before you cut anything. You may be able to readjust your layout if you are a little short of fabric. So, always lay out the entire pattern before you cut any of it. Then, too, if you have a choice in organizing or rearranging the pattern pieces for cutting, do it in such a way that any leftover fabric will be in one usable piece at the end.

If a trial layout reveals that there is not enough fabric for your pattern, there are many things you can do:

1. Plan for a narrower hem.
2. Piece a facing or other inconspicuous area, or make the piecing an interesting line or detail.
3. Use a different fabric for facings or trimmings.
4. Combine with another fabric.
5. Eliminate or change some detail.
6. Get another pattern with fewer pieces or less detail.

For most garments, if you tear or pull threads and cut your fabric into skirt-length strips, for cutting, you will be more certain of having your fabric on grain perfection.

Circle on the instruction sheet the cutting layout to follow with the view, size, and fabric width to be used. Pin the pattern pieces according to the layout. In using the dressmaker's ruler to measure the straight of the grain, place two pins to hold the grain correctly, before placing any along the outer edges of the tissue. When placing a tissue on the fold, pin that edge first before the others. Pins should pick up only a few threads of fabric, and should be placed at right angles to the edge of the tissue, with points turned out. Too many pins will distort the edges; they can be used in corners and 6 or 8 inches apart on long edges. If the margin is left on the pattern (see p. 49), always place pins inside the cutting line, never on it. The pattern should be perfectly smooth and flat on the fabric.

Never cut with pinking shears. Use cutting shears with a bent handle. Slide the scissors along, and make long, smooth, firm strokes but never quite close the shears. Cut curves with short strokes. Do not lift the fabric from the cutting table; keep it in place with your left hand near the edge of the pattern. For accuracy in cutting, keep the shears to the right of the pattern. To complete your cutting, walk around the table whenever possible, rather than moving the pattern and fabric, to prevent the fabric from slipping or shifting. Never cut a straight edge — place a straight edge of a pattern down to a selvage, a torn edge, or to one where you have pulled a thread and cut.

Do not unpin the pieces; leave them in place for marking.

Marking with perfection

Using tracing paper and tracing wheel. This method works on most fabrics. However, it cannot be used on sheers, which will show the markings on the right side, or on heavy or napped woolens on which the markings will not show. See succeeding photographs for method for those fabrics.

Choose a color of tracing paper that is one shade lighter or darker than your fabric. A convenient size is a folded piece, 4 by 10 inches, coated sides together.

A sample dart or other construction detail on a scrap will determine the amount of pressure needed to give an adequate marking for a particular fabric.

Do not remove the pattern from the fabric pieces being marked. Remove just enough pins so the tracing paper can be placed between pattern and fabric. Slip one end under the fabric and the other end between pattern piece and fabric. Both wrong sides of fabric will then be marked at once. If you need the mark on the right side of the fabric, for the placement of a pocket, for example, you can bring it to the right side later with a line of basting thread. With the wheel, always use the dressmaker's ruler to mark construction details that are straight lines. Use the tracing wheel away from you and always mark the middle pickup line before you mark the two outside lines. With any of the softer, thicker fabrics, it is helpful to place a piece of wax paper under the tissue, and to mark every other inch so that there is less chance of tearing the tissue.

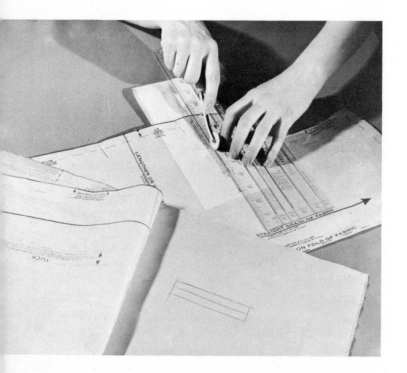

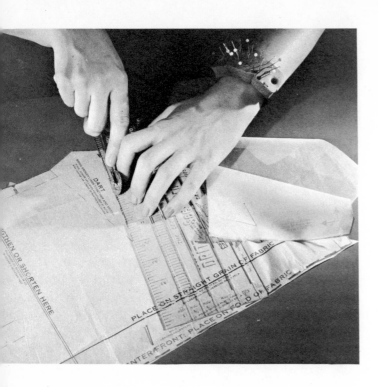

Marking sheer fabrics. A sheer fabric is marked with the ruler and wheel, but without any tracing paper.

Marking nap fabrics and tweeds. With nap or thick fabrics and with multicolored tweeds, mark one layer at a time. When marking the top layer, place a cardboard (A) between the first and second layers of fabric. A single layer of tracing paper is placed under the tissue (B).

Using the wax paper under the tissue, and marking every other inch helps in marking this type fabric. However, if further help is needed to prevent tissue from tearing, place cellophane tape over the construction lines before using tracing wheel on them.

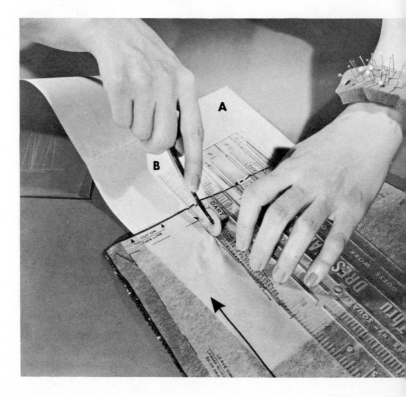

To mark the second layer, unpin the tissue at area being marked. A single layer of tracing paper is placed under the second layer of fabric (C). Using markings on top layer as a guide, transfer the markings to the second layer of the fabric.

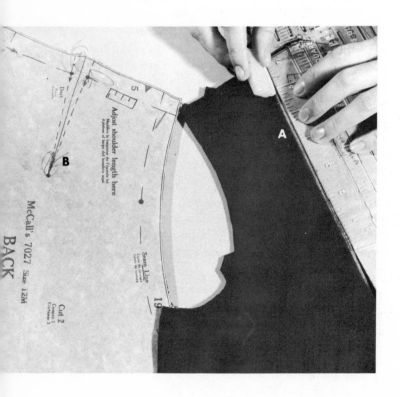

Another technique (A in photograph) for marking these fabrics is to place pins in center of dart to hold tissue in place. Fold back tissue on one of the dart-stitching lines. Use transparent ruler and mark dart line with chalk. Fold back tissue and repeat for second stitching line of dart. Remove tissue and place on second section of garment piece to mark dart or other construction detail.

A chalk pencil is even better to use at times than the tailor's chalk. It can be sharpened to give a much more accurate, thin line.

Still another technique (B in photograph) is to take a stitch several places on the marking line, leaving thread ends extended about an inch. Remove pattern and mark dart lines from thread points with chalk and ruler.

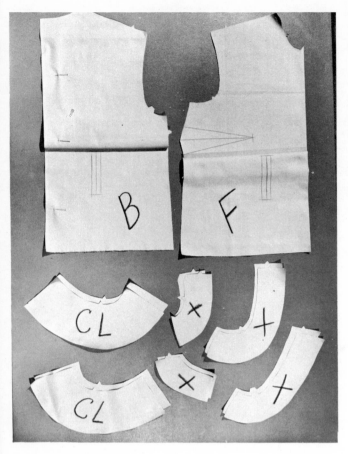

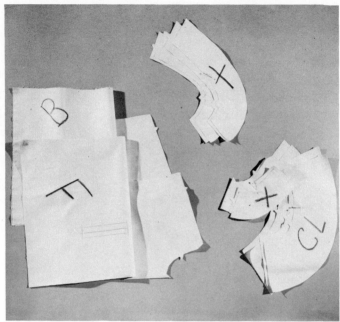

Placing a garment in units of work

The pattern can now be removed, and pieces of the garment laid in units of work. When there is seemingly no right side or wrong side to a piece of fabric, always keep the same side for the wrong side on every part of the garment. If there is no tracing wheel mark to identify the wrong side, mark X with chalk. More specific chalk markings can be used to identify confusing pieces as well as the wrong side of the fabric. Examples are F for front of skirt; B for back; SF for side front; CL for collar; and CF for cuff.

Next, the pieces of the garment are placed in units of work in the order to be constructed. For a skirt, all the front pieces will make up one unit, and the back pieces will make up a second unit. The number of units in a garment and the number of pieces in a unit depend entirely on the style of the garment. A dress will have four major units — bodice front, bodice back, skirt front, and skirt back. If a dress has facings, the facings will be a unit that is completed before it is attached to the dress. These may be folded with the larger pieces on the outside, and will include any interfacings or underlinings, as you will learn to use in more advanced projects.

Unit method of construction

The unit method of construction is an organized way of making a garment unit by unit. Assemble the sections of a garment that make a unit, and as far as possible, complete all stitching and pressing before joining the unit to another completed one. It is one of the basic principles of the Bishop method.

In this manner, excessive wrinkles, stretching, and a handled, shopworn appearance are avoided. It is a much more organized way of working, and you will always know what you are doing.

Short periods of time for sewing can be used to advantage, because a unit can be completed and laid aside until there is another opportunity for sewing.

Your interest in sewing will increase because you will have a feeling of accomplishment when a unit is completed.

Note how the units are planned in the garments which follow in this book, because unit construction follows the same plan for each garment you are making.

Bishop method teaches all of the principles of making a garment. However, if you have an unusual style line or feature, you can keep the pattern instruction sheet and pattern pieces in a convenient place in case you must refer to them.

SELVAGE

SELVAGE

SELVAGE

SELVAGE

58

Chapter 6

Making two skirts

Beginner's first skirt

This first skirt is simple, easy to make, and is not too complicated for the novice. Gathers, a waistband, and a zipper placket can be difficult in a beginner's first skirt. This one eliminates all of them, and could be included with the torn projects in Chapter 2.

Make it of cotton — plain color, stripe, small check, or flowered print but not a plaid that has to be matched at the seams. Use broadcloth, chambray, poplin, gingham, or percale. Do not use fabric such as denim that is so bulky it does not gather easily.

After you have made this skirt, make the first blouse in Chapter 7 to go with it. The steps are as easy as they are with this skirt.

If your fabric is approximately 36 inches wide, use 3 strips for the skirt of the average-size girl. If it is approximately 45 inches wide, 2 strips will be enough.

Measure length of strip, clip selvage with scissors, and tear across fabric to opposite selvage. Cut through second selvage. If fabric will not tear, clip selvage, pull a thread across fabric to second selvage, and cut on puckered line (see p. 41).

Prepare your fabric to grain perfection as directed on page 43 or page 44. The fabric should form perfect square corners when folded in half; the lengthwise threads must run up and down, and the crosswise threads straight across at right angles.

Staystitch each skirt section ¼ inch from lower and upper edges. Staystitching is a row of permanent machine stitching with matching thread, and it will act like a rod on which to turn the fabric to finish it.

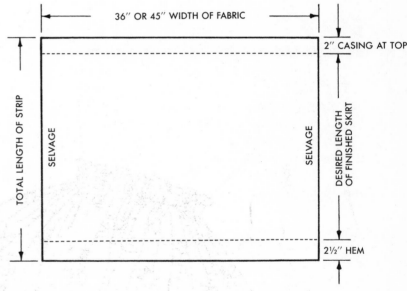

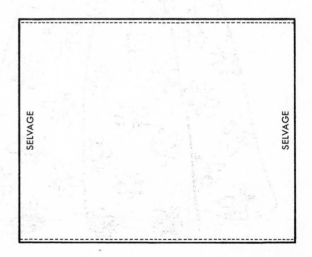

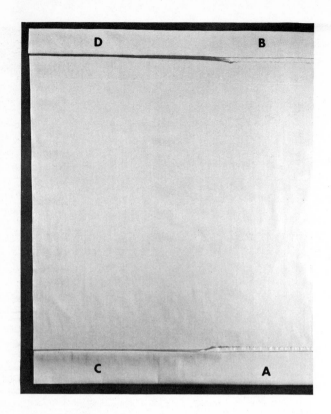

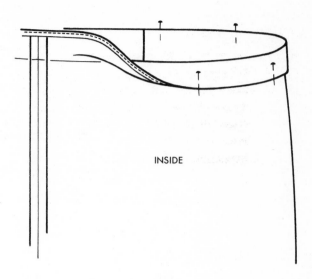

Then, using a hem gauge, turn up hem 2½ inches and press (A). If you are not certain of desired skirt length, wait and turn up the hem after remainder of skirt is completed.

Turn down casing 2 inches at upper edge and press (B). Next, turn under the raw edges on the staystitching and press (C and D).

Press seams along stitching line and then press open seams with point of iron. Press first with dry iron and then again with steam turned on. Press to restore hem and casing lines at seamlines.

Use a few pins to hold casing in place at top of skirt.

SKIRT SECTIONS

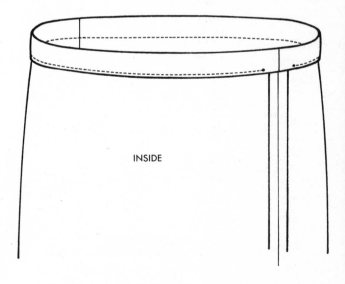

INSIDE

Open out the hem and the casing, and with right sides of skirt sections together, stitch selvages into seams ⅝ inch wide. At the machine, use the seam guide shown on page 7.

Stitch turned edge in place, leaving an opening for 2 inches at one seam. Fasten threads securely at beginning and end of stitching (p. 7). Remove pins before stitching over them. Through this opening a piece of elastic will be pulled later.

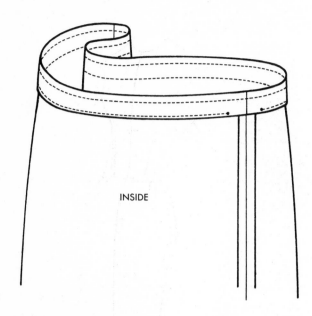

Now stitch completely around skirt ½ inch from top fold. This forms a heading and is worn above the waist.

To make the skirt fit at the waist, use ¾-inch elastic and measure your waist snugly but not tightly. Cut elastic desired length plus one inch extra for overlap to sew together. Use a large safety pin at one end of elastic to pull through opening in skirt. Pin a spool of thread at second end of elastic to prevent it from being lost as you pull.

Overlap ends of elastic for one-inch allowance. Pull the overlapping ends out of skirt and fasten them securely with machine stitching.

Push aside all gathers at opening in casing so it will lie very flat. Stitch it closed, being careful not to catch the elastic.

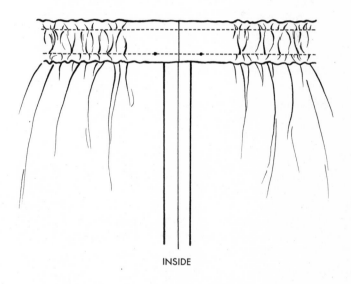

INSIDE

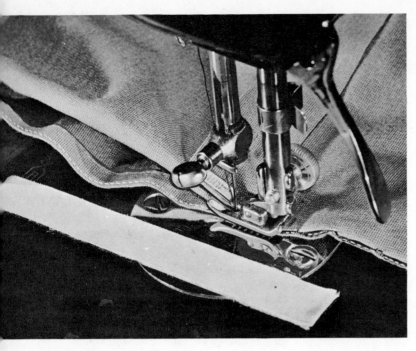

The hem may be completed in one of two ways.

To hem by machine, fold the hem under as shown. A few pins may be used at right angles to edge of hem. Take 4 or 5 stitches along the underside of the hem. Then, take one stitch into the fold of the hem. Continue around the entire hem.

If fabric has a firm, stabilized finish and will not ravel, raw edge does not need to be turned in at top of hem. Pink raw edge above staystitching. It may then be hemmed as shown in the photograph above, or by hand as shown here.

Clean-finish turned edge of hem by machine stitching near folded edge. Then, pin hem to skirt with pins at right angles to edge of hem. Fold back hem so that you can work from its underside.

Using a fine needle and a single thread, take a stitch through clean-finishing. Move ahead a scant ½ inch and take a tiny stitch in skirt fold. Continue around hem. On the inside, the threads will be concealed to protect them from catching and breaking in the iron or in jewelry and to prevent wear on the thread when the garment is worn. Hems should be inconspicuous on the outside of the garment, also.

Using a steam iron, press entire skirt, including the hem, on up and down grain of fabric. Have skirt right side up.

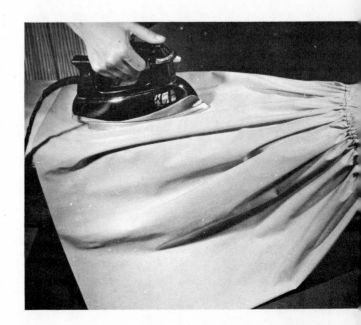

FOLD

SKIRT FRONT

WAISTBAND

SKIRT SIDE FRONT

FOLD

SKIRT BACK

SKIRT SIDE BACK

Beginner's second skirt

In making this second skirt, it will be the first time a commercial pattern is used. The style of the skirt is simple and requires very little fitting. If any change is necessary in cutting length or width of skirt, refer to Chapter 8. You will need to use the necessary information from Chapter 3 on buying your pattern correctly, from Chapter 4 on preparing your fabric for cutting, and from Chapter 5 on cutting and marking.

In making the skirt, however, you are not only learning to make one skirt, but are acquiring techniques for making many other skirts and parts of many other garments.

Select a fabric with enough firmness to hold the gores nicely. A limp fabric such as dimity does not have the self-supporting firmness for this style of skirt. Denim, cotton suiting, Indian head, or corduroy would be a good choice.

In carrying out our previous learnings about the unit method of construction, this skirt will have four units; namely, skirt front unit, skirt back unit, complete skirt unit and zipper, waistband unit.

In cutting the skirt, the notches on the pattern at the top of the skirt need not be cut, because in the Bishop method the skirt is sewn to the band according to measurements.

Before cutting waistband, see page 68 on waistband.

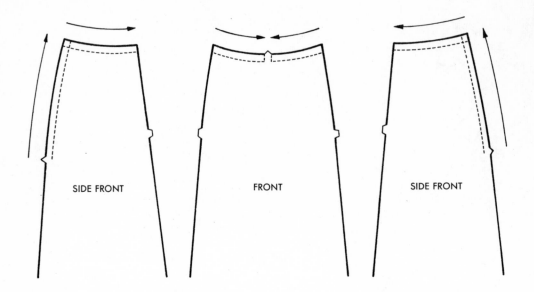

SIDE FRONT   FRONT   SIDE FRONT

The skirt front unit. Staystitch waistline edge and sides of skirt side front from notch up just outside the seamline and in direction shown with arrows on the sketch.

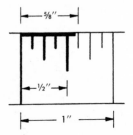

Staystitching is your very first step. It is a line of regulation machine stitching with matching thread, and is done through a single thickness of fabric. It is not lockstitched or secured at the ends. Sew from cut edge to cut edge; do not pivot on corners. It is placed just outside the seamline or ½ inch from the edge, unless another width is specified for a special purpose. Use the seam guide on machine as shown on page 7.

Staystitching is important because it holds the grain threads in position, and prevents off-grain edges from stretching or garment pieces from being pulled out of shape. Staystitching preserves the pattern line. The photograph below shows how much a shoulder that is not staystitched can stretch. Note the under one. The correct direction for staystitching is necessary in order to hold the grain in place. It is done in the direction threads lie down or point, and are not roughed up. Arrows on the sketches throughout the book indicate the correct direction and the places staystitching is needed.

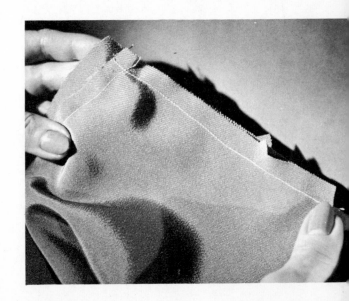

With right sides together, stitch skirt front to skirt side front from lower edge to upper edge. Repeat for second skirt side front. If the sides of the skirt are straight of grain, as in the previous gathered one, they can be stitched in either direction and will not stretch out of line.

However, when the sides are cut at a slant or off grain, they must be stitched from the bottom up to hold the line with perfection.

Further discussion of sewing seams on grain line will be found on page 165.

If fabric requires a seam finish, pink edges with pinking shears. If fabric does not lie smoothly, press seams first along the stitching line, and then press open with point of iron. They must be pressed on grain line from bottom up, exactly as they were stitched on grain line. Press first with dry iron and then with steam turned on.

For photographic clarity, the completed front unit is shown, but for real sewing efficiency, when this unit is completed, it may be laid aside until the back unit has also been completed, so that the two units may be pressed at the same time.

This completes the skirt front unit as far as possible at this stage.

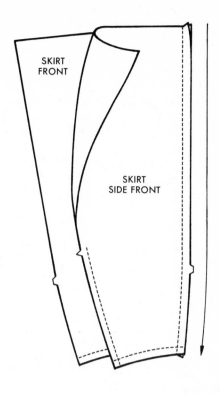

Making two skirts

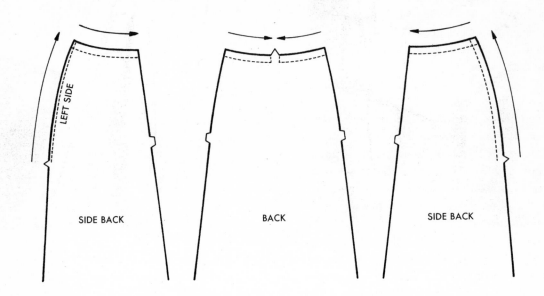

LEFT SIDE

SIDE BACK   BACK   SIDE BACK

The skirt back unit. Staystitch waistline edge and right side of skirt side back from notch up just outside seamline and in the direction shown with arrows on the sketch. The left side of skirt side back is staystitched ¼ inch from the edge from notch up, because the wider width of staystitching would show on the finished zipper placket.

Join skirt side backs to skirt back exactly as you learned to do with the front unit above.

If you know the correct finished length of your skirt, it will be easier to press up the hem in the skirt front unit and the skirt back unit before the side seams are sewn.

Unless you are certain of the fit of this skirt, you will want to machine-baste the seams and the band to the skirt for a fitting. Leave the left side open above the notch where the zipper will be used. To fit this skirt see page 93. To permanently stitch the seams and remove the machine-basting, see page 134.

The complete skirt unit and zipper. Stitch skirt front unit to skirt back unit at side seams on seamline from lower edge to upper edge.

Before you begin to stitch the left side seam, measure the placket opening for the exact length of the chain of the zipper with the tab turned up, plus the waist seam allowance. Mark the needed opening (A) from the bottom-stop of zipper (B). When sewing this seam, lockstitch the threads at A.

Then, change stitch regulator to basting stitch and baste-stitch opening for placket on seamline. Do not make a knot at top of skirt (C).

Pink and press open both side seams as you have just learned. For easy removal later, snip first baste-stitch at A.

Stitch from bottom to top of opening in every step. It is not necessary to remove the garment from the machine between steps.

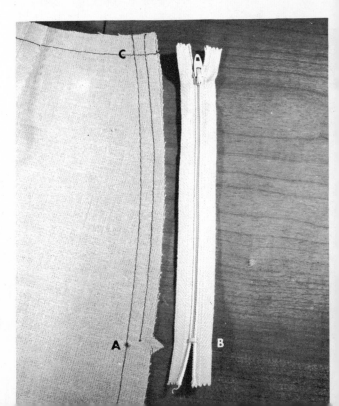

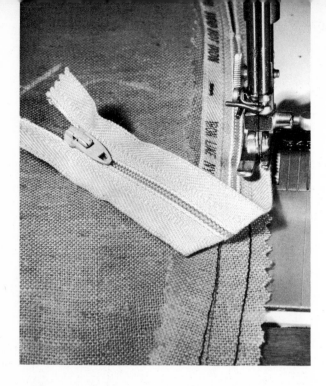

To sew zipper to back seam allowance, place the zipper face down full width of chain on back seam allowance and place the left edge of chain along seamline. Stitch with regular presser foot, left edge of foot against right edge of chain. Pause in stitching every 2 or 3 inches to check position of chain. Work by rolling chain forward. Always start and end your stitching at the very ends of the tape.

An alternate method for the first step of sewing zipper to back seam allowance is to open the zipper.

Use the zipper foot adjusted to right of needle. Place zipper face down with teeth along seamline, and baste-stitch along the heavy sewing guide line woven in tape. When stitching is completed, close zipper. (Photo: above, right)

Adjust zipper foot to left of needle. Turn zipper face up. Smooth out fabric close to zipper chain, making a narrow fold in back seam allowance. Using a permanent stitch, topstitch on fold beginning at bottom end of tape. (Photo: below, left)

Arrange garment with zipper face down over front seam allowance, forming a pleat at placket end. Draw toward front when pinning in place. Keep zipper tab up. Stitch across bottom and along zipper, close to chain, following woven-in stitch guideline. Tie threads by hand at seamline at lower edge of placket after drawing the upper thread to the underside. Make certain that the baste-stitching is removed from underside of back seam allowance.

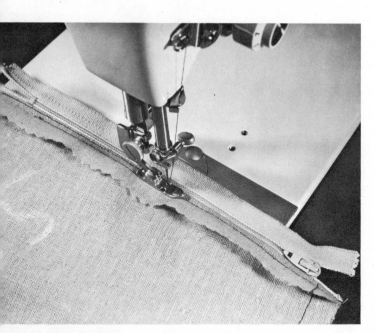

Making two skirts

A beginner may do a first zipper as shown here with the cotton skirt. However, as the student becomes more advanced, hand-picking one or both edges of the placket will be taught (see pp. 158 and 244). Hand-picking is softer in appearance, gives a fine quality look, and is more desirable in linens, silks, and woolens.

Keep zipper closed, and press finished placket on a press cushion on right side of garment. Use iron on crosswise or lengthwise grain of fabric. The chain of the zipper must be well concealed.

The waistband unit

Making the waistband. The waistband (to finish 1¼ inches wide) is made from a lengthwise torn strip 4½ inches wide and about 3 inches longer than individual waist measurements. With a crosswise-ribbed fabric such as bengaline, tear a crosswise strip for the band.

With an automatic hem gauge, make a lengthwise fold to the inside 1½ inches deep, and press. Stitch close to raw edge (B) of folded section. This forms the band's own interfacing.

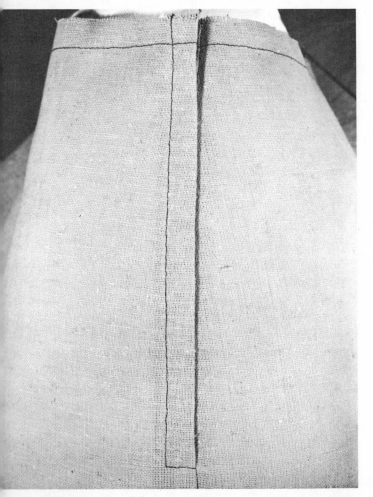

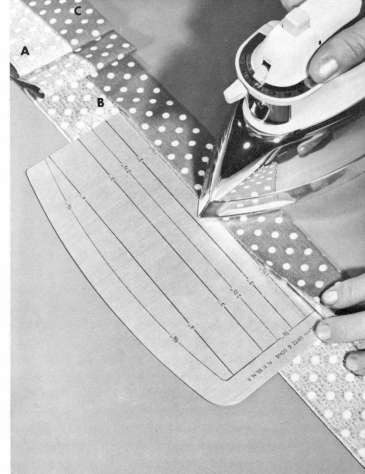

Attaching the waistband to the skirt. To attach the waistband to the skirt, place the right side of band (edge A) to the wrong side of skirt. Pin first at center front (R), allowing enough additional band to extend to front placket opening plus 1¼ inches extra (S).

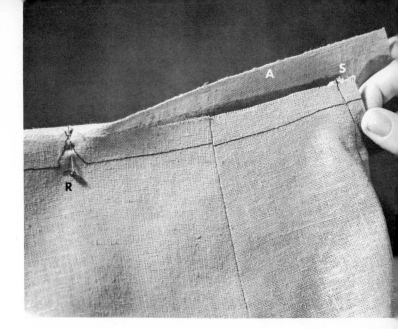

Measure one-half of waist measurement and allow that much band to center back of skirt (T). Pin in place. The size is accurate for center front to center back. For example, if the waist measures 28 inches, the amount of band from center front to center back would be 14 inches. (Teachers find it helpful to sew a tape measure to a sample band. The students can place this around their waistlines to determine size of band needed.)

The pattern manufacturer has given tolerance on a skirt to allow it to fall softly over normal body curves (usually one inch). Pin skirt to band at intervals, distributing ease evenly.

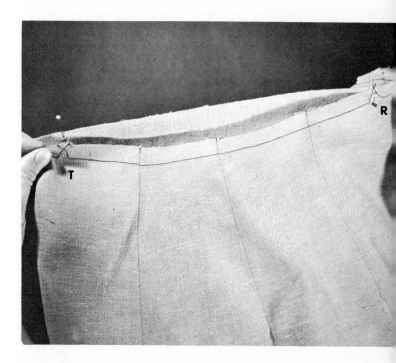

To measure the amount of band needed for the second half of the skirt back, fold loose end of the band carefully back to the side seam (marked with a pin U). With a pin, mark the exact seamline on the band (U). Place the pin on seamline of zipper edge of other half of skirt back (V). Distribute ease evenly and pin band to skirt at intervals. Repeat for second half of band front and skirt front.

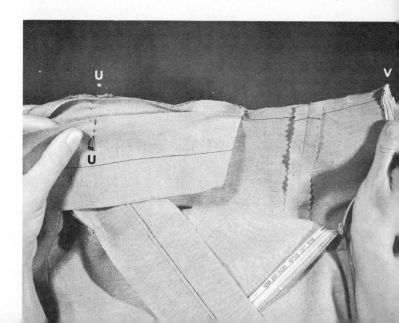

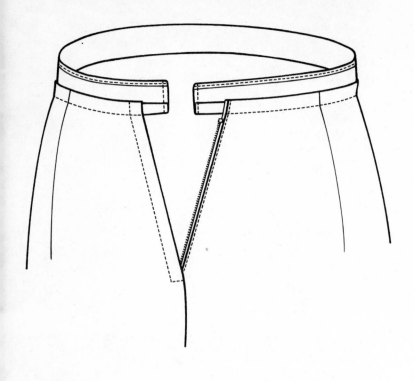

Finishing the waistband. With band side up, sew band to skirt. Ease will always stitch in more easily if it is on the underside. (If it is a gathered skirt, keep gathers up, and stitch through a row of gathers.) Press seam up. In some fabrics, trim seam to ¼ inch. To stitch ends of band, fold right sides together.

It is easier for the beginner to stitch front edge to extend one inch beyond the edge of the placket. It is more difficult to end a band with a point or parallel with the edge of the placket.

The back end is stitched to extend one inch or more. Stitch a ¼-inch seam with small stitches, and see page 152 for turning corners.

Turn band to outside of skirt and pin in place. The band is already turned in with perfection (edge C from p. 68) and is ready to topstitch on lower edge over skirt seamline. Final-press band.

Finish ends of band with two buttons and two machine buttonholes, or with two sew-on type, flat, heavy hooks and eyes.

When measuring for placement of hooks and eyes or buttons, overlap band so that zipper tapes will meet at top of placket.

The hem.   A flared skirt should not carry a hem deeper than 2 inches, so trim off any excess fabric. Staystitch raw edge ¼ inch from edge.

Using automatic hem gauge, turn up hem to correct finished length and press. Press a pleat where there is fullness at top of hem; it will show area where extra staystitching plus is needed in the next step to ease out fullness. Garments will hang with grain perfection at the lower edge and will not need to be marked with a hem marker. This has been an amazing step in the Bishop method, but the method is based on grain perfection.

The only exceptions that will require marking with a hem marker are garments from bias-cut or problem fabrics and garments with severe fitting problems. In these cases turn up hem and press on indications from hem marker. Mark and trim off excess fabric.

Staystitching plus is a technique whereby the fabric is manipulated so that the threads are crowded together to eliminate fullness at the top of the hem.

To do staystitching plus, press the index finger of the right hand very firmly against the back of the presser foot, so that the fabric piles up against the finger, while stitching for several inches with a permanent stitch. Release the fabric. Repeat until entire edge where ease is desired has been stitched.

Staystitching plus takes time to master. But it is a technique that can be used in other places that require easing, such as the back of some shoulder seams and the one side of the seam at the elbow. If tucks or darts were to be placed at the top of a full hem, the garment would lack a quality look.

Finish hem with one of two ways shown on page 62.

Finally, press the entire skirt (Chapter 9). In final-pressing, always press on lengthwise grain. Give special attention to the seamlines, band, and hem, and always keep zipper placket closed for pressing.

You may have a fabric that will hold creases very well in pressing. In that case, for a different look, you may prefer pressing the seams of your skirt in a fold on the right side. These folds are commonly called "milk carton folds."

BLOUSE
FRONT

FOLD

BLOUSE
BACK

FOLD

Chapter 7

Making two blouses and a jerkin

Blouse with cut-on facings

This blouse is easy to make. There are no facings to sew on, no collars or buttonholes to make, and no sleeves to set in. It requires little, if any, fitting and may be worn inside or outside the skirt. If you make this blouse to wear with the gathered skirt in Chapter 6 before you make the second skirt in that chapter, it will be your first experience with a commercial pattern. Then, you must follow directions in Chapter 3 on buying your pattern correctly, in Chapter 4 on preparing your cotton fabric for cutting, and in Chapter 5 on cutting and marking.

Make this blouse of cotton fabric. The same types that were suggested for the gathered skirt are good choices because they cut, sew, and press easily. If you are planning the blouse and skirt as a complete unit, the fabric should be chosen at the same time. The fabrics should harmonize in color, design, and type.

This blouse will have three units; namely, blouse front, blouse back, and complete blouse unit.

Blouse front unit. Staystitch ¼ inch from top edge and armhole edges. This stitching will act like a rod on which to turn the fabric to finish the edges. Staystitching is done with a permanent machine stitch and with matching thread.

On the inside of the fabric, turn under exactly on the ¼-inch staystitching line and stitch close to folded edge. This is called clean-finishing and is used to finish raw edges of facings in many fabrics.

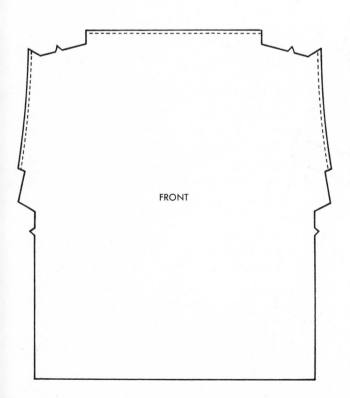

FRONT

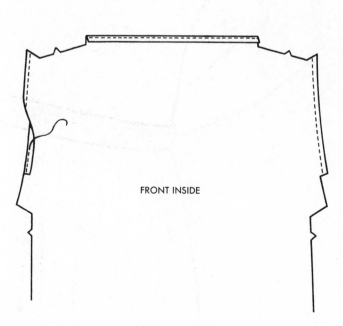

FRONT INSIDE

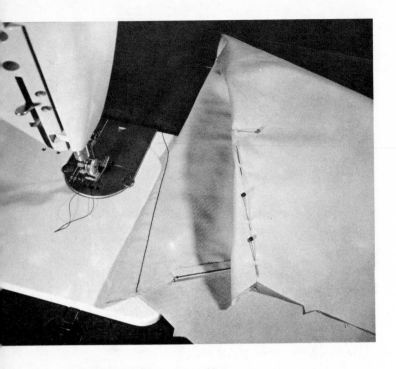

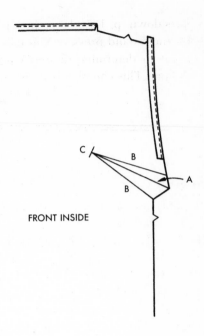

FRONT INSIDE

You learned on page 50 to mark three lines for a dart. The center one (A) is called the crease line or pickup line. The two outside lines (B and B) are the stitching lines. The crossline at the point of the dart is called the termination line (C) and the dart must end there.

On the inside of the blouse, crease on the center line (A). Begin pinning at point of dart. As you put in the pins, check that the two outside stitching lines (B and B) are together. Later on, when you sew with heavy, bulky, rolling fabrics, press fold of dart at pickup line to make it easier to stitch it.

Place dart-line to be stitched straight at machine, and fabric always to the left. Stitch from wide end of dart to the point. Remove pins as you go along; never stitch over them.

In many fabrics, it is helpful to change to very small stitches for last half inch of dart. At end of dart (termination line C) stitch beyond fabric for an inch, and leave tightly twisted threads one inch long when threads are cut away with scissors (see top, left photograph). A second technique for finishing the point of a dart is illustrated with this photograph. Release presser foot at point of dart to stitch back into the body of the dart about ½ inch; then lock-stitch and cut threads up to lockstitching.

Press darts down (p. 135). Using hem gauge, turn up hem 1½ inches and press, or you may prefer to try on blouse to determine desired length before turning up hem. This completes the blouse front at this stage.

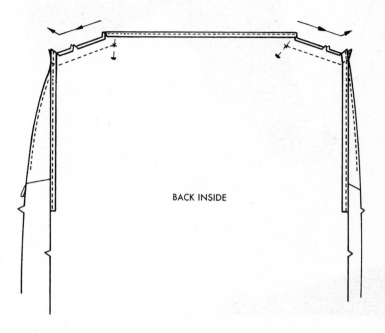

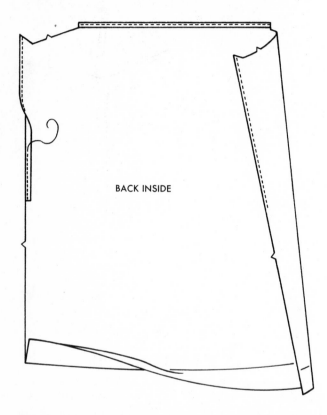

If your fabric will fray, pink the edges with pinking shears and press open in the same direction in which they were stitched.

At the neck edge and armhole edges, turn back on fold line of pattern and press with a hem gauge. Clip into seam at fold of sleeve hem so that the hem will lie flat.

Blouse back unit. Staystitch and clean-finish top edge and armhole edges of blouse back just as you did on blouse front. Turn up hem 1½ inches and press unless you are going to wait to try it on first.

Complete blouse unit. Find the crosses at the neckline on front and back of blouse. Put a pin through them so that they meet and hold together with perfection.

With right sides together, stitch blouse back to blouse front at shoulders in direction shown with arrows on sketch. You learned how to fasten threads at both ends on page 7. In stitching one of the shoulder seams, the back of the blouse will be on top; in stitching the second one, the front will be on top. It does not matter which one is on top, because the correct direction for stitching is most important. You will learn more about stitching on the grain of fabric in Chapter 10.

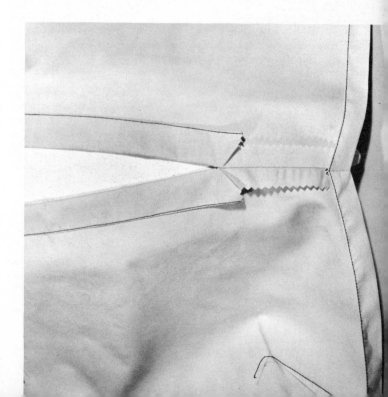

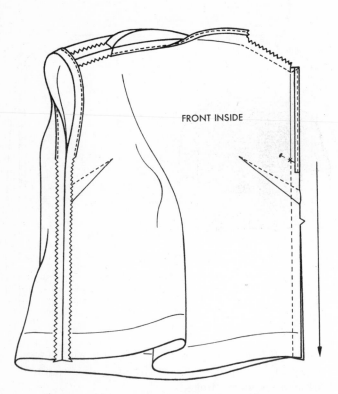

FRONT INSIDE

Open out pressed folds at armholes, match crosses with a pin the same as you did at the neckline, and stitch side seams from the top down. If your fabric will fray, pink the seams, and press open (p. 135).

Then, finish neckline and armholes with hand sewing as shown on page 62.

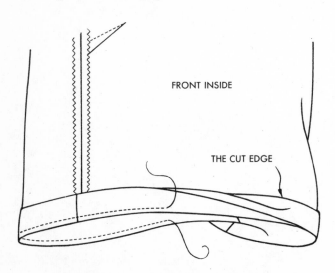

FRONT INSIDE

THE CUT EDGE

The hem may be finished in one of two ways. Staystitch raw edge ¼ inch from edge. Turn in on staystitching and hem by hand or at machine as shown on page 62.

If the blouse is to be worn outside the skirt, you may prefer this simulated band finish. The hem has already been turned up 1½ inches; exactly at cut edge of hem, turn up again 1½ inches as if making a double hem.

Press and stitch ¼ or ⅜ inch from lower edge fold. You will enclose the cut edge of the hem.

Turn hem down, and stitch ¼ or ⅜ inch from remaining fold.

To avoid any ripples from stitching in opposite directions, make both rows of stitching in the same direction (A and B). Follow this rule whenever you make two rows of parallel stitching, because the fabric will feed through the machine more evenly when sewing in the same direction.

The upper tuck is pressed up.

As a variant in completing the bottom of this blouse you may prefer a bloused version as shown on page 18. Leave one of the side seams open double the width of the hem; machine hem the seam allowance to finish the opening. Encase the raw edges at top of hem like sleeve on page 157. Insert a drawstring; or you may prefer to use elastic like the skirt on page 61, with or without a heading.

Even though you have pressed the details of construction during the making of the blouse, an overall final pressing from the right side will help to give it a final professional look. See Chapter 9 on pressing.

Always press on the lengthwise grain of the blouse. Care should be taken to retain the original shape of the darts and shoulder seams.

FRONT NECK
FACING

FOLD

BACK NECK
FACING

BLOUSE
BACK

POCKET

BLOUSE
FRONT

FOLD

Blouse with separate facings

Now that you have made a first blouse without separate facings or a neck opening, try to make one that utilizes these learnings. If your blouse has a collar, see the learnings on pages 150 to 154. This blouse pattern still does not have too many pieces for a beginner, and there are no set-in sleeves, buttonholes, or difficult details. A beginner should never attempt too much too soon.

However, these learnings are far more than a guide to help you make this blouse, for they teach you the techniques and a method of working whereby you can make any number of blouses and parts of many other garments.

A firm cotton fabric, such as broadcloth, poplin, gingham, or percale is still a good choice for a beginner and for this blouse.

This blouse is attractive with the gored skirt in Chapter 6. If you are going to make them to wear together, the fabrics should be chosen at the same time, if possible. They should either be the same for the blouse and skirt, or at least harmonize in color, design, and type.

This blouse will have four units; namely, blouse front and sleeve, blouse back and sleeve, neck facing and zipper, and complete blouse unit.

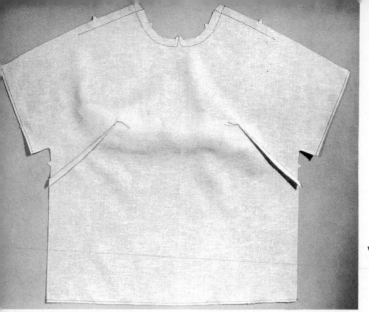

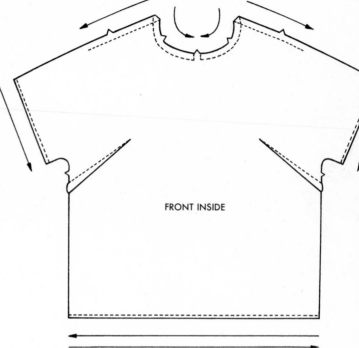

Blouse front and sleeve. Staystitch neckline and width of shoulders just outside the seamline and in direction shown with arrows on the sketch. Staystitching is explained on page 64.

Staystitch lower edge of blouse and sleeve edges ¼ inch from edge. This stitching will act like a rod on which to turn the fabric to finish the edges.

Stitch and press bust darts as shown on page 74.

This completes the blouse front unit at this stage.

You do not need to get up from the machine to press this unit until the back one is completed. For photographic clarity, it has been pressed to be shown here.

Blouse back and sleeve. Repeat staystitching at neckline, shoulders, sleeve edges, and lower edge of blouse exactly as you learned on blouse front.

Stitch shoulder darts and press toward center back.

FRONT INSIDE

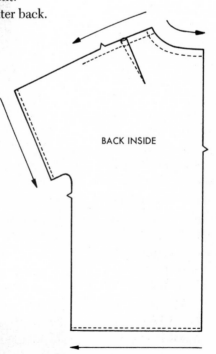

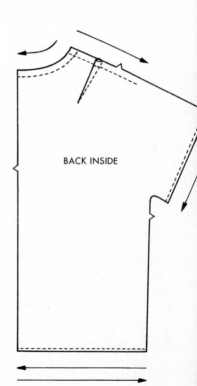

BACK INSIDE

BACK INSIDE

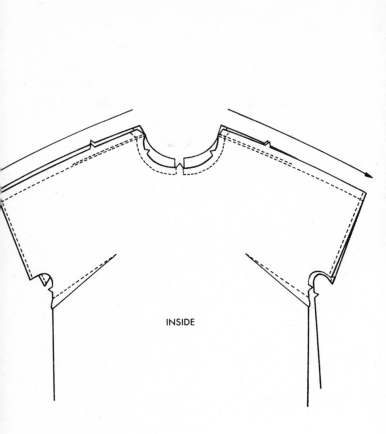

INSIDE

It is worth mentioning at this point that the techniques shown on a given garment are right for the suggested fabric for the garment. However, not all facings are clean-finished. With a garment made of heavy linen, wool, or corduroy, staystitch neck and outside edges as you have learned. Stitch both shoulder seams and press them open. Topstitch the seam on both sides of the seamline, then trim close to eliminate the bulk as shown at A. The untrimmed bulk can still be seen at B.

Entire blouse unit. With right sides together, stitch shoulder seams, easing back to front, in direction shown by arrows. In stitching one of the shoulder seams, the back of the blouse will be on top; in stitching the second one, the front will be on top. It does not matter which one is on top, because the correct direction for stitching is most important. You will learn more about sewing with the grain of fabric in Chapter 10.

If the fabric requires a seam finish, pink the edges with pinking shears and press open the seams on a cushion in the same direction in which they were stitched.

Neck facing and zipper unit. The neck facing will be put on the neckline in exactly the same way — with or without the collar. If your blouse pattern has a collar, see pages 150 to 154.

Staystitch the neck edges of the front and the back neck facings just outside the seamline in the same direction in which the blouse was staystitched. Next, staystitch outer curves ¼ inch from edge.

Stitch both shoulder seams. Trim to ¼ inch and press open. Clean-finish outer edges of facing. To clean-finish, turn under on ¼ inch staystitching line and stitch close to folded edge.

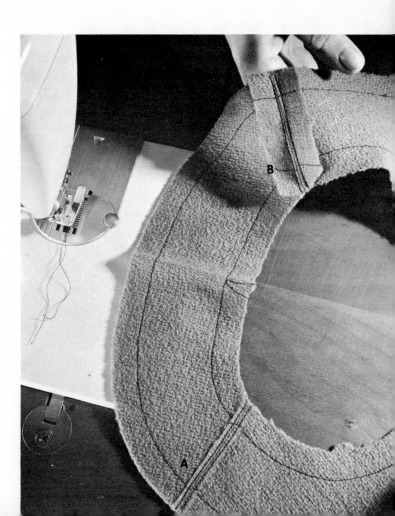

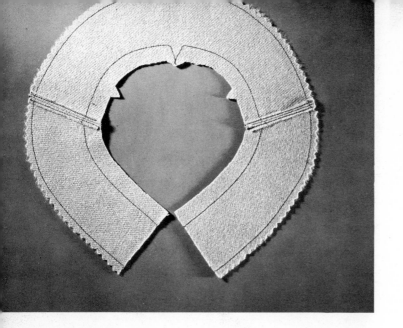

Pink the outer curved edges near the staystitching. The fabric would be too bulky to turn double as you do with clean-finishing. Always let the fabric guide you as to how to finish it.

Turn back facing 1⅛ inches on overlap side of placket and ½ inch on underlap side. Set creases with the iron. These edges are not unfolded again.

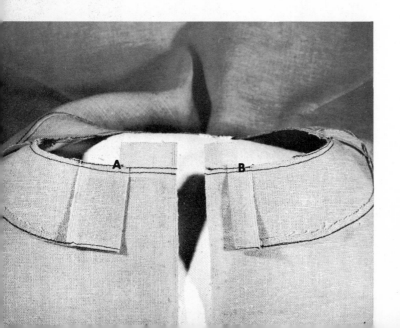

With right sides together, key facing to blouse at center front and shoulder seams. Verify that the facings lie ½ inch from one center back edge and 1⅛ inches from other one. With garment side up, stitch facing to neck edge of blouse. Trim seam to scant ¼ inch, beginning ¼ inch from folded edges of facing (A and B). Facing may be trimmed off all the way to the folded edge.

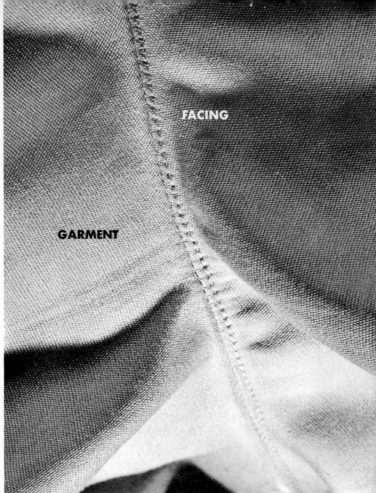

Beginning approximately one inch from folded edge of facings (A and B), understitch neck edge of facing. Press facings in place going all the way out to raw edges at center back. Press this curved line of the neck on a cushion.

Understitching is a row of machine stitching along the neck edge of the facing that catches the trimmed seams to the facing. It is of great help in keeping the facing in place.

Before you begin to stitch the center back seam, measure the placket opening for the exact length of the chain of the zipper with the tab turned up. Mark the needed opening (A) with a pin; determine its position from the bottom-stop of zipper (B).

Baste-stitch center back seam from top down to pin; change to regulation stitch before making lock-stitching at this point. Then, continue to permanently stitch seam for remainder of blouse.

The reason for stitching from the top down is that the two seams are folded down at C, and these two turned edges must be keyed with perfection.

If fabric requires a seam finish, pink and press open seam. This blouse had selvage at the center back.

Snip first baste-stitching at A for easy removal later.

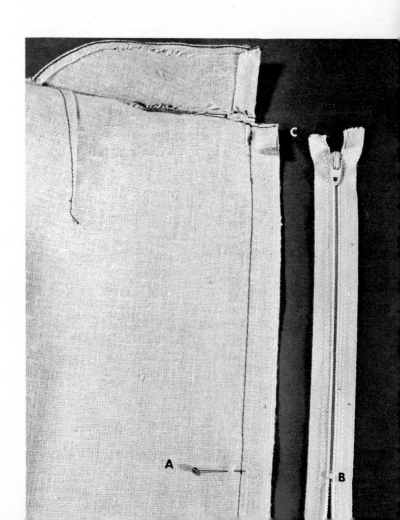

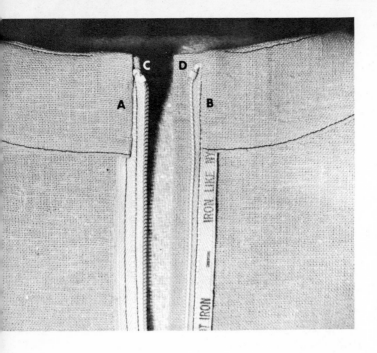

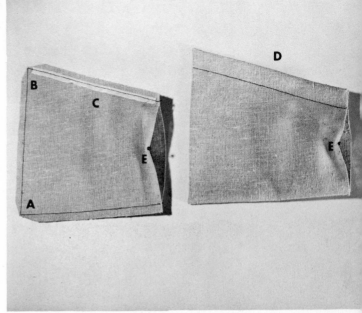

Insert zipper at neckline exactly as you learned with the skirt on pages 66-68. The lap is turned the same as it is in the skirt — as if the zipper in the side of the skirt were to be moved around to the center back.

Slant out raw edges of tape at top of zipper; tack these raw edges by hand. Bring facings into position over zipper tape and tack the facings by hand at A and B.

The only other places to which the outer edges are tacked are at the shoulder seam allowances. Blindstitching or tacking the entire edge of the facing to the garment gives it a non-professional look.

Close zipper for final-pressing. With some necklines and some fabrics, a hook and eye may be sewn at C and D or a snap may be used. Sew snap through one hole at C, and have remainder extend to fit under second half of snap sewn at D.

Many photographs have been taken of this fine technique because it has been a constant problem spot in clothing construction, especially with heavy fabric.

Complete blouse unit. With the hem gauge (p. 139), press up the hem at the lower edge 1½ inches, and while sleeves are still out flat, press one-inch hem in place on both sleeve edges. Then, clean-finish the lower edge and sleeve edges. To clean-finish, see page 73.

The edges of pocket were left open (E). Including the pocket in a seam whenever possible gives a smoother line.

When sewing two right sides together, use small stitches for ½ inch at either side of corners (A and B).

A piece of seam tape was cut in half and included in the seam at C to reinforce this very bias-cut edge. You can use this technique in many other places in sewing; it has also been shown on pages 83, 198, and 250. Sometimes the ½-inch tape is just folded in half, or ¼-inch cotton twill tape or satin ribbon is used.

In some fabrics, instead of trimming off corners at A and B, the technique shown on page 152 may be used to better advantage.

The pocket is turned right side out and pressed. Topstitching at D is completed before pocket is sewn on blouse.

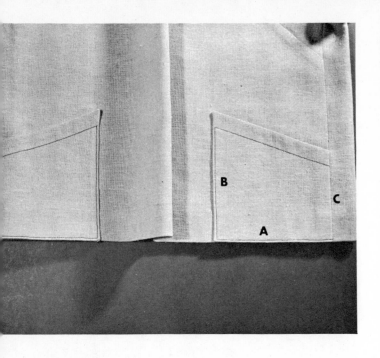

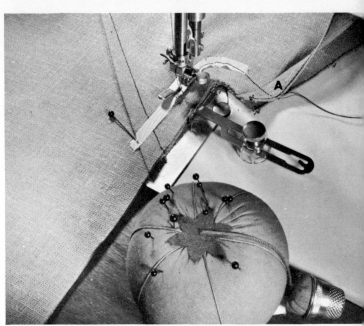

Topstitch pockets to blouse at B and A ¼ inch from edge to side of blouse at C before side seams are stitched and hem turned up. The pocket was placed to line up with the folded pressed edge of hem.

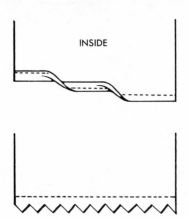

Open out pressed edge of sleeve hems shown at A. With right sides together, stitch side seams in the direction shown. To reinforce the underarm curve, cut a 2-inch long strip of seam binding, and then cut it in half lengthwise, or you may use ¼-inch cotton twill tape or satin ribbon. Pin the center of the strip over seamline at underarm curve. With a shortened stitch at machine, stitch on tape in regulation seam. This seam must also be clipped at intervals up to stitching line to release curve, and to have the seam lie properly. If fabric requires a seam finish, pink edges with pinking shears and press seams open.

Press to restore hemlines at seamlines and hem sleeves by hand as shown on page 62. Hem blouse as shown on page 62.

If the blouse is made to be worn inside the skirt, it may be finished in one of the two following ways: On lighter-weight fabrics, staystitch ¼ inch from lower edge. Turn in raw edge on staystitching line, turn up narrow hem, and stitch at machine along upper edge. On heavier fabrics, such as corduroy and jersey, or on firmly woven cottons, stitch ⅝ inch from cut edge and pink with pinking shears.

Final-press blouse. Follow the directions on pages 140-141. When you are top-pressing the neckline facings, do this lightly so that the edges of the facings will not mark the fabric and show on the outside. Keep zipper closed for pressing area over it.

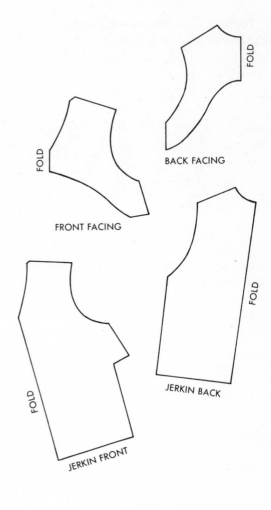

Jerkin with neck and armhole facing unit

The interesting learning on the jerkin is applying the facing all in one for the neckline and armholes. Instead of on a jerkin, you may wish to use this learning on a blouse, a shift dress, or a jumper, because this learning applies to all of these garments when sleeveless. See photograph on page 89. Even if a pattern does not give facings cut in one for neckline and armholes, you may cut it yourself from the garment pattern. Just make certain that facings are cut on the same grain as the garment is cut. This jerkin will have three units; namely, front, back, and neck and armhole facing.

Front unit. There is nothing new to learn about the staystitching, except that a V neckline, to follow grainline, is staystitched in the opposite direction of almost all other necklines. This time you also have armholes to do. Always staystitch armholes, whether you are going to finish them with a facing, with a binding, or with set-in sleeves. They would never have a quality look without staystitching.

A discussion of staystitching was given on page 64. Staystitch neckline, shoulders, and armholes in direction shown just outside seamline, and at lower edge, ¼ inch from edge.

Then, stitch the darts (p. 74) and press down. A wide dart, as this jerkin has, will lie and press better if part of it is pinked away and left as a ½-inch seam. Using hem gauge, turn up hem 1½ inches and press (p. 139).

Back unit. Except for the neckline being staystitched in the opposite direction from the front unit, the back unit is prepared exactly as the front.

The hem is pressed up 1½ inches.

This completes the front and back units at this stage.

Neck and armhole facing unit. Staystitch the front and back facings just outside seamline along neck, shoulder, and armhole edges in the directions shown. Staystitch ¼ inch from lower edges. Clean-finish the lower edges of the facings. To clean-finish, turn under on ¼ inch staystitching line and stitch close to the folded edge.

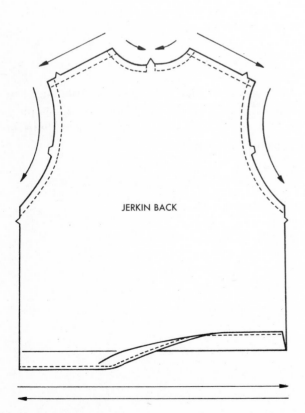

JERKIN BACK

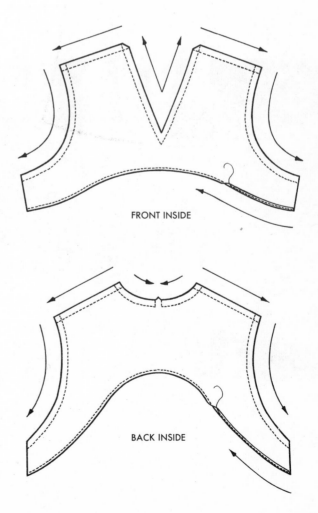

FRONT INSIDE

BACK INSIDE

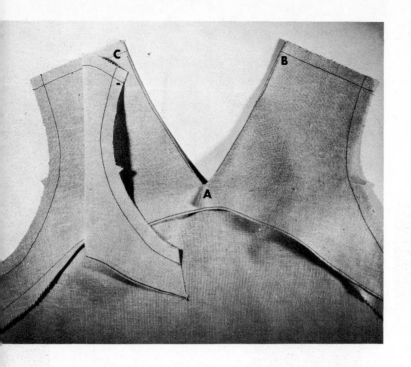

With right sides together, and garment side up, stitch the front facing to the front of jerkin at the neckline. Use small stitches for ½ inch at either side of A. Trim seam to ⅛ inch, and down to stitching at point (A). Understitch as explained on page 81, beginning one inch from shoulder edge (B and C) and ending ½ inch from point (A). Repeat for neckline of jerkin back.

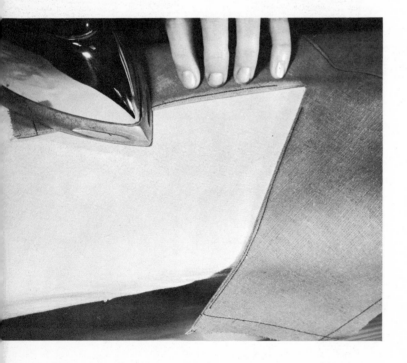

To press any edge that has understitching, first shape edge with fingers and then hold edge in place with fingers of left hand. Press on underside to set edge with perfection.

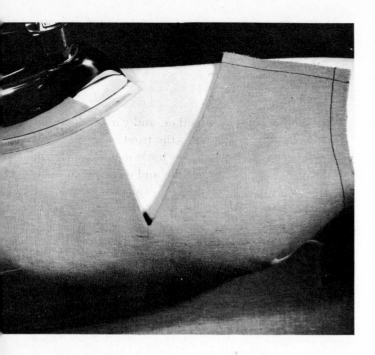

Next, turn to topside to final-press facing and edge.

Turn facings and jerkin inside out, right sides together, and stitch facings to armholes. Baste-stitch for approximately 3 inches down (A to B); change length of stitch to a permanent one; lockstitch the threads, and sew to side of jerkin. Using an edge presser, press open baste-stitched area of armholes (A to B), and remove baste-stitching. Below this opening, trim armhole seam to ⅛ inch. If you sew on the facing with a small stitch, you can trim closely, and clipping curves to stitching line will not be necessary. Understitch this lower part of armhole, beginning one inch from the side edge. Press as directed with neckline facing.

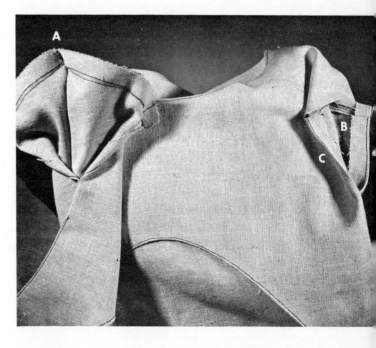

To join front and back of garment, closing shoulder seams will now be a continuous operation that includes the garment and facings (A). On an edge presser, press the seam open and trim to ¼ inch (B). Slipstitch the pressed armhole edges of the jerkin and facings (C), or they may be done on the machine from the underside.

This last step may be understitched by hand with a short running stitch. See photographs on pages 88-89.

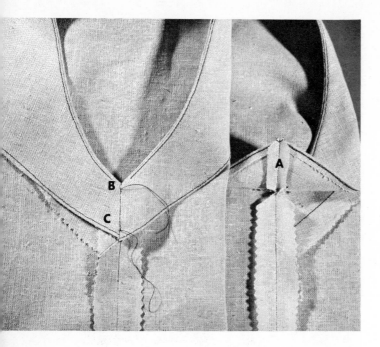

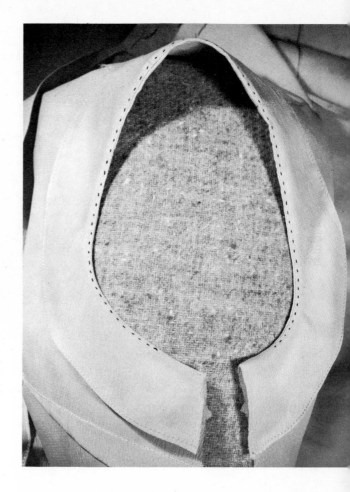

Stitch facings and side seams together from top down. If the fabric requires a seam finish, pink the edges, and press open. Trim facing seam (A) to ¼ inch. Turn facings to inside and anchor in place by stitching at machine or by hand through well of seamline of jerkin with jerkin turned up. Begin stitching ¼ inch from edge (B) and end stitching ¼ inch from edge (C).

To complete jerkin, restore hemline at seamline in pressing, and complete hem in one of two ways shown on page 62.

Final-press jerkin as discussed on pages 140-141.

If the style of the garment has a facing only at the armhole, the facing is applied and understitched, beginning and ending one inch from the edge, before side seams of blouse and facing are sewn, as you have just learned.

Note that in this dacron blouse the understitching was done with a small running stitch by hand. In softer fabrics hand understitching may be more desirable. In addition, for a softer finish in this fabric, the staystitching was made ⅜ inch from the edge, so that it could be trimmed off, when seam is trimmed down.

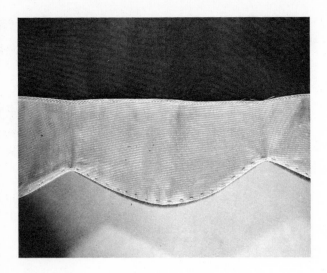

With many areas that are difficult to reach with the sewing machine, hand understitching may also be desirable. It was used with the scallops on the bottom of this overblouse.

It is worth mentioning that the facings of this velveteen overblouse were made of rayon twill, so that the velveteen blouse would hang freely over the velveteen skirt. A velveteen facing would have had a tendency to cling to the velveteen skirt.

At the same time you learned to make a jerkin, you learned every step of making this shift (or it could be a jumper) shown in the photograph above, right.

This shift has a long zipper in the back. Put that in the same way as on the second blouse, pages 80 to 82.

There are many patterns you could choose that would be as simple to make as these two blouses and jerkin, and still need just the basic learnings presented here.

If you would like to make a reversible jerkin or vest, follow the directions in Chapter 5, *Fashion Sewing by the Bishop Method.*

Chapter 8

The fine art of fitting your clothes

When you are first learning to sew, it is ideal to begin with several garments that require little or no fitting, until you have learned some basic principles of sewing, and have developed some skills. Up until now, in making some torn projects and several blouses and skirts, the only parts of this chapter on fitting you may have needed are lengthening and shortening a skirt, adjusting it at the hipline or waistline, or changing a bust dart.

Now, you are ready for a harder project, but do not try to go into all of the chapter yet. Begin with the more simple learnings, perhaps just those that may apply to you. It is just as important in fitting as it is in sewing not to attempt too much too soon.

You have been learning about the grain of the fabric on your first torn projects, in preparing fabrics for cutting, and in cutting, sewing, and pressing. See how easy it will be to apply this *magic key* in the art of sewing to *fitting magic with key grain lines*! The section on pages 94-95 is the most important part of this chapter. Once you begin to see this, you will be able to solve any fitting problem that ever comes your way. After you have studied these fitting techniques you should have *the feeling for what is right*!

This chapter discusses some standards for a well-fitted garment, some rules to follow when you are going to try on a garment, and the concept of using grain lines in fitting.

Standards for a perfect-fitting garment

Statistics show that 20 million out of 62 million women cannot wear garments off the racks in stores, because they do not fit. Yet, you can have a perfect fit when you sew. Your goal will be to meet the following standards for a perfect-fitting garment:

1. The garment looks smart and feels comfortable. No matter what the fitting problems are, the garment is in perfect balance in relation to the individual figure. It fits smoothly without wrinkles, strain, or bulges, and without sagging. It hangs gracefully and smoothly from the shoulders for the bodice, and from the waistline for the skirt. The garment should never have to be pulled into place.

2. The shoulder seam falls exactly on top of the shoulder, one inch behind the lobe of the ear.

3. The neckline lies smoothly at the base or curve of the neck, where the neck joins the body. It should not ride up.

4. The garment should hit the neckline and shoulders at the same time.

5. The front armhole line should fall in a straight line from the top of the shoulder to the front notch underarm. In a traditional set-in sleeve, the front armhole line should not drop onto the arm.

6. The armhole should fall one inch below the armpit.

7. The arm does not touch the sleeve, or seemingly push into the line of the fabric at any area.

8. The elbow dart falls at the bend of the elbow.

9. The cuffline or hemline of a long sleeve should fall at a point where the hand ends and the wrist begins. (In order to determine the correct length of a long sleeve, the elbow should be bent at a right angle.)

10. On a fitted garment, one buttonhole should always fall at the natural waistline. One should also be in line with the crown of the bust.

11. The waistline seam falls at the natural waistline, which is the smallest part of the figure, or where the body creases when you bend sideways. (An exception to this standard would be for the per-

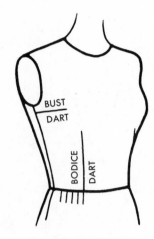

2. Poor features in the figure should be concealed rather than revealed. Accept your good points and play down your poor ones.

3. In analyzing a garment for a perfect fit, and later in fitting, start at the shoulders and work down. The fit of the upper part affects the rest.

4. To get a good fit at the neckline, tie a string around your neckline to simulate a perfect jewel neckline for the shape and length of your neck. A wide or low neckline should be cut to conceal a bony structure or to reveal an attractive one.

5. If the garment has a lapel, the top buttonhole should be analyzed for placement in relation to length of neck, depth of desired opening, etc. Determine carefully the number of buttonholes, the space between them, and the size of the buttons in relation to the proportions of the figure.

6. Before deciding on the length of the jacket or sleeve hems on a suit or overblouse, the hem on the skirt should be turned up.

7. For the figure that has a roll above the waistline or that has a large rib cage, the use of tucks, dart tucks, or gathers would be preferred at the waistline to the use of bodice darts there.

8. On the skirt front, darts or tucks (1, 2, or 3 on each side) should be placed where there is fullness in the figure. This often varies from the pattern. Frequently, a round figure looks best with as many as six ⅛-inch tucks (see sketch above, left) stitched on the outside, inside, or hand-picked on the outside. A staystitch plus line (p. 71) will help a full figure above or below the waistline. Never be hesitant about gathers.

Fine fitting is one of the main differences between poor and good dressmaking. The success of any garment should always be judged by how it looks on the wearer.

The ability to recognize a well-fitted garment is necessary not only in sewing one, but also in choosing ready-made clothes successfully.

These general standards for a perfect-fitting garment remain the same indefinitely, regardless of fashion changes, because they are based on the structural lines of the human figure. Fashion may influence some variation, but the basic characteristics remain the same.

son with a short waist or large bust or large hips where appearance would be improved if the waistline were lowered an inch or two.)

12. The bodice length is correct and the waistline seam fits snugly.

13. Front bodice and bust darts stop short of the crown of the bust, but are in line with it.

14. Back hip darts stop short of the fullest part of the hips. Darts always give room, so the size and number of them must be controlled by the size of the hips.

15. The side seam hangs perfectly straight from armhole seam to hemline. This vertical line is also known as the plumb line.

16. The skirt should be the most flattering length for your figure within the fashion range.

In addition to the aforementioned standards for a perfect-fitting garment, consider the following:

1. A perfect fit is not possible unless you learn:
   a. How to choose right size and type of pattern for the individual (Chapter 3);
   b. What is the right style for the figure and its proportions (Chapter 2, *Fashion Sewing by the Bishop Method*);
   c. What are the proper foundations for your figure and style of garment;
   d. Correct cutting, sewing, and pressing techniques;
   e. About proper underlinings.

Various ways to alter patterns

As you learned in Chapter 3, you will take your measurements and determine the correct size and type pattern to buy. When you have purchased your pattern, you can compare your bust, waist, hip, length of bodice, and length of skirt measurements to those given for your size on the pattern size chart. If you vary from the chart, you will have to make basic changes in cutting to allow for these variances.

Ways to proceed with altering patterns for a perfect fit may vary with experience.

For the beginner. When you are learning to sew and are making blouses and skirts as you have just learned, or the shirtwaist dress to follow in Chapter 10, you can make the easy alterations listed below from your pattern directly on your fabric in cutting after comparing your measurements to those of the pattern. See the photographs on pages 128 and 129.

1. Length of bodice, page 96;
2. Long waisted, page 96;
3. Short waisted, page 97;
4. Large bust, page 106;
5. Large waistline, page 110;
6. Length of skirt, page 118;
7. Large hips, page 118.

These are all that a beginner needs.

For the experienced seamstress. An experienced seamstress, having but minor alterations for the size pattern, can always make them, as recommended above, right from the pattern when the garment is cut out. The garment then can still be tried on for any minor changes, such as relocating darts or tucks. Many other types of alterations, besides those listed above, are described in the section from page 96 to page 127.

Making a fitting shell. If you have some severe fitting problems, you can master what needs to be done for your figure by making a fitting shell (a basic type garment) from percale or broadcloth. A woven check is a good choice, because the straight lines of the check help you to see grain problems and how to correct them (p. 94). Unbleached muslin is not recommended for the basic dress, because it does not conform to the lines of the body and does not have the same draping quality as fabric used in making clothing. There is no point in beginning the shell, unless you at least attempt to cut the above

seven alterations into it before you first try it on. If you don't, you may not even be able to get it over large hips, for example, to begin to check other needed skirt alterations. Then, you will baste-stitch the shell together and observe the changes needed to make it fit your figure perfectly.

When it has been fitted to perfection, do not take it apart and lay it on future patterns to determine alterations needed. The lines of the two patterns may not be alike at all. Instead, make special notes in your sewing notebook of the necessary cutting-to-fit alterations; these alterations will then be made in each new tissue pattern that is purchased to make a garment. Thereafter, you will apply the same adjustments to any dress, and to suits and coats as well.

It is worth mentioning that these alterations would usually apply to any pattern you buy of the same type but not of another type. For example, if your shell is a Misses' 12, the alterations will apply to any 12 Misses' pattern, but not to a 12 Teen or 12½ Half-size.

The fitting shell helps you to know your own figure, and serves as a logical guide for all of your fitting. It is also a practical way to learn about the key grain lines discussed on pages 94-95. A day spent on a fitting shell is a day well spent, and once you learn what is needed for your figure, you are ready for success in fitting.

Master patterns of pellon. If you make a shell from whatever basic lines or garments you wear frequently, you could cut pellon master patterns for them. Garments made from such a master pattern would fit you perfectly, and could be made up without trying on the garment (see photograph, p. 130). Master patterns that seamstresses re-use constantly are:

1. For straight skirt (see photograph, p. 130);
2. For any other becoming skirt line, such as a six gore skirt;
3. For a bodice top with various necklines (see photograph, p. 130);
4. For a bodice top with cut-on sleeves;
5. For shorts or slacks;
6. For a sheath or shift dress.

The master pattern for the bodice top could be made sleeveless or with sleeves. A master sleeve pattern could also be made, in various sleeve lengths. The master pattern for the bodice top with cut-on sleeves could be made with various tested necklines.

Pretesting fit and style. A pretest of a pattern may be made for style as well as for fit. It can even be made from old bed sheets. Tracing wheel markings for center fronts and buttonholes can be made on the outside. You can eliminate hems in cutting. Omit facings and the top collar. If you are pretesting a coat, you may prefer to cut it from corduroy, denim, or similar material. Later it may be completed as a short robe.

This is helpful when you begin to make coats, etc., and are cutting into expensive fabric. You can see very quickly if the style is right for you. Study the pretest for line, proportion, fullness, and style details. No matter how attractive the design may be, it must be right for you.

If you are going to use stripes, plaids, or unusual designs, you may roughly simulate them with pencil on some areas of the pretest to observe the directional flow of the design. It will be an invaluable aid in placing the pattern on the fabric later, and will save you disappointment if you find on the pretest that the pattern is not a good choice for the design of the fabric.

With the underlinings in today's fashions, especially in tailoring, pretesting a pattern makes it a pleasure to put the garment together permanently with underlining.

Trying on a garment, shell, or pretest for a fitting

1. Make certain that you are wearing the proper foundations for your figure and style of garment. Remember there is nothing worse than shapeless undergarments.

2. The band is always baste-stitched on a skirt before it is fitted. If you are completing your skirt with bias binding (p. 244), then baste-stitch seam tape at the waistline (p. 146) before the skirt is fitted.

3. The bodice and skirt of a dress are always baste-stitched at the waistline with tape in the seam, before a dress is fitted.

4. In stitching a garment together for a fitting, part of it can be permanently stitched, as are the seams in a gathered skirt; but the areas where some alterations may be expected are always baste-stitched, as are bust darts and bodice darts or tucks.

5. Sleeves are always baste-stitched into armholes for a fitting. Unless you have shoulder problems, one sleeve may be enough to try. Collars, facings, cuffs, pockets, or any other details are not put on the garment until the fitting is completed. They may be pinned on, however, to analyze the style lines for the individual figure.

6. Center lines are marked, overlapped, and pinned to meet for a try-on. Buttonholes are marked to check their placement and their number in relation to the figure.

7. The placket opening is pinned together exactly on the seamline.

8. A staystitch that is cut away in a fitting alteration should be replaced immediately.

9. Start at the shoulders and work down to analyze the garment. Then ask yourself:

First, are the style lines within the pattern right for you and for the fabric? Remember that you do

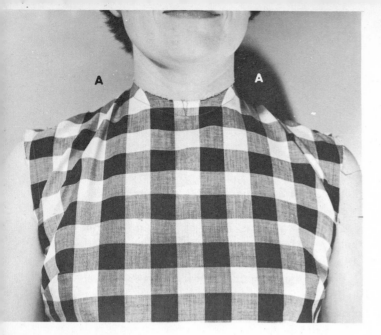

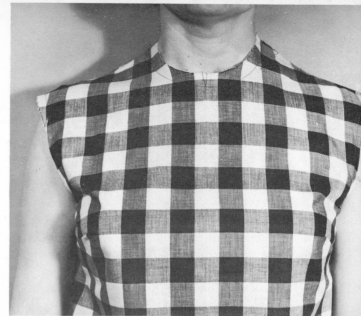

not have to be a slave to a pattern. Individualize it for you and your fabric. If bodice darts are called for but are not becoming to the figure or in the fabric, make tucks. If pocket placement does not give a good proportion to your figure, try to find the correct placement for your figure.

Second, does it meet the standards for a perfect-fitting garment (see pp. 90-91) which are your goals in fitting?

Successful fitting with the magic key grain lines

This section is the most important part of the entire chapter. Everything up to this point has been in preparation for this section. Everything from here on is based upon it.

Key grain lines are lines that actually relate from pattern to fabric to body. For a garment to be fitted perfectly, both the lengthwise and crosswise grain of the fabric must be in correct relation to the structural lines of the body. On every garment, there are grain lines which may be called key grain lines, because they indicate whether or not the garment is fitted perfectly. These lines are the basis for both judging the fit of a garment and correcting it. They are the key to fit, and they are marked on basic shell patterns you buy from the pattern companies. Yet, they are imaginary lines on everything else you make. You can train your eye to see them on any fabric, even though they are not actually marked. A woven, checked fabric was suggested for a basic shell on page 92, because it has true lengthwise and crosswise grain lines showing right on it (see photo).

Now, study the illustrations about them. It won't take you long to be able to see through every alteration in relation to grain. For example, if the number one grain on the front bodice pulls up and there are

wrinkles pulling up (number 5, p. 98), it will tell you to allow fabric on the shoulders, so the grain can come down. If you look where the point of the wrinkle is headed (A in photograph), you can find the source of trouble. The grain thread will tell you every time. Remember if there is a pull going up, the grain must come down; if there is a downward pull, the grain must go up.

A pattern is perfect in line when it is manufactured, and that perfection must be retained. The pattern must be made grain perfect now on the individual figure. A standard, perfect figure is practically a myth; nearly everyone needs some clothing alterations for a perfect fit.

Some other styles of garments are popular besides the ones the sketches represent. The sketches presented are basic, and the corrections and use of key grain lines remain the same on any style of garment.

This chapter presents 47 alterations. Some of them may not be the combination of alterations that you need, but you will find your problems as you study the group, and can combine the alterations.

You can readily see that the pattern has not been slashed, for you can accomplish the same thing without it. Moreover, you will be retaining grain perfection, and you will not have to be working with a slashed tissue (see p. 121). Another thing you will note is that an even tuck is always used for shortening an area (see photograph, p. 128). You may say that you do not need to take out fabric all across the back, for example. However, to retain grain perfection, you must add extra to the edge where you did not want to shorten with the even tuck.

These same key grain lines are used in Chapter 9, *Fashion Sewing by the Bishop Method*, to alter women's slacks and shorts, and in Chapter 3 of that book on altering ready-to-wear.

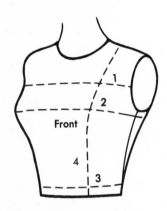

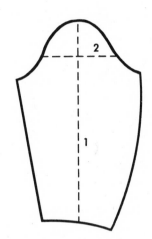

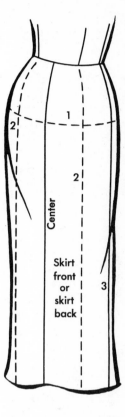

Bodice front

On the bodice front, there are 4 key grain lines:

1 Chest: about 4½ inches below the shoulder line on the crosswise grain.
2 Bust: across the crown of the bust on the crosswise grain.
3 Waist: about 1½ inches above the waistline on the crosswise grain.
4 Lengthwise key grain line: about halfway between the center front and side seam, from shoulder line to waistline, over the crown of the bust on the lengthwise grain.

Bodice back

On the bodice back, there are 4 key grain lines:

1 Shoulder: about 4½ inches below the shoulder line on crosswise grain.
2 Underarm: about 1½ inches below the armhole, across the shoulder blades and on crosswise grain. This corresponds with the bust key line in bodice front.
3 Waist: about 1½ inches above the waistline on crosswise grain.
4 Lengthwise key grain line: about halfway between center back and side seam, from the center of the shoulder line to the waistline on lengthwise grain.

Sleeve

In the sleeve, there are 2 key grain lines:

1 Halfway mark: from shoulder line to side of hand at wrist bone on lengthwise grain.
2 Sleeve cap: straight across sleeve cap at right angles to the halfway mark, about 3 inches below the shoulder line on crosswise grain.

Skirt

In the skirt, there are 3 key grain lines:

1 Hipline: about 7 inches below the waistline, following the curve of the waistline. It is parallel to the floor but not necessarily on grain.
2 Halfway mark: halfway between the center line and side seam on the lengthwise grain.
3 Side seamline: must hang straight up and down. This is not on fabric grain.

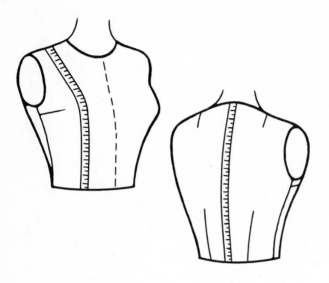

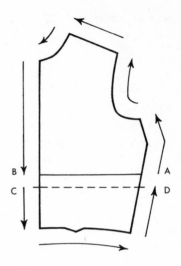

CUTTING-TO-FIT ALTERATIONS ON PATTERNS

Alterations on bodice

Many of these cannot be separated from sleeves (see pp. 113-117).

1. Measuring length of bodice

If the person for whom the garment is being made is long-waisted or short-waisted in the front or back, or both places, measure the length of the individual, and check the pattern at the same place and in the same way. On the pattern, one must allow for seam allowance, for any extra length desired for the bodice on a fuller figure that best wears a bloused bodice, and for soft fabric like voile that suggests a soft-looking bodice. On a fitted bodice, there is a standard ¼ to ⅜-inch ease on the back waist length. A blouson style will have more length than a fitted bodice, and this is known as design ease. Therefore, these given amounts of ease are not used for needed extra length.

The length of the front is measured from the middle of the shoulder seam, over the crown of the bust, to the middle of half the front at the waistline.

The length of the back is measured from a bone at the base of the neck straight down to the center of the back waistline. However, you may prefer to measure the back length exactly as shown for front length, depending upon the shoulders.

If you need to lengthen or shorten a pattern piece, the alteration must be made where it will do the most good. For instance, if length is needed in the bodice front, is it needed from the bustline up or from the bustline down? If needed to shorten the bodice back, should it be like the correction shown under number 11 or under number 12 on pages 103-104.

2. Figure problem: long-waisted

Correction

This is usually needed on both front and back bodice. If needed on back only, see number 13, page 105; if needed on front only, see page 107.

Do not slash the pattern to add extra length. There are many disadvantages to doing that. Simply pin the pattern to the fabric on true grain; cut from A to B (at the line given on pattern for lengthening or shortening). Then, chalkmark or place a pin at C and D according to measure of extra length needed. Move A and B line on pattern down to C and D, and complete cutting from B around to A. This is the same technique generally used in the Bishop method any time extra length is needed. In this way you are always using your pattern outline to make alterations to perfection.

3. Figure problem: short-waisted

You may need to shorten the bodice front as well as the back as shown with number 11, page 103 or with number 12, page 104. No one book could ever cover all the problems and solutions that would come up for all figures. If you can be given a feeling or perception for correct fit and for applying it by working with true grain, you can then begin to see what your own figure really is and what it needs for a perfect fit.

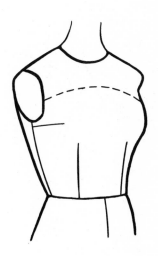

4. Figure problem: narrow sloping shoulders

Fitting problem: Back and front shoulder key grain lines drop as they approach the armholes. Front shoulder line is too long. For today's fashion the armhole line is straight down, as shown in the sketch.

Correction

A. Cut front shoulder line shorter at armhole, tapering to nothing at notch or underarm, depending upon amount cut away.

B. Instead of following the procedure in A, a seam or dart at the shoulder can be taken in deeper, if there is one on the garment. If there is no dart, one may be added.

C. Increase dart in back shoulder line (or add dart) the same amount as cut off front. Back shoulder line can also be eased to front. There should be ⅜ of an inch given on patterns for ease to front shoulder. Some figures with a full back usually need more. Use staystitching plus first (p. 71) to hold in the fullness.

If you cut off the extra width at the back armhole, the garment cannot have a quality look, because the sleeve will have no fullness at the top, and cannot hang on grain.

D. Recut back shoulder line using pattern piece.

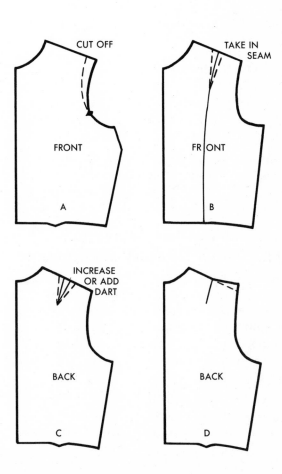

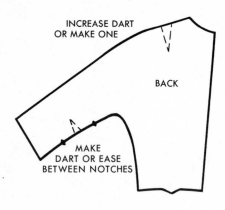

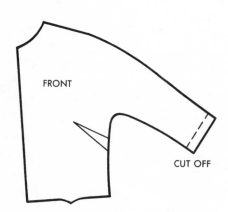

Correction for sleeve and bodice cut in one

Stitch a dart in back shoulder line (or increase dart if one is there, or make two on some figures).

To shorten front: Cut the front sleeve section shorter at lower edge by the same amount as was taken in by the shoulder dart.

To stitch shoulder and overarm sleeve seam: Match neck edges and lower edges of sleeve. They will match perfectly.

To stitch underarm seam: Match notches at underarm curve and lower edges of sleeve sections. Take up excess fabric in back sleeve section with dart or ease at the elbow.

5. Figure problem: fullness or roundness at base of neck extending into upper shoulder line

Fitting problem: bodice front. Chest key grain line swings up as it approaches center front. A tape measure across the front will show how much the key grain line swings up at center front. The distance between the tape and the key grain line is the amount to be added at shoulders.

There is a pull from neckline to underarm.

Bodice is shorter at center front. A coat front or jacket front is shorter at center of lower edge. On a coat or jacket, the need for this alteration is also evident from the way the coat or jacket hangs from the shoulder.

This alteration may be necessary for the bodice front only. On some figures it is also necessary for the bodice back. It is not uncommon for figures to need this alteration on one shoulder only.

In its displacement of grain line and type of alteration, this problem is similar to the problems of the high hip line discussed on page 124.

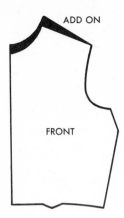

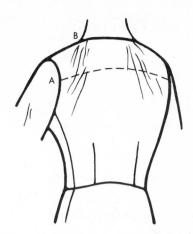

Correction

Cut on needed amount of fabric, starting at neck edge of shoulder line and tapering to nothing at armhole edge.

Move pattern piece and cut neckline following pattern outline.

Neckline may have to be lowered.

Sometimes, when fabric is laid double, it is easier to add extra to both layers even if wanted on one side only. After cutting out, move the pattern back to its original position, and cut off layer that isn't needed.

Alter collars and facings the same way. Collars have the shoulder line marked, so that you would know where to shift and add extra needed as was done for shoulder.

6. Figure problem: fullness at base of neck extending into upper shoulder line

Fitting problem: bodice back. Although this alteration usually is necessary for bodice front only, on some figures it may also be necessary for bodice back.

Shoulder key grain line swings up as it approaches center back.

There is a pull from neckline to underarm.

Bodice may be shorter at center back.

The amount of tuck you can pick up and pinch with your fingers at A helps you to determine the amount of fabric needed at B.

Correction

See directions just given for bodice front.

Correction for sleeve and bodice cut in one

See directions just given for bodice front.

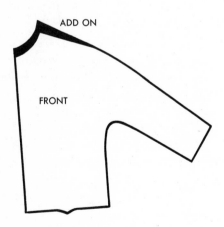

Correction for sleeve and bodice cut in one

Cut on needed amount of fabric, starting at neck edge of shoulder line and tapering to nothing at the point of the regulation armhole. This is usually about one inch beyond the shoulder notch. Then, follow all the other corrections just given.

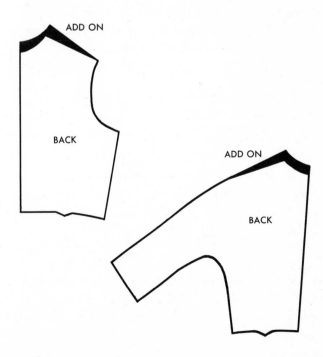

7. Figure problem: square shoulders

Fitting problem: Shoulder key grain line swings up as it approaches the armhole.

There are wrinkles across the back below the neck.

This is very common for square shoulders.

Fitters often cut the neckline deeper. This temporarily eliminates the wrinkles and the discomfort, but it does not eliminate the problem.

Correction

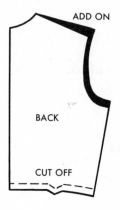

Cut on needed amount of fabric at armhole edge of shoulder line, tapering to nothing at neck edge. Move pattern up to new shoulder line to cut armhole, side seam edge, and waist edge.

The waist edge will be shorter all the way across, or it may be cut off the side back, but left on at the center back. This alteration may be needed on the front of the figure as well as the back. If needed on back only, ease extra width at shoulder to front by making staystitching plus (p. 71) before sewing seam.

Alter collars and facings the same way.

Correction for sleeve and bodice cut in one

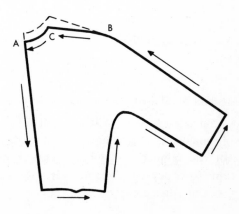

To shorten the bodice back, cut back of bodice from A all around to B (point of regulation armhole).

Move pattern piece necessary amount (pivoting at regulation armhole point B). Cut shoulder line to neck edge C.

Move pattern piece to match center back and point C with the pattern and cut neck edge from C to A. In this manner, the grain line of the pattern will not be lost.

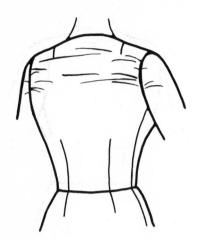

For broad or rounded shoulders use the shortened curved dart. The curved dart is stitched with an inside curve to give more fabric where it is needed across the wider part of the shoulders.

This technique is recommended for other places where there is roundness in the figure, such as a rounded hipline.

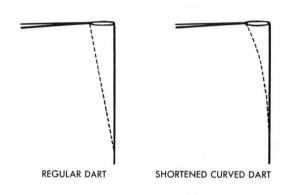

REGULAR DART   SHORTENED CURVED DART

8. Figure problem: broad shoulders or knob on top of shoulders

Fitting problem: Bodice back is too tight through shoulder section. There is a pull across the shoulders.

This problem may be evident on the front, also. Because of a knob on the top of the shoulder, the sleeve will be pulled up on it.

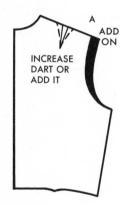

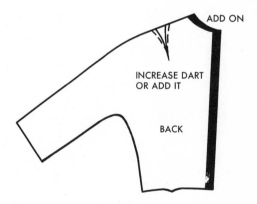

Correction

Add needed amount of fabric on back armhole, starting at shoulder line and tapering to nothing at notch or underarm seam.

Increase the back shoulder dart (or add dart) the same amount as added to the armhole so that the front and back shoulder seams will match.

This may also be needed on the front shoulder. Then, the two will key together with perfection. A little extra height at A has occasionally been needed for the knob. Add as in previous problem.

Correction for sleeve and bodice cut in one

Add needed amount of fabric at center back.

To do this cut center back line and neckline. Then move pattern piece and continue to cut the sleeve section.

Increase shoulder dart (or add dart), taking out of the shoulder line the same amount as added to the center back. Again, use shortened curved dart. Alter facings the same way.

9. Figure problem: round shoulders

Fitting problem: This problem is often termed "the dowager's hump." The shoulder key grain line swings up as it approaches center back.

The bodice is too tight across upper shoulder section, and it is shorter at center back.

It is not uncommon for figures to need this alteration on one shoulder only. The neckline will be tapered down to the normal shoulder line on opposite side. Alter collars and facings the same way.

Correction

To widen shoulders, add needed amount of fabric on armhole, starting at shoulder line and tapering to nothing at notch or underarm.

Add needed amount of fabric at neck edge of shoulder line, tapering to nothing at armhole. Cut normal neckline from pattern.

Increase the back shoulder dart (or add dart) the same amount as added to armhole so that the shoulder seams will match.

See page 101 for an explanation of shortened curved dart.

Correction for sleeve and bodice cut in one

Cut normal neckline and move pattern to add needed amount of fabric at center back.

Add needed amount of fabric at neck edge of shoulder line, tapering to nothing at regulation shoulder point.

Use shortened curved dart to take out of shoulder line same amount of fabric as added at center back.

See page 101 for shortened curved dart.

10. Figure problem: sloping shoulders

Fitting problem: The shoulders of the garment do not slope as much as the shoulders of the individual. Any garment should hit the neckline and shoulders at the same time. This is a common alteration with sleeveless clothing.

Correction

Use pattern to lower the shoulder line the desired amount. Place pattern at new shoulder edge A, and recut armhole following the pattern.

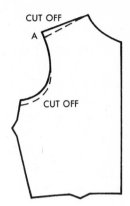

11. Figure problem: short back

Fitting problem: Underarm and waist key grain lines swing down toward center back. Bodice back is too long.

The straight back needs less fabric in length of bodice back. The high chest needs more fabric in bodice front length. Since the side seams must match with perfection, the difference in length between the front and the back will determine the size of the underarm dart or darts. Whether two bust darts are used, or one with increased depth, depends upon the figure and the amount of alteration.

Any shoulder alterations should be made before this alteration is done.

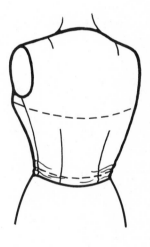

Correction

Back: Shorten bodice back by making an even fold on pattern grain, about 1½ inches above waistline.

Front: Increase underarm dart, or make two instead of one, by the amount folded out of back, so underarm seams will be the same length.

Many times people will say that they need to take out length only at the side or at the middle of the back. In the Bishop method, we would *never* take an uneven fold or tuck in the pattern. If you bring down your shoulders like number 5 or number 6, then you will have enough fabric to make an even fold, and your alteration will be *on true grain.*

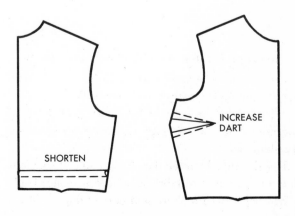

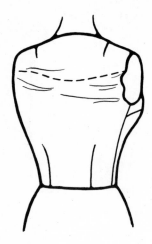

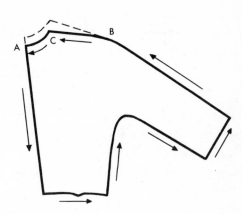

12. Figure problem: short back

Fitting problem: There is excess fabric across the upper back and there are wrinkles. Length of underarm seam is correct.

Correction for sleeve and bodice cut in one

To shorten the bodice back, cut back of bodice from A all around to B (point of regulation armhole).

Move pattern piece necessary amount (pivoting at regulation armhole point B), and cut shoulder line to neck edge C.

Move pattern piece to match center back and point C with the pattern and cut neck edge from C to A. In this manner, the grain line of the pattern will not be lost.

Correction

Shorten back length between shoulder line and underarm with an even fold about halfway down the armhole. To correct the sleeve to fit the new armhole, only one-half the amount of the tuck in bodice back will be made in the sleeve cap (see no. 27, p. 113). When the sleeve is set in, it will be moved toward the front.

Note the last paragraph in previous alteration about making this an even tuck or fold in pattern.

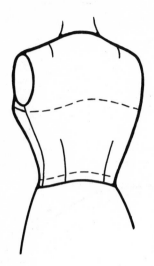

13. Figure problem: long back

Fitting problem: Underarm and waist key grain lines swing up toward center back.

14. Figure problem: long back

Fitting problem: All key grain lines are in correct position, but the waistline of bodice is slightly shorter at center back.

Skirt rides up over the waistline in center back.

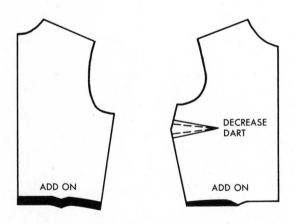

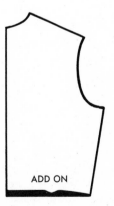

Correction

Cut needed amount of fabric on lower edge of bodice back. Cut lower edge of bodice front on straight grain from the center of dart to side seam, eliminating the natural curve to the waistline seam. Decrease underarm dart the amount necessary to match side seams of front and back bodice.

Correction

Cut bodice back on straight fabric grain along waist edge, eliminating the upward curve toward center back.

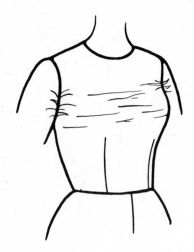

15. Figure problem: unusually large bust and upper arm

Fitting problem: Blouse pulls and is tight across front and upper arm.

Correction

Add uniform amount of fabric on side seam from underarm to waistline (B to C).

Cut lower edge of bodice on fabric grain, eliminating the natural curve to the side seam (C to D).

Pivot out the pattern and follow its outline, to add extra in the curve of the armhole (A to B). Some figures may not need this extra height in the armhole.

On front sleeve seam cut on the same amount of fabric as was added to the side seam on bodice, tapering to nothing at the lower edge.

Fabric is added the same way for any sleeve length, unless more width is needed at lower edge. Then, add the same amount all the way down. This may be especially needed for short sleeves.

Match the lower and top edges of the side seam of the front and back bodice, and distribute the added ease over the fullest part of the body; or the figure may be improved with a bust dart or two (B to C).

Bustline and arms can vary so much with the individual figure. Many times extra height is needed from A to B, and only extra at the waistline as shown in the sketches on the next page from G to F. Other suggestions for large arms are given on pages 113 to 116. See number 20 for line on page 110, also.

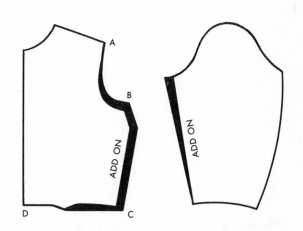

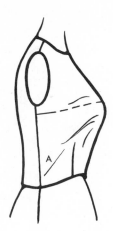

16. Figure problem: large bust or large low bust

Fitting problem: Bust and waist key grain lines swing up toward center front. Bodice front is too short. A diagonal wrinkle from bust to underarm side seam (A) indicates that you need to add on at the side seam (E to F) from the dart down.

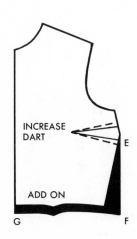

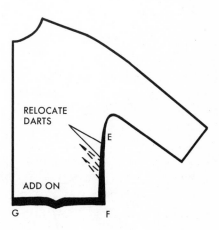

Correction

Cut on needed amount of fabric at lower edge of bodice front (F to G).

Cut side seams on straight grain from underarm to waistline (E to F).

Increase bust dart or make two or three smaller darts to keep grain straight across the figure at the bustline. If added fabric is not needed at waistline, make two or three small bodice darts.

Correction for sleeve and bodice cut in one

Cut on needed amount of fabric at lower edge of bodice front and on side seams as in basic bodice (F to G and F to E).

Relocate underarm darts or make two or three smaller ones, *keeping darts pointed toward crown of bust.*

If bust is very low, it is often more flattering to eliminate the waistline dart or darts, and to take up fullness at waistline (F to G) with gathers, tucks, or dart tucks. This will give a softer shaping for the bust.

17. Figure problem: small flat bust

Fitting problem: Bust and waist key grain lines swing down toward center front. Bodice is too long at center front.

Correction for sleeve and bodice cut in one

Shorten bodice front by making an even fold on pattern grain, about 1½ inches above waistline. Decrease underarm dart the same amount as the fold so side seams of front and back bodice will match.

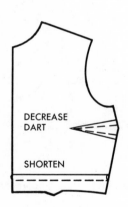

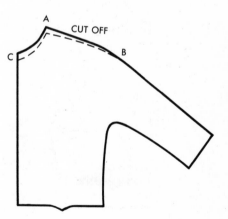

Correction

Shorten bodice front by making an even fold on pattern grain, about 1½ inches above waistline. Decrease underarm dart the same amount as the fold so that side seams of front and back bodice will match.

Correction for sleeve and bodice cut in one, without underarm dart

Shorten bodice front at shoulder line of overarm seam, by starting at the neckline, and tapering to nothing just below the regulation armhole point (A to B).

Cut normal neckline (A to C), after moving pattern down to new shoulder line.

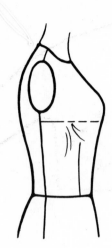
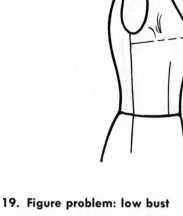

18. Figure problem: high bust

Fitting problem: The bust key grain line drops below the crown of the bust. There is a bulge under the bust at the point of the dart. Any shoulder alteration should be made before darts are corrected.

19. Figure problem: low bust

Fitting problem: The bust key grain line rides over the crown of the bust. There is a bulge over the bust at the point of the dart. Any shoulder alterations should be made before darts are corrected.

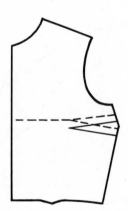
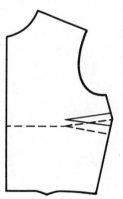

Correction

Raise the underarm dart so that the point is in line with the crown of the bust. If you raise the bust dart, you raise the bust key grain line (number 2 key grain line on p. 95).

Correction

Lower the underarm dart so that the point is in line with the crown of the bust. If you lower the bust dart, you lower the bust key grain line (number 2 key grain line on p. 95).

20. Figure problem: perfecting line of bodice darts

Any shoulder alterations should be made before darts are corrected. The entire bust dart can be made higher or lower as needed and as shown above. It is usually better to keep these darts running upward to give a younger and more youthful lift to the bustline for the full-busted figure. The crosswise key grain line (A to B) should be at the crown of the bust.

The next step is to adjust the bodice dart to the right or left, so that the lengthwise key grain line (C to D) also extends over the crown of the bust. It is number 4 on bodice front on page 95.

The lines from A to B and from C to D cross each other at the crown of the bust. The bodice dart may also need to be raised or lowered, increased or decreased, or made into 2 or 3 smaller darts, but at no time is it stitched long enough to be over the crown of the bust.

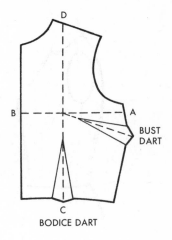

BUST DART

BODICE DART

21. Figure problem: large waistline

Fitting problem: front and back.

The front and back need more fabric at the waistline on the bodice and the skirt.

Correction

Cut on one-fourth the needed amount of fabric on side seam of both front and back, starting at the waistline and tapering to nothing at the armhole. Refer to page 126 for directions about adding to waistline of skirt. See photograph on page 129.

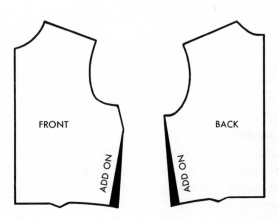

FRONT   BACK

ADD ON   ADD ON

22. Figure problem: large waistline, front only

Fitting problem: front only.

The side seams swing toward the front at the waistline. This indicates that more fabric is needed at the waistline on the front of the bodice.

23. Figure problem: narrow back

Fitting problem: Bodice back is too full lengthwise. This figure is often a size smaller in bodice back than bodice front.

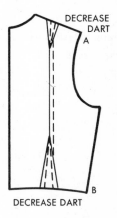

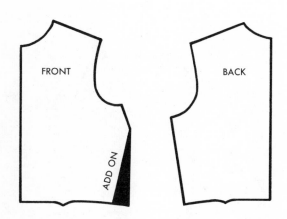

Correction

Cut one half the needed amount of fabric on side seam of bodice front, starting at waistline and tapering to nothing at the armhole. The bodice back may need no additional fabric (see photograph on p. 129). Refer to number 45 for directions about adding to waistline of skirt.

Correction

Narrow down bodice back by making an even fold on pattern grain at about the middle of the shoulder line.

A ¼-inch tuck decreases the back one inch, or one pattern size.

Decrease the waistline and shoulder darts the same amount as the fold, or some additional width may be added at A and B as you learned in number 8 and number 21. The important thing is that this alteration be done on true lengthwise grain.

This is seldom done to the front. If it is needed, it usually indicates that the pattern could have been purchased a size smaller.

24. Figure problem: wide back

Fitting problem: Bodice back is too narrow length-wise. This figure is often a size larger in bodice back than bodice front.

Correction

Do not slash pattern to add extra width. Draw a line midway out on shoulder on lengthwise grain of bodice. Then, cut from A to B. Measure and chalk-mark extra width needed. Move pattern out to chalk marks and cut from B to A.

If the extra width is not needed at shoulders and waistline, it can be eased in or stitched into darts.

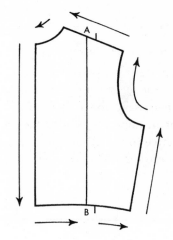

25. Figure problem: low neckline is too large for the figure

Fitting problem: The bodice front is too wide at the neckline for the small frame, hollow chest, or line of the bust.

Correction

If this alteration is anticipated, first try the bodice front in a sample, as it is sometimes impossible to recut the dress.

Narrow down the bodice front by making an even fold on the pattern grain at about the middle of the neckline. Cut neckline up to shoulder (A to B).

Unpin tuck and cut the remainder of the bodice front. If the front shoulder line is too wide, refer to number 4 on page 97.

Alter collars and facings the same way. This alter-ation has proved quite successful.

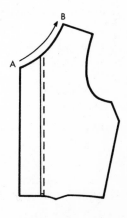

Alterations on sleeves

26. Figure problem: short arm or long arm

Fitting problem: The pattern will need to be shortened or lengthened for the length of the arm.

The alteration may be necessary above or below the elbow, or at both places, depending upon the proportion of the arm relative to the elbow dart.

A short sleeve may be shortened at the lower edge.

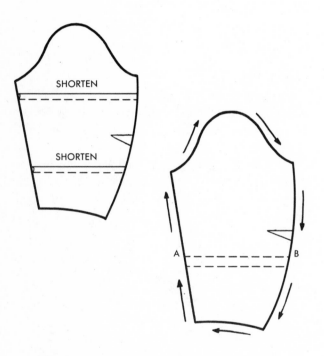

Correction

Shorten sleeve by making an even fold on pattern grain where needed. To lengthen sleeve below the elbow, cut from A to B; move down tissue necessary amount to lengthen, and cut from B to A.

To lengthen sleeve above the elbow, choose A and B above the elbow dart; then follow same procedure.

27. Figure problem: full or large upper arm

Fitting problem: There is a pull across the cap of the sleeve. The cap of the sleeve is too long and too narrow.

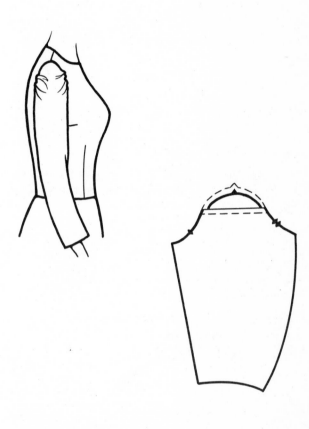

Correction

Make an even fold across the cap of the sleeve above the notches.

The width of the fold depends on the additional width needed in the cap. If one inch is needed, fold out an inch in a ½-inch tuck.

Cut the sleeve, continuing around the cap from the alteration fold about ½ inch from pattern edge of the sleeve cap as shown.

The sleeve cap will be one inch wider and ½ inch shorter. It will fit the armhole perfectly.

With this, the armhole may need to be raised in the front and back, or just the back, as shown in number 29 on page 115. If you raise the back armhole only, the sleeve will have to be moved forward in the armhole to have it hang to grain perfection.

28. Figure problem: muscular arm

Fitting problem: The sleeve is too tight over the muscle on the upper arm. It feels uncomfortable when the arm is moved forward.

Correction

Add needed amount of fabric to the front sleeve seam, tapering to nothing at bottom of any length sleeve, unless more width is needed at the lower edge.

If sleeve is too large for armhole, make one or more darts in front underarm section near the seam. They are tiny and will not show in the finished garment.

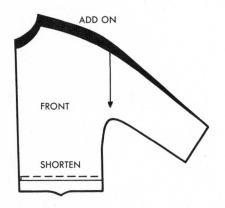

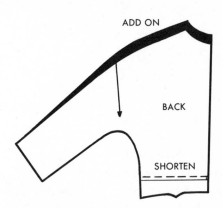

Correction for sleeve and bodice cut in one

The arrows point to the section where more fabric is needed.

Cut on needed amount of fabric along shoulder line and upper sleeve section, tapering to nothing at wrist. Move pattern piece and follow the outline of the pattern. Be certain to cut normal neckline.

If this added length at shoulder line makes the bodice too long, shorten by making an even fold in the pattern piece just above the waistline.

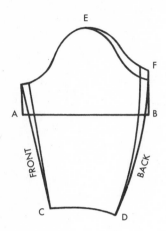

30. Figure problem: large fleshy arm

Fitting problem: Often, the way in which you handle a sleeve problem will depend upon one or more other fitting problems that are connected with it; for example, a large bustline. This one is for the arm alone.

If an arm is fleshy at the back, or if the pattern itself does not give much ease in a back sleeve seam through ease or a dart, this correction is merited at all times. A back sleeve seam must always be full like the back shoulder seam, but never the front.

Correction

Cut back of sleeve longer. Ease the length between arrowheads for the fleshy arm at the back. Also add dart if pattern does not have one, or ease back sleeve seam over elbow.

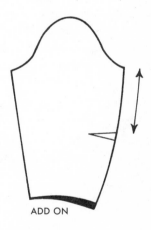

ADD ON

29. Figure problem: large and muscular arm

Fitting problem: The sleeve is too narrow to wear, and the arm bulges out into the sleeve. The sleeve should always hang free of the arm, and feel comfortable when you move your arm in any direction. You may need more allowance than the one just described.

Add to the front and back edges of sleeve, tapering to nothing at lower edge, C and D. On a short sleeve, it may be needed all the way down as shown at A and B. These amounts usually vary — for example, you may need ⅝ inch on the front edge and 2 inches on the back edge.

Only a part of this addition may be needed on the bodice, or the bodice would be too wide and full at the underarm. The remainder of the fullness on the sleeve can be stitched into tiny darts underarm at the front and back, as shown in number 28.

One of the best things to do is to cut the back cap higher, as shown from E to F. Patterns give some extra height here, but you may need more. A large figure, a size 42 for example, may achieve the most comfortable sleeve by adding 1½ inches gradually from E to F. This is just one of several ways of handling this problem. Another suggestion follows. Number 28 on page 114 is a modified version of the same technique. In that case, extra was added on the front which made the cap higher. Try folding the sleeve in half and you will see that this is so.

31. Figure problem: small back — large bust and arm

Fitting problem: This is another bustline and sleeve alteration that may be the right one for you. On a larger figure with erect posture, size 44 for example, more room is needed on the front of the bodice and sleeve, at the same time that fabric may have to come off the back. This is another kind of alteration that should be tried first on a fitting shell to determine what is best.

Correction

You may have to add as much as 1¼ inches on the front, and take off ½ inch from the back both on the sleeve and on the bodice. If you get a pull or diagonal wrinkle at the front armhole, as shown with the arrow, you will need to add more height in the front armhole (A to B, number 15, p. 106). This is common with adults.

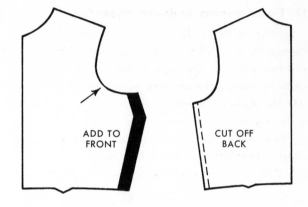

ADD TO FRONT

CUT OFF BACK

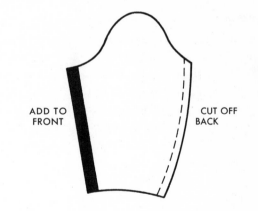

ADD TO FRONT

CUT OFF BACK

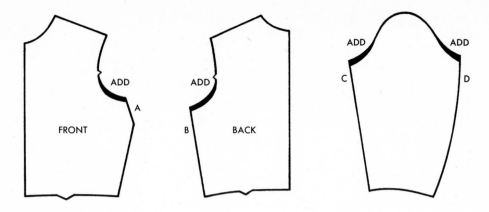

32. Figure problem: underarm discomfort

Fitting problem: If you do not seem to have enough room to lift your arm, and your sleeve pulls and binds when you do, you will get more action room by raising the armhole seam. This correction acts like a hidden gusset, and does not affect the fit of the garment elsewhere.

The armhole seam should be one inch below the armpit, therefore, this alteration will not be satisfactory if it brings the underarm seam too close to the body.

Small women who have gained weight will often find the armholes are too large for their figures, and will need this adjustment.

Correction

You may add as much as, but not more than, ½ inch up to the notches on both the garment and the sleeve. This may be needed only on the front of the garment. The seam may need to be let out slightly and gradually at the points marked A, B, C, and D, or additional fabric may be added in cutting.

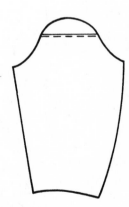

33. Figure problem: puff or ease in sleeve cap

The ease in a sleeve cap varies on patterns from ⅝ to 1½ inches. The more ease, the more puff will appear at sleeve cap. You may desire to decrease the cap fullness for a thin arm, style change, or a firm fabric that does not ease too well.

Correction

Even an ⅛-inch tuck on crosswise key grain line (number 27, p. 113) will decrease ease in cap ½ inch.

Alterations on skirts

34. Figure problem: tall or short

Correction: shorten pattern

A small amount (up to 2 inches) can be taken off the lower edge of the tissue. The amount must be measured to perfection to retain the curve of the tissue across the lower edge. If the pattern needs to be shortened more than that amount, the remainder should be taken out by making an even fold on pattern grain at the hipline. This method maintains the style of the garment.

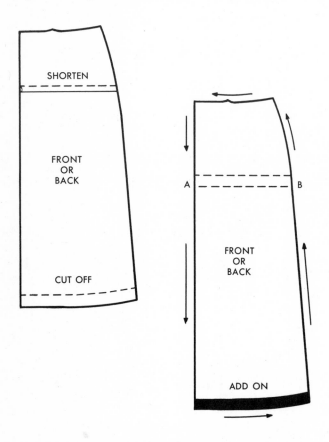

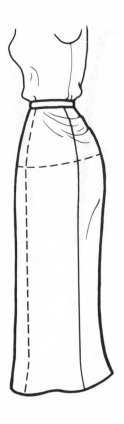

Correction: lengthen pattern

A small amount (up to 2 inches) can be added to the lower edge of the tissue. The amount must be measured to perfection to retain the curve of the tissue across the lower edge.

If the pattern needs to be lengthened more than that amount, cut from A to B, move up tissue necessary amount to lengthen, and cut from B to A.

This method maintains the style of the garment.

35. Figure problem: large hips, normal or small waistline

Fitting problem: Skirt is too tight over the hips. There are wrinkles, and the skirt does not hang gracefully and smoothly from the waistline.

Correction

Cut on one-fourth total amount of fabric needed the entire length of the side seams, both front and back. As an example, if an additional 2 inches are needed, add ½ inch to each side seam, both front and back (see photograph, p. 129). Fit in excess fullness at waistline with 2 or 3 short darts in both side front and side back (see p. 96 for variances in front). These darts are always placed toward the side (A and B) in relation to fullness in figure, and not toward the center. Attempting to take the skirt in a little at C and D from the notch up, in most cases, would emphasize the size of the hips, because of the severe off grain created from the notch upward. If there is a large amount to take out at the waistline, besides extra darts, the center back seam or other

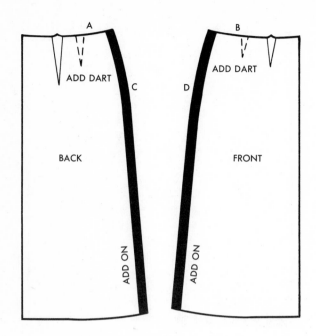

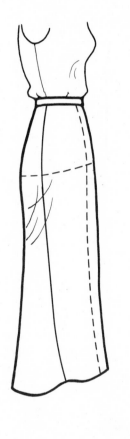

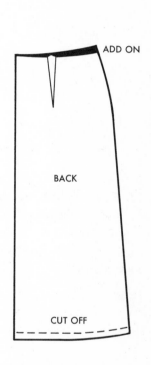

36. Figure problem: flat hips

Fitting problem: Side seams swing toward the front. Hip key grain line swings down toward center back. There are diagonal lines from hipline to center back, and skirt is longer at center back.

gore seams on the pattern may gradually be taken in a small amount. If a hip needs much width, it must also have height at A and B (see number 39 on p. 122).

If the hips are large in back and not in front, then add the fabric to the back side seams only. As an example, if an additional 2 inches are needed, add one inch to each side seam of the back only. The reverse is true if the hips are large in front and not in back; in this case, add to the side seams of the front only.

If extra width is needed at both hipline and waistline, then the excess at the waistline would not be fitted in with extra darts. This is a common alteration. It is important to remember that the additional fabric needed at the hipline must be added to the entire length of the side seam. If fabric is added only at the hipline and tapered to the waistline, a curved off-grain line will produce "pull" and emphasize the hips. It gives the same effect as taking in the skirt from the notch up, mentioned above.

See page 127 for a discussion of the problem of large thighs and adding to one-piece dresses such as sheaths.

Correction

On top of skirt, cut on needed amount of fabric at side back, tapering to nothing at center back, to straighten number one key grain line (p. 95) at hipline. The same amount that is added to side back at top of skirt is cut off all across lower edge. Many people still mark skirts with a skirt marker to get them straight, but there is no need to do this if they are fitted to grain perfection.

On a one-piece dress, the only way this alteration can be handled is to create a seam at the waistline on the back. It may be covered, if desired, with a belt across the back.

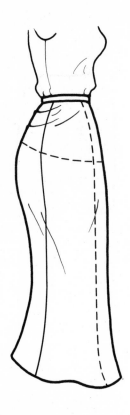

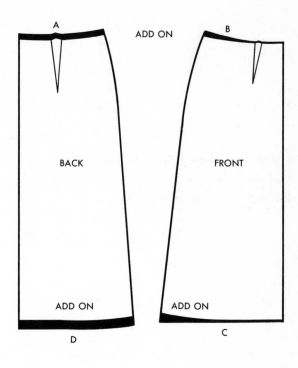

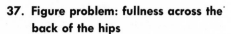

37. Figure problem: fullness across the back of the hips

Fitting problem: Side seam swings toward the back. Hip key grain line swings up toward center back. Skirt is shorter at center back. It is just the reverse of grain from preceding problem.

Correction

Back: Cut on needed amount of fabric evenly at lower edge of skirt back D, following pattern outline.

Front: Cut lower edge of skirt from C on straight of grain, eliminating the upward curve to the side seam. This can be a drawn thread line to help the front meet the back.

To stitch side seams, start at lower edge, matching skirt front and back, and stitch toward the hipline.

Match waist edge of skirt front and back, and ease in the added length over the fullest part of the hip. The ease over the hips will not be noticed in the finished garment. Notches on side seam will not match.

If above alteration was not sufficient, it may be necessary to add to the front waist edge from the side seam to the dart (B).

It may also be necessary to add to the waist edge across the back, either as shown at A, or in the same manner as shown at B. The most practical thing for you to do with these more severe fitting problems is to make a skirt shell or two to determine what is exactly right for your figure.

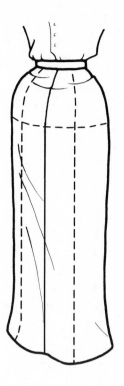

38. Figure problem: fullness below waistline

Fitting problem: Skirt fits at hipline and waistline, but it pulls or wrinkles below the waistline.

Correction

Stitch shortened curved darts below waistline to allow more fabric to fit over fuller parts of the hip.

This figure looks best with two or three of this type dart on each side of the skirt front and back (see p. 101 for shortened curved dart).

A staystitch plus line (p. 71) from side of skirt front A to dart B may be more becoming and hang more gracefully than other darts or tucks. On some figures, a staystitch plus line looks better all across the front without any darts or tucks.

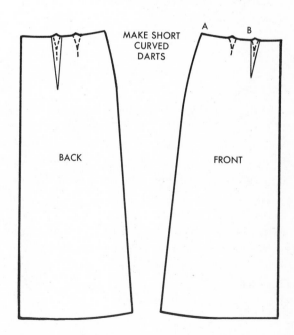

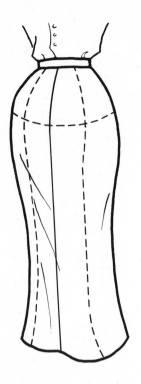

39. Figure problem: fullness at side hipline

Fitting problem: Hip key grain line swings up at side seams. Skirt is shorter at side seams. This is a very common problem.

Correction

Add needed amount of fabric on waist edge of both skirt front and back, starting at side seam and tapering to nothing at center front and center back.

If you are using a basic pattern that has the key line marked at the hipline (number 1 on p. 95), use yardstick to measure from the floor, and check if it is out of line. The amount that it is out of line is the amount that would be needed to be added to the top of the skirt. After this addition, even though this key line may not necessarily be on grain, it is parallel to the floor.

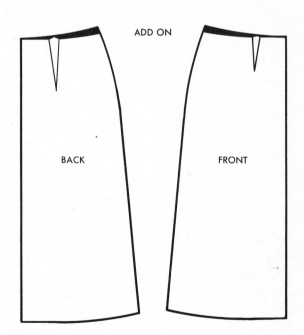

ADD ON

BACK

FRONT

40. Figure problem: sway back

Fitting problem: Skirt wrinkles above the hipline on the back. Skirt cups in below the hipline.

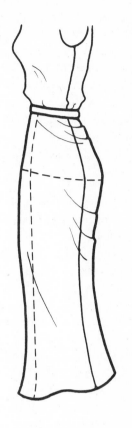

Correction

Skirt front: Cut lower edge on straight of grain, eliminating upward curve to the side seam. It may be necessary to add a little on the front waist edge from the side seam to the dart.

Skirt back: Add half the amount as cut on lower edge of skirt front, or as much as 1 inch, at waist edge of skirt back, tapering to nothing at center back.

Add as much as ½ inch all the way across the lower edge.

The sway-back is a common alteration, especially among teen-agers.

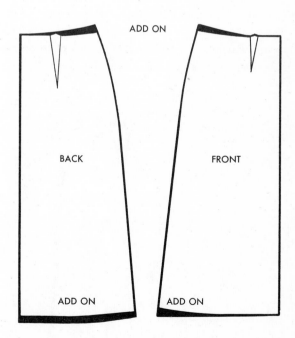

41. Figure problem: large hip, high hip, or both

Fitting problem: Center front and halfway key grain lines swing toward large hip side. Hip key grain line swings up on large hip side.

Skirt is shorter on large hip side.

In its displacement of grain line and type of alteration, this problem is similar to the problem of the one high shoulder discussed on page 98.

Correction

To straighten halfway key grain lines, cut on needed amount of fabric entire length of front and back side seam for large hip.

If it is just a high hip, then add only to the notch at the hip from waist down, like number 44, page 126.

To straighten hip key grain line, cut needed amount of fabric on waist edge at side seam of front and back (high or large hip), tapering to nothing at center or at dart section of opposite side. If you are just adding ½ inch, it can end at the center. If more is needed, taper to dart section of opposite side.

Sometimes, when fabric is laid double, it is easier to add extra to both layers. Then, move pattern back to position and cut off layer that isn't needed.

Take out excess fabric at waistline of high or large hip side with short curved dart, or see problem number 38, page 121, about staystitch plus line.

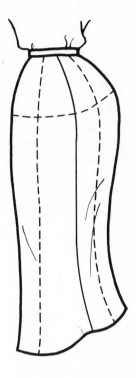

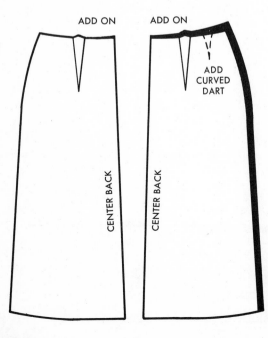

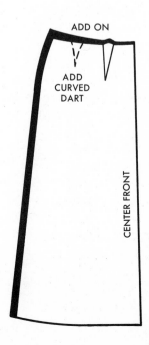

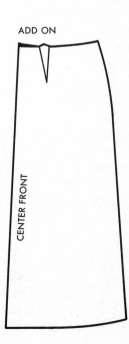

42. Figure problem: small back

The skirt does not fit the figure below the darts and shows fullness. There is too much hip room given with the darts for the small hips of the figure.

Correction

The back skirt darts are made smaller, or 1 dart instead of 2 is used. The difference is cut off the side seam of the back. On some figures, when the darts are minimized, the difference is eased at the waistline across the back.

At the same time that the difference may be cut off skirt side back, some additional fabric may be needed on skirt side front. If the individual has fullness in the front of her figure, the extra may be needed to have skirt hang gracefully and conceal front fullness.

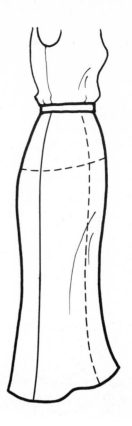

Correction

Cut on needed amount at waist edge, starting at center front and tapering to nothing at side seams. Often enough fabric is needed so that the waist edge of the skirt front can be cut on the straight of grain, eliminating the natural curve at the waist edge of skirt front. If you are in doubt, cut on the straight of grain. Then, proceed to check the hip key grain line.

On this figure, a staystitch plus line on part or all of the front may be becoming (see number 38, p. 121) or the fine tucks stitched ⅛ inch wide (see p. 91).

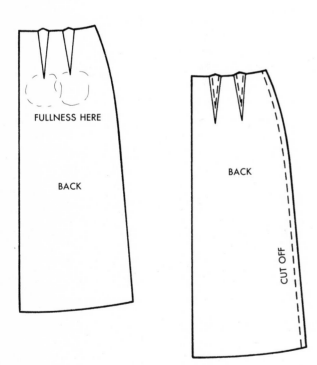

FULLNESS HERE

BACK

BACK

CUT OFF

43. Figure problem: fullness at front waistline

Fitting problem: Hip key grain line swings up as it approaches center front. Skirt is shorter at center front.

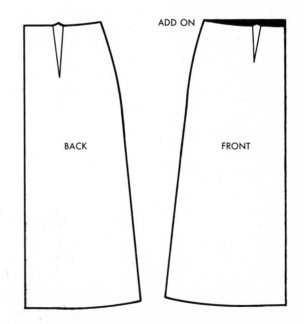

ADD ON

BACK

FRONT

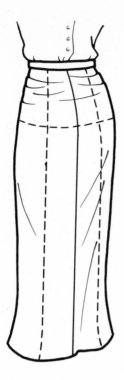

44. Figure problem: large waistline

Fitting problem: front and back. The front and the back need to be increased at the waistline on the bodice and the skirt.

Correction

Cut on one-fourth the needed amount of fabric on side seam of both front and back, starting at the waistline and tapering to nothing at the notch.

Refer to number 21, page 110 for directions about adding to waistline of bodice.

See number 45, also.

45. Figure problem: large waistline — front only

Fitting problem: The side seams pull to the front. Only the front needs more fabric at the waistline.

Correction

Cut on one-half the needed amount of fabric on side seam of skirt front, starting at waistline and tapering to nothing at the notch.

Refer to number 22, page 111 for directions about adding to waistline of bodice.

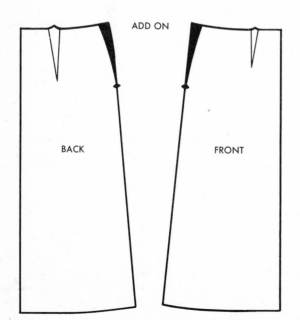

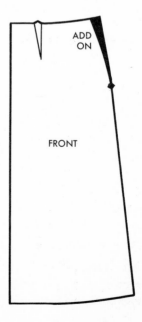

46. Figure problem: small waistline

Fitting problem: Figure is smaller at the waistline than the pattern.

Correction

Side seam of bodice can be taken in deeper gradually from armhole down, or bodice darts may be adjusted. A second dart may be added, if only one is given.

Skirt side seams are seldom taken in deeper from notch up. Excess fabric at waistline of skirt front and back will be taken out by hip darts. Often the center seam or gore seams are gradually tapered deeper at the waistline.

If necessary, side seam can be taken in deeper all the way down to lower edge of skirt.

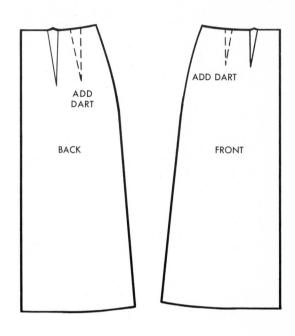

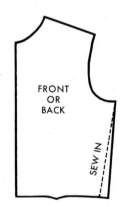

47. Figure problem: large hips for one-piece dress

Correction

If a one-piece sheath or shift-style dress pattern is purchased to fit the bustline, it will be too small in the hipline for this figure. To add extra, on both front and back of dress, cut from A around to C; then, the pattern can be moved out the necessary amount at A and B (notch at hipline), and cut from A to B. Then, move pattern back to original line at C and complete cutting from C to B. If this adds too much extra fabric at the waistline, darts may be deepened, or an extra one added. You may not want to fit the garment too tightly here.

If the figure has extremely large hips, two other learnings are essential. Up to a certain amount, needed fabric could be added at each side seam (approximately one inch). If the figure needs more, a pattern style should be selected with gore seams, so that some additional width could be added to them.

A style pattern with a little flare or flange at the side seamline would be a better choice for a figure that has full thighs or hips.

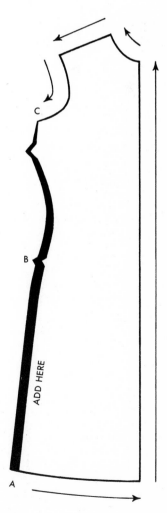

Methods for doing alterations

We have learned that the grain line of the fabric is your key to success in altering your pattern. Therefore, you must preserve the grain line of the pattern piece no matter what change is made.

It is important that you do not change the outline of your pattern. Successful alteration is changing the size but not proportions or lines of the design of the pattern.

There are three ways you will make cutting-to-fit alterations in the paper pattern. The first is made within the pattern, but the second and third are made in cutting.

1. Pin an even tuck on lengthwise or crosswise grain according to suggestions for use throughout the chapter.

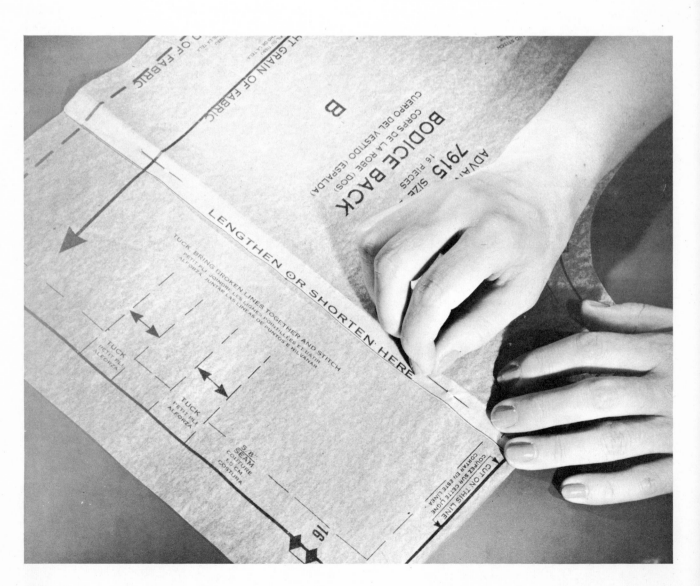

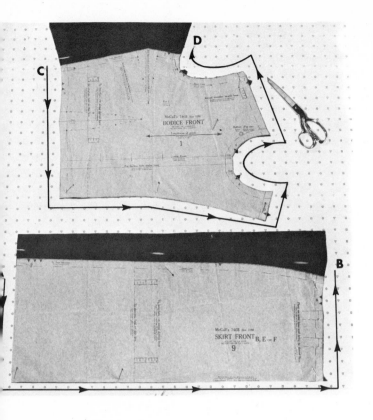

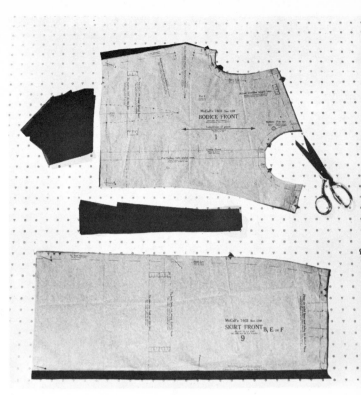

2. Slide all of the pattern to add needed extra fabric. Here are the steps to follow:

   a. Lay and pin pattern piece in place.

   b. Cut the area of the piece (A to B in left photograph) that does not need alteration.

   c. Measure and chalkmark additional width needed.

   d. Slide all of the pattern to give desired change.

   e. Pin pattern to fabric and complete cutting from B to A (see right photograph).

   f. Transfer the construction markings.

3. Pivot one corner of pattern piece to add to one end only. Here are the steps to follow:

   a. Lay and pin pattern piece in place.

   b. Cut the area of the piece (C to D in left photograph) that does not need alteration.

   c. Measure and chalkmark additional width needed at one end only (see C in photograph).

   d. Pivot one corner of pattern piece to give desired change (C), but do not move the end of the pattern (D) where alteration is not needed.

   e. Pin pattern to fabric and complete cutting from D to C.

   f. Slide pattern to original position (see right photograph) to transfer the construction markings.

If more than one change is needed on a piece of a pattern, then two or more pivots or slides will be necessary.

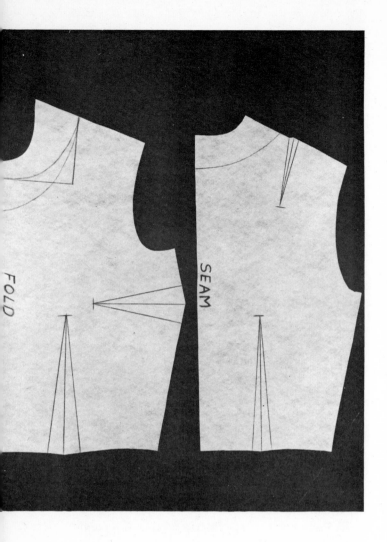

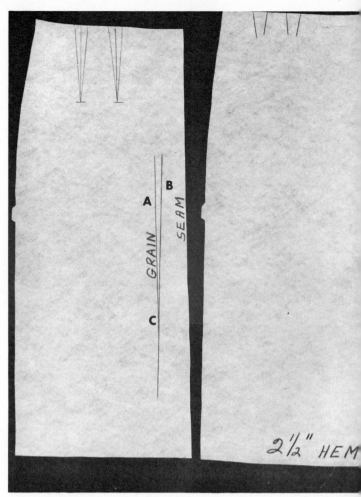

These two photographs are the master pattern discussed on page 93.

This one had been fit to perfection in percale from a basic pattern and then cut of pellon. Pellon is durable to use for repeated cutting and marking. Notice the four tested and attractive necklines on the bodice.

Also, note the two different grain lines on skirt back. The A or straight one can be used for most fabrics, but the B or one slightly off grain would be a better choice for stripes, checks, ribbed fabrics, etc. It is ¼ to ½ inch closer to center back at B than at C, and eliminates the possibility of stitching together two straight design or rib lines.

Chapter 9

Pressing Techniques

The art of pressing is essential to the art of clothing construction. The various processes at the right stages are fascinating. Many seamstresses, through the years, have considered pressing a chore, because they had little or no proper equipment. They did not develop it as an integral part of the art of clothing construction, and it has not always been taught as a part of sewing.

To be able to iron is not necessarily to be able to press. Ironing is using the hot iron in a lifting, sliding, pushing motion with long strokes across washable fabrics to smooth and dry them. Pressing is using the iron in a lifting and lowering motion to smooth or block an area, or to flatten edges. Pressing exerts pressure down on fabric; ironing carries pressure across the fabric. Pressing is the method or the skill you use most when you are sewing.

Much time has been spent preparing the fabric to grain perfection, cutting the fabric on grain, stitching on grain, and fitting with grain perfection. Following the grain line in pressing is as important as it has been in every step of constructing the garment.

In developing the art of pressing, you must learn not only to press on grain, but also when and how to press each part of the garment, and how to handle various types of fabric. The learnings will be a building process from a torn project through to a tailored garment — from cotton fabric through to silks and woolens. All the skills cannot be learned on one or even several garments, but to help assure the final success of your sewing, you must begin to develop professional pressing techniques.

Proper equipment

The proper equipment is described in Chapter 1 on pages 4 to 6. Try to have in your home the equipment on that list as soon as possible. One other item for pressing darts is shown on page 191.

The press board on page 5, and shown throughout this chapter, completely replaces an ironing board. Used on top of any table or desk, or on the press table (see photograph below), it supports the weight of the garment, so that it will not pull or stretch out of shape.

A padded press table is a convenience. The press board, sleeve board, cushions, can be brought up on it from the lower shelves as needed. It is padded and then covered with denim and is also used as a pressing area to straighten and press pieces of fabric, and to press large parts of a garment such as a coat back. The dimensions can vary somewhat to suit room area and individual height, but these may serve as a guide:

A to B — 31 inches
B to C — 28 inches
B to D — 54 inches

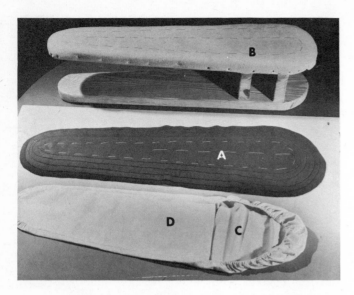

To pad a press or sleeve board, cut enough layers of wool to have padding ⅜ to ½ inch thick. They should be staggered in size so that all of them do not go over the edge of the board. Each of the five layers in A varies ½ inch in size. Tack together by hand to keep layers from slipping.

When they are nailed on the board, the largest layer is on top (B). The removable cover is made of unbleached muslin. The top (C) is on the bias, and the under section (D) is straight of grain. For a good fit, elastic is used at back edge of top (C).

When you have collected the proper equipment for pressing, organize it in convenient relationship to your sewing machine, so that you can turn from sewing to pressing and back again with the least amount of lost motion. For a right-handed person, it should be placed to the right of the machine.

Factors to be controlled

The amount of pressure, moisture and heat that can be used with safety and for professional results will vary according to the type of fabric.

Pressure. Certain fabrics require very little pressure to press flat at construction details and to retain texture of weave. Keep the weight of the iron in your hand so that pressure on the fabric is light, and you are pressing with less than the weight of the iron. A very careful placing-down and lifting-up motion is needed in the use of the iron.

Crease-resistant and worsted fabrics require more pressure because they are also resistant to easy pressing.

To prevent flattening nap or pile on such fabrics as fleece, velveteen, and corduroy, press with one of the following that will absorb the nap or pile on the outside of the fabric and keep them standing on end.

1. A piece of its own fabric is often acceptable. A rectangle of corduroy, for example, can be placed with corduroy, right sides together. Note pressing the seam on underside with a piece of its own fabric, bottom photograph, page 135.

2. A remnant of mohair upholstery makes a durable and successful press cloth for nap fabrics.

3. A needle-board looks as if a million tiny needles were stuck straight up in it. Lay pile side against the needles, and press lightly, lifting and lowering the iron. A piece of velveteen was not used to protect the facing of this overblouse, because the facing was made of rayon twill, so it would hang freely over velveteen skirt (see p. 89).

A stiff clothesbrush will act like a needle-board to press short or small areas.

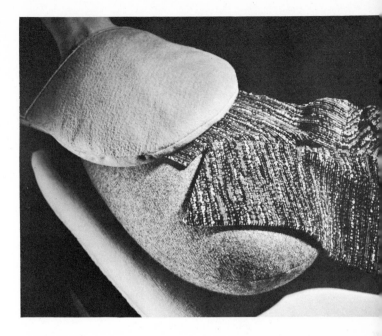

4. A cloth mitt to pound nap fabrics aids in flattening facings and other areas. Hold mitt up to steam iron to get it hot and filled with steam. Hit fabric with hot mitt.

Moisture. The incorrect amount of moisture can be as harmful to professional pressing as improper pressure can be.

Certain fabrics, like some silks, may press beautifully without any moisture at all. If moisture is needed, it will have to be controlled with one or two layers of drill cloth on the fabric before the steam iron is used. This will be necessary in top-pressing as well as in underpressing.

Many fabrics, like cottons, will press professionally with the steam iron or a dampened cheesecloth directly on them.

No fabric needs a wet cheesecloth. Dip about one-third of the cloth in water and wring it out. Roll or fold the rest of it around the damp third until the entire cloth is uniformly damp.

For added steam on fabrics that will not take moisture directly on them, a dampened cheesecloth is placed over the drill cloth, or a wet sponge is rubbed over the drill cloth to moisten it.

Another technique that works on small, concentrated areas like buttonholes that need additional moisture is to use a one-inch brush to add moisture. Dip it in a container of water, and apply to drill cloth or directly on fabric as desired. The moisture is precisely where needed.

Iron shine. At the same time the drill cloth is used to control moisture on outside of fabric, it also prevents iron shine on certain ones. The steam-iron cloth (page 4) is designed for this purpose, also, when less protection is needed. You can see through it.

Very heavy brown paper (supermarket bag cut open) does an excellent job of protecting fabric from shine when pressing on right side — with or without steam. In some cases, it gives better protection than a drill cloth.

The steam-iron shoe (pp. 140, 141) is used on topside to prevent shine, also. Two good features of it are that it permits you to see what you are pressing, and it forces you to use the lowering and lifting motion of pressing. It cannot be pushed along as in ironing.

To protect the soft texture of wool, as well as to prevent iron shine, on topside of some wools, you will need to press wool with a piece of wool. This is often sewn on a piece of drill cloth and is used double.

Glossy fabrics such as chintz and polished cotton are pressed on the right side without a pressing cloth to retain or restore their luster.

Heat. As long as you are aware of the importance of the correct heat settings on irons, and are cautious about following them, heat should be no problem in pressing.

A beginner must have this stressed, however, because some fibers are very sensitive to heat and will deteriorate under excessive heat. Some become harsh and brittle.

Techniques for specific fibers

1. Cotton. It is the easiest fabric to press. Cotton usually requires moisture, but, then, it should be pressed until dry to complete it. Use steam to press it; then, turn the steam off, and press again. White or light colors can be pressed on either the right or wrong side, but dark colors or dull finishes require a dry cheesecloth or steam-iron cloth on the right side to prevent shine.

Sheer cottons require a slightly lower heat; too hot an iron will scorch them.

2. Linen. Linen, like cotton, is easy to press. It requires moisture, but should be pressed until dry to complete it. Use steam to press it; then, turn the steam off, and press again. Ironing or pressing produces a shine, so the linen fabric should be protected on the right side with a dry cheesecloth, steam-iron cloth, drill cloth, or brown paper.

Pressing techniques

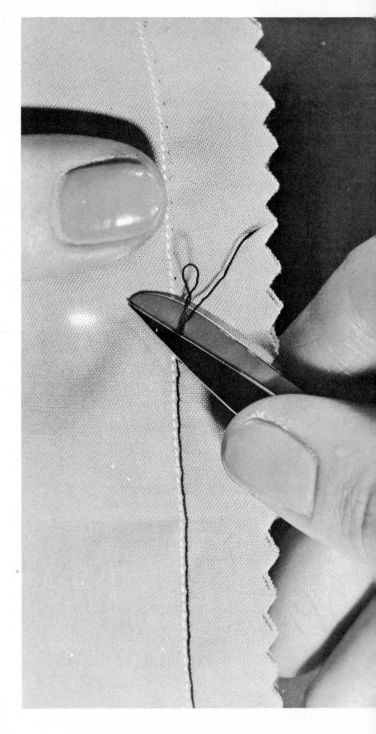

3. Wool. It is the easiest fabric to mold or block. Do no subject it to excessives of heat, moisture, or pressure. Wool requires moist heat for pressing; dry heat makes it harsh and brittle. Do not press wool until completely dry. In the section above, you learned that a piece of woolen fabric or wool sewn on drill cloth makes an excellent press cloth for soft textures of it. One side of the press cushion is made of wool to use for pressing this fabric. Then, too, the wool cushion cover gives the best redistribution of steam through this fabric.

4. Silk and man-made fibers. Silk and some of the man-made fibers are among the most difficult to press. They require great care to protect their delicate and often raised surfaces. Many of them are pressed dry, and may still need the protection of a press cloth. If any moisture is needed, before it is applied, care should be taken to see if the fabrics water-spot. If they do, a piece of tissue next to the fabric prevents water-spotting.

Some man-made fibers require little pressing and a warm iron.

Construction pressing and blocking

There are two types of pressing. The first is construction pressing and blocking, and, as its name implies, is the pressing being done on the garment while it is being constructed. It is the underpressing done on the inside of the garment to seams, darts, pleats, and other construction details. It is also the blocking which gives shape to the garment. A garment may be given contour with a dart, a curved seam, a seam with ease, a curved hem; blocking over a cushion further shapes these areas.

Do not wait until an entire garment is stitched together to begin pressing; it is easier to press in smaller areas. Have the iron heated all the while you are sewing, and *press as you sew*.

Finishing seams. Never stitch over a seam or dart with another seam until the former is completed (unless, of course, it is baste-stitching). Completing it includes permanent stitching; removing baste-stitching, if there; finishing seam, if necessary; and pressing.

Note that the permanent stitching is placed one thread away from the baste-stitching.

To remove the baste-stitching, hold ripping scissors with the tips of your fingers at the lower end of the blades. With the upper and under threads held securely in the scissors, and the scissors laid parallel to the fabric, pull along the line of stitching toward you in one quick motion. A section of the baste-stitching will pull out before the threads break. Repeat the operation until all baste-stitching is removed, picking out one or two stitches with the point of scissors, when necessary, so as to always pinch the loop and the single thread before pulling to rip.

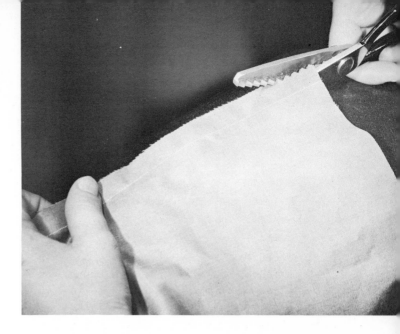

If the seam requires a finish, pink edges with pinking shears near the edge of seam, before it is pressed open. Other seam finishes are discussed on pages 256 and 257.

Directions to press seams. Before you actually start pressing, you will need to know in which direction seams, darts, and tucks should lie. All seams are pressed open with the following exceptions:

1. Seams stay together at the back of a pressed or an unpressed pleat.

2. Waistline seam stays together and is pressed up toward the bodice.

3. Yoke seams lie together away from gathers. Press any seam that joins a gathered edge to a flat edge with both seam allowances turned toward the edge that has no fullness. Press an edge of fabric thoroughly before gathering, because it is not as easy to get into it afterward.

4. From one notch to the other in the underarm area, the armhole seam is not pressed at all. From one notch to the other over the top, it lies together into the sleeve, but is not pressed flat (see p. 138).

Directions to press darts and tucks. Vertical darts, such as shoulder, waistline, and skirt darts, are usually pressed toward the center front or center back. Horizontal darts, such as bust and elbow ones, are pressed down.

Trial pressing. Though we have given some generalizations on pages 133-134 for pressing various types of fabric, the only way you can be certain of the proper techniques for an unfamiliar fabric is to do some trial pressing on a scrap or on an inconspicuous area of a garment. If the test result is not entirely satisfactory, find out what will correct it before proceeding with the garment. These are your aims:

1. Preserve surface texture of fabric.
2. Determine correct amount of moisture, if any.
3. Avoid shine on fabric.
4. Prevent seam or dart imprints, iron marks, or a groove or well in a seamline.
5. Determine best heat setting on the iron.
6. Find best method to flatten seams and edges.

Techniques in action. 1. Some seams need to be pressed along the stitching line before being pressed open. This will smooth the stitching, and will give a smoother seam to press open. As always, this pressing should be done in the same direction the seam was stitched.

Take time to place your garment carefully in position for pressing; place it on the board on grain. Many times it will take longer to press a part of a garment than it will to stitch it; pressing is the invaluable part of clothing construction.

Pull the seam apart before pressing by placing your hands to the right and the left of the seam and smoothing fabric; then, open the seam allowance with your fingers. On most fabrics, press the seam open first without any moisture, using the iron on the line of stitching only. If this results in a wrinkle in the fabric, or a well or groove at the stitching line, it is easier to correct before applying moisture. Certain fabrics press more professionally if a seam or dart is underpressed only slightly, and then completed with top-pressing.

Always press on grain just as stitching is done on grain. Exactly as there is directional stitching, there is directional pressing. Refer to arrows on page 165 if you have any doubts about which way to press.

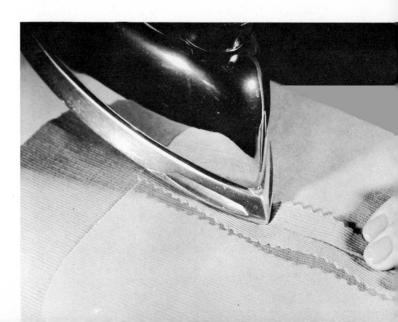

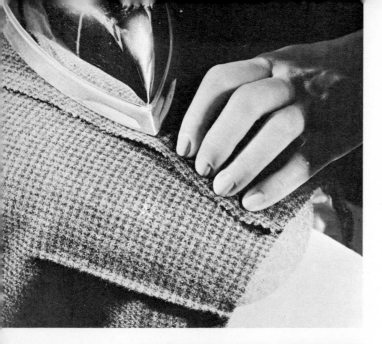

2. Areas that are to be blocked on the cushion are carefully placed over the cushion on grain, and on a section of the cushion that the area fits properly. The following parts of a garment are never pressed flat on a pressing board, but are molded or blocked to the figure on a cushion: (In the photographs note that the iron is being used on fabric with grain of fabric.)

  a. Curve of side seams on a straight skirt above the hip notches.

  b. Waistline seam — For smaller size, and for some styles of dresses, it is better to press this seam on the edge presser.

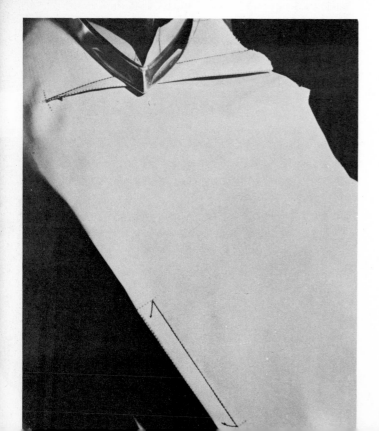

  c. All bodice darts or tucks and back skirt darts are pressed and blocked on a cushion. In many fabrics, first press dart flat in same position as it was stitched. This will smooth the line of stitching and will crease the center fold.

  When placing dart on cushion, the point of dart will be placed at end of cushion. Press dart crosswise from wide end to point to eliminate well at stitching line. When top-pressing, if the imprint of the dart shows at all, turn back to the wrong side, and remove the imprint by pressing under edge of dart with point of iron. Before blocking, to lie flat, double-pointed darts must be clipped at widest part to within ¼ inch of stitching.

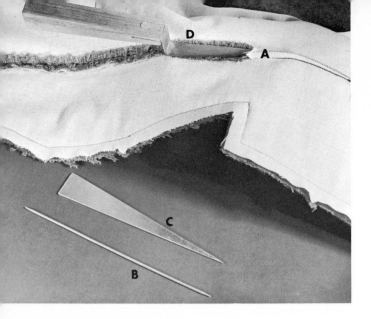

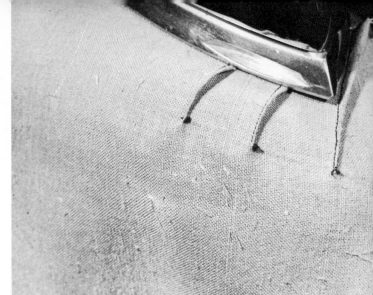

d. On heavy fabrics, trim dart away to a ⅜-inch seam as far down as it is that wide. At end of slash, cut into dart at an angle (A) halfway to stitching line. Press open seam. Below seam, use a metal knitting needle (B) or a piece of metal cut to a point (C or D) to continue to divide dart. Press on each side of stitching line all the way to the point. This is a dart seam in the photograph from coat, page 191.

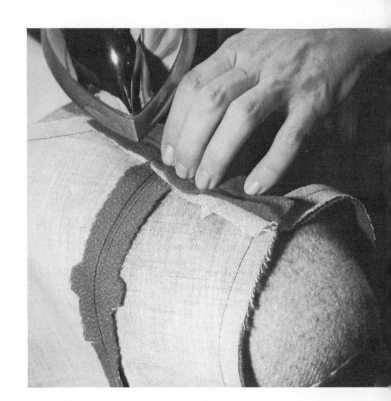

e. Elbow darts are pressed on lengthwise grain of sleeve as shown. However, if there is ease at elbow instead of darts, press the sleeve seam crosswise to mold out fullness at elbow roll.

f. The same technique should be followed for blocking a shoulder roll. First, on underside, press open seam from neckline to armhole. Then, on topside, mold and press the back shoulder line on lengthwise grain around the edge of the cushion as it will naturally fit the curve of the back shoulder. A diagonal sleeve seam with a cut-on sleeve needs to be held firmly on the lengthwise grain as it is being pressed open.

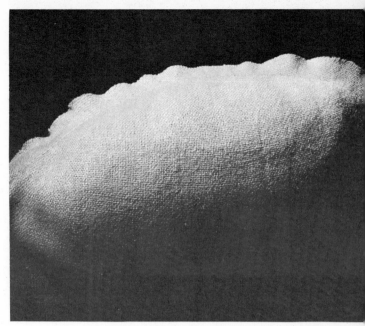

g. Shrink out the ease on the sleeve cap on blunt end of cushion or on end of sleeve board. Steam press with point of iron at seamline to form a smooth, rounded cap ⅝ inch beyond seamline. There can be little pleats in seam allowance but never at the line of stitching.

h. From one notch to the other in the under-arm area, the armhole seam is not pressed at all. From one notch to the other over the top, lay seams together on the cushion (or edge of sleeve board) away from the garment, and having sleeve on top. Press with point of iron at seamline. When completed, seam will turn and lie into sleeve, but is not pressed flat into sleeve. This gives the arm-hole a rounded, rolled look at the cap of the sleeve.

i. Blocking a tailored collar to fit the neckline is shown on page 229.

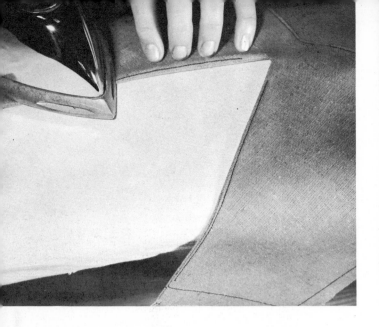

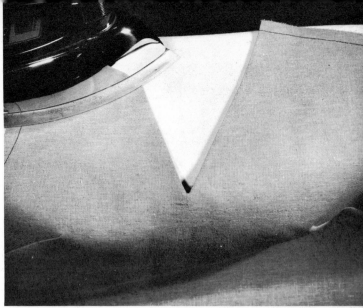

3. When a facing has been understitched (pages 86 and 87), then, it falls into place almost automatically for pressing. Shape and work the area in your fingers to perfect the line of the faced edges. No basting or pinning is needed. In fact, never press over pins, except lightly for one technique as shown on page 182.

Always set the edge of a facing on the underside before turning to topside to final-press as shown in second photograph. When first pressing on underside, keep fingers ahead of iron to hold edges to perfection, as shown in first photograph. For both underpressing and final or top-pressing, use the iron on the crosswise or lengthwise grain of the fabric.

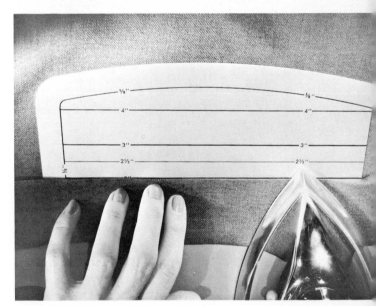

4. Use the automatic hem gauge to turn up hems desired amount and press. Use straight edge of gauge for straight hems and curved edge for flared hems (see photograph, page 2). Never push the iron along the folded edge of the hem. Press on grain from folded edge to hem edge.

When fashion calls for a softer look at the edges, do not press a sharp hemline in silk or similar fabrics.

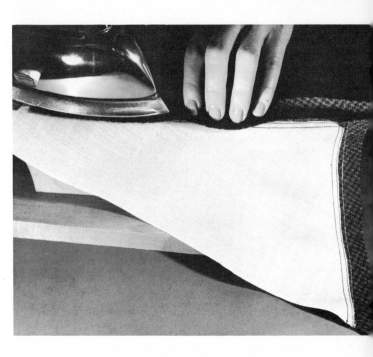

5. The edge and point presser is used to press open seams on such parts of a garment as collars and facings, before they are trimmed, turned, and closed. When they are pressed on the outside, the edges will lie smooth and flat without a well or groove at the stitching line.

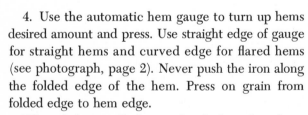

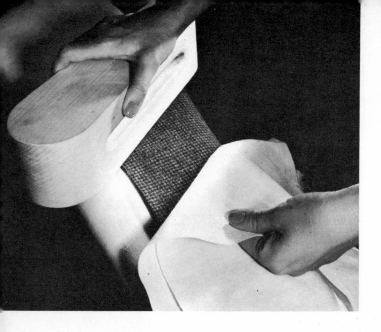

6. After edges have been set in place with the iron (page 139), the pounding block is used on the outside of the garment to obtain sharp, thin edges without iron shine on wool and other heavier fabrics. Steam an area the exact length of the block, quickly remove iron (and steam-iron cloth or drill cloth and cheesecloth, if used), and slap garment with the block. This forces out the steam and leaves flat, sharp edges. Repeat if necessary. The pounding block is used mainly in tailoring on buttonholes, lapels, collars, facings, hems, pleats, pockets, but never on the zipper. It is not used extensively in pressing when fashion requires a softer look at edges.

If fabric has pile or nap, a cloth mitt aids in flattening these areas (see page 133). Certain pile or nap fabrics may be pounded with a piece of their own fabric on top (right sides together). It is placed before applying steam and is not removed until the pounding is completed.

Final pressing

By the time you have completed a garment, you will already have completed some of the final pressing. You do this in construction pressing. How much final pressing a garment needs will depend upon the quality of work done in construction pressing and the care and respect given the garment during construction, such as keeping it hung perfectly on a hanger.

The final pressing is done on the outside of the garment, so it may need an overall pressing, or it may need just a touch-up here and there.

In any case, the pressing is done on grain. Notice how the iron is being used on grain in all of the photographs. Lift a gathered edge with your left hand as you press into the gathers to keep from forming creases.

Follow the directions in construction pressing for moisture, pressure, heat, preventing iron shine, and use of press cloths. It is an art not to press too little nor too much, nor to destroy shape in a garment but rather to build it, nor to destroy the chief interest and beauty in the texture of a fabric.

Have a zipper closed for any pressing in the area of it. If the zipper is in a curved area of a garment, the pressing should be done on a cushion.

Final-press all the same parts of a garment on a cushion as was done in construction pressing. A collar and lapel are always molded and shaped as one unit in a final pressing on a cushion. Notice that the wool side of the cushion is turned up for the woolen garment. Also, note that the iron is carefully being used on lengthwise grain of collar.

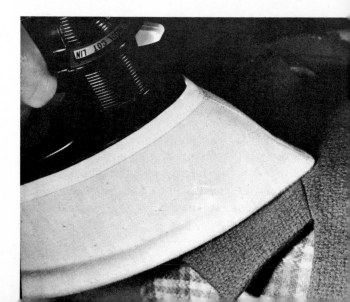

There are no creases in sleeves. The lower edge is pressed up and down on lengthwise grain of sleeve. To mold the lower edge to perfection, several soft-covered magazines often make a perfect roll. They are not taped together, so they can adjust themselves to size of sleeve.

Be certain to press the hem of the garment on the grain of the fabric. Use the iron up and down, never across. A narrow skirt will be placed over the edge of the press board, while a garment will be pressed to better perfection when a wider area of the hem can be laid out on the length of the press board. Baste-stitching is removed from pleats. Use block again where necessary as shown in construction pressing.

Press a garment in the following sequence: collar; sleeves; shoulders; facings; bodice front; bodice back; and skirt.

Holding the steam iron ½ to 1 inch away from fabric, allowing the steam to penetrate it, is an effective method to remove shine, to raise nap, and to remove an overpressed look.

WHITE vinegar is also excellent to remove shine and creases in fabric, such as hemlines that are let down. The white vinegar can be painted on these areas with a narrow paint brush. Steam press after it has been applied.

Place garment on hanger, close zipper placket, and button where necessary to hold garment on perfect grain.

In ironing a garment that has been laundered, these same final-pressing techniques will be applied. It will be necessary, however, to begin ironing on the underside to open seams, set darts correctly, maintain the roll in the sleeve cap, and so on.

When turning garment to outside to complete ironing, many fabrics will shine if iron is used directly on them. Place a dry cheesecloth on dampened dress when using iron on right side of such fabrics.

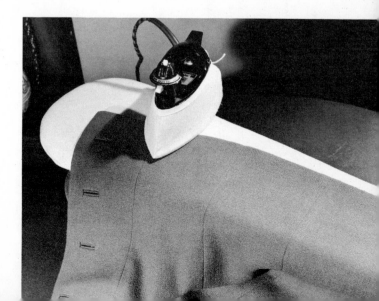

For the final success of your garment, the art of pressing is one that takes time; patience; experience; the right equipment; knowledgeability about grain line, various fabrics, and the contour of garments; and finally, the recognition of high standards. A fine seamstress cannot turn out a professional-looking, high-quality garment without this significant art of pressing. Keep working to develop your skills in pressing just as in sewing and in fitting.

FOLD

BACK
NECK FACING

FOLD

COLLAR

SLEEVE

FOLD

FACING

BACK

FRONT

SKIRT BACK

SKIRT FRONT

142

Chapter 10

Making a dress

You have come a long way in learning the fine art of sewing from the first torn projects, blouses, and skirts. Oddly enough, making dresses is actually making blouses and skirts. You will be repeating these learnings and experiencing a few additional ones. The new experiences you will have on this project are the waistline seam, dress placket zipper, set-in sleeves, interfacings, and putting on a collar. Many of these could apply to blouses as well. For the first dress, we have selected a skirt style that still has little or no fitting. Remember that in making this dress you are not only learning to make one dress, but are learning techniques and methods for making any dress.

Give some thought to whether you would prefer fabric which falls into soft folds for a soft silhouette, or a more crisp fabric for a bouffant silhouette. Use cotton, a crisp or spun rayon, or a new blend.

This dress will have six units: namely, skirt, bodice, collar and facing, sleeve, complete dress, and belt. Of course, you know how to follow all the previous learnings in Chapters 4 and 5 on preparing fabrics, cutting, and marking. Refer to page 92 for any necessary alterations in cutting, and to pages 93 and 94 for the way you will go about fitting your dress.

As you develop the art of sewing, constantly work to improve every technique each time you do it. Do not get into the habit of doing anything carelessly or inferiorly, but try to show improvement in each garment you make. Aim to develop the highest standards of workmanship.

Skirt unit

Importance of staystitching. From the first torn projects, blouses, and skirts, you have been learning about staystitching. It will carry over into every garment you make. Let us review what you have learned about it.

When beginning to work on each unit (see p. 64 on unit construction) staystitching is the very first step. It is a line of regulation machine stitching with matching thread, through a single thickness of fabric placed just outside the seamline (see sketch), unless stated another width.

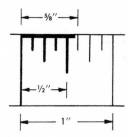

Staystitching is important because it holds the grain threads in position, prevents fabrics from stretching, and preserves the pattern line. It eliminates many self-caused sewing and fitting problems.

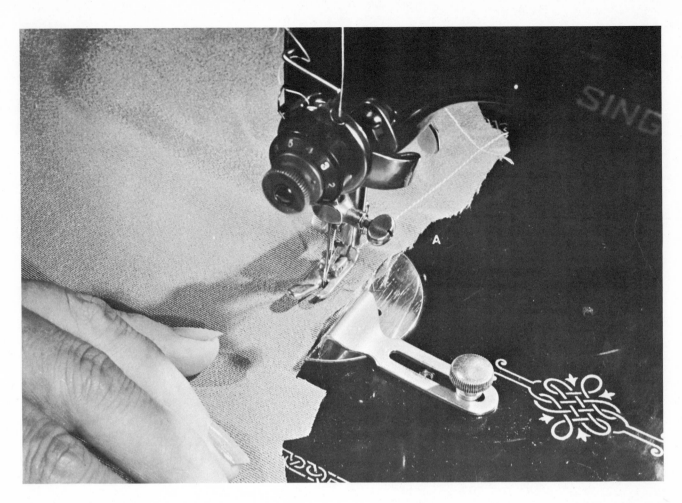

The correct direction for staystitching is important to hold grain in place. It is done in the direction that the threads lie down naturally (or the greater length of the area lies correctly). Note how threads lie down at the edge in the photograph (A). In the sketches in this chapter, the arrows indicate the correct direction and the places in which staystitching is needed.

Skirt front unit.   Staystitching waistline edge just less than ½ inch from edge (seam tape to be used in seam, p. 146, is only ½ inch wide). Staystitch sides of skirt from notch up just outside seamline. Follow arrows on sketch for correct direction.

With right sides together, stitch center seam in correct direction shown at A. Pink with pinking shears, if necessary, and press open seam. Refer to pressing chapter for help as needed in construction and final-pressing.

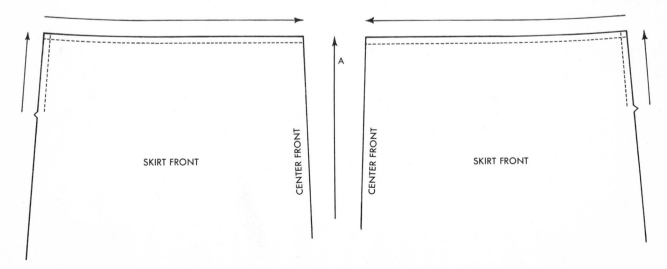

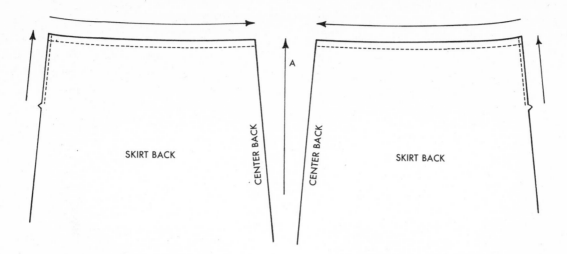

SKIRT BACK   CENTER BACK   CENTER BACK   SKIRT BACK

A

Skirt back unit. The back unit is prepared exactly as the front unit, except that the sides are staystitched ¼ inch from the edge from the notch up. The wider width would show on the left side on the finished zipper placket. It is simpler to staystitch both edges ¼ inch from the edge rather than stopping to pick out the left side.

Complete skirt unit. With right sides together, stitch skirt front unit to skirt back unit at side seams from bottom up, leaving left side open above notch for zipper placket. Unless you can be certain of exact length of zipper placket, do not fasten threads at notch. Leave them about an inch long as you can see at A in bodice photograph, page 149. When correct length for placket is determined, these threads can be tied by hand and cut off.

Pink seams with pinking shears, if necessary, and press open in same direction in which they were stitched.

Pleat lines are marked on inside of garment with tracing wheel and tracing paper. From the inside, it is very confusing to fold pleats in correct direction according to pattern markings for outside of garment.

Hand-baste pleat lines through to top of skirt. Some may prefer to use pins, but the basting permits you to make certain the fold is perfect in each pleat, and you can press the top of the pleat with the basting in it.

Line up raw edges at the top of skirt and the basting lines, as pleats are folded in place, according to pattern markings. Make certain that pleats fall to perfection to the floor.

Press pleats in place for 1 to 1½ inches down from raw edge; pin in place. Stitch in place at waistline through staystitching line. Remove hand-basting. On some fabrics, you may want to place a second row of stitching ¼ inch above the first row to help hold pleats in perfect line.

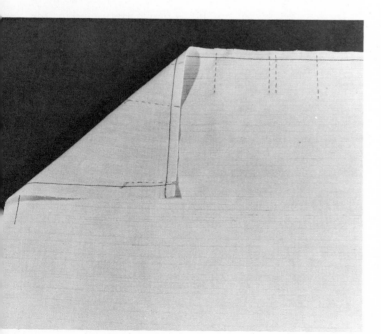

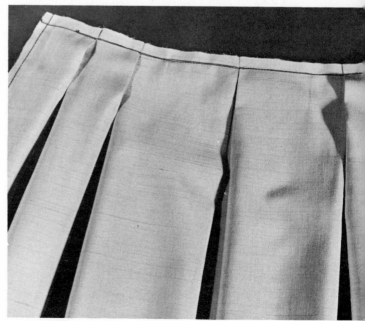

Taping waistline of skirt. Tape the waistline of the skirt before joining dress bodice and skirt to achieve a well-fitted waistline, and to control the crosswise grain at the waistline. Use a rayon seam tape; or, on cotton dresses, a cotton twill tape.

Take waist measurements, allowing for any ease you may like in the fit of clothes. With tape laid on inside of skirt, pin in place with the same series of steps you learned with the cotton skirt on page 69.

Stitch tape to skirt along lower edge of tape. If style of garment requires a fitting, baste-stitch at this point. Make this seam only ½ inch wide, because that is the width of the tape.

At front placket edge, cut down on pleat to ½-inch seamline before stitching on tape. Pin pleat out of way of seam for ease in applying zipper. This is the same technique used to remove a pocket from a side seam with a zipper placket (p. 148).

This completes the unit as far as possible at this time. Place the skirt on a skirt hanger so it will not become wrinkled while you make the bodice unit.

Straight skirt. The dress you are making may have a straight skirt. If so, you may choose to put a back drum in it that is recommended for a washable dress. This is shown on pages 46-47, *Fashion Sewing by the Bishop Method*. If the dress is to be dry-cleaned, use the full drum shown in the next chapter (pp. 178-179).

Gathered skirt. A gathered skirt may be constructed from 2 to 4 widths of fabric, depending upon width of fabric, type of fabric, and individual figure. A quality-looking skirt is always made from a lengthwise piece of fabric instead of a lengthwise piece being used crosswise. Tear pieces of fabric, seam together and press; fold to divide into quarters for making gathering threads. Always have a seam at placket edge for ease in applying zipper.

The gathering threads are made in four groups — from side placket edge to center front, center front to side, side to center back, and center back to side placket edge again. Two rows of the longest stitch at the machine are needed, one on seamline and the other ¼ inch from it toward raw edge (see sketch, p. 87, *Fashion Sewing by the Bishop Method*). Use heavy duty mercerized thread; it will withstand pulling better than regular mercerized thread (see photograph, top p. 94, *Fashion Sewing by the Bishop Method*). Adjust gathers to fit tape at waistline. While you work, the thread ends may temporarily be fastened by winding them in a figure 8 around a pin placed in fabric.

The hem of a gathered skirt should be made on true grain line of the fabric; if the hem hangs unevenly because of a figure problem, adjustment should be made at the waistline.

It may be necessary to eliminate excess fullness at the waistline; and this is accomplished by stitching darts intermittently. Fold the top of the skirt on lengthwise grain, and every 6 to 8 inches make a dart ½ inch wide at the top, and 5 to 6 inches long. Continue making gathers, stitching through the top of the darts also. Often a firm fabric or a design such as stripes would be smarter made up in unpressed pleats rather than in gathers.

With a zigzag machine, you may gather by zigzagging over kite string or fine, strong string. Then, pull up skirt on string.

Skirt with pockets in side seams. Complete the skirt front unit (p. 144). With right sides together, stitch front pocket pieces along the side seamlines from the notch to the waist edge. Lockstitch securely and precisely at notch or other pattern marking for pocket opening.

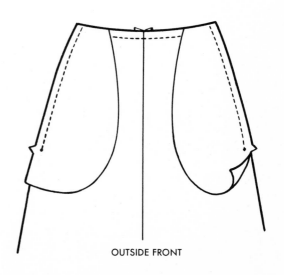

OUTSIDE FRONT

Complete the skirt back unit (p. 145). With right sides together, stitch right back pocket piece along the side seamline from the notch to the waist edge. The left one remains open the desired amount for inserting the zipper. Lockstitch securely and precisely at notch or other pattern marking for pocket opening.

OUTSIDE BACK

Join skirt units by stitching both side seams from lower edge up to pocket opening; this connects the stitching line of the pocket pieces. Then, place the skirt away from pocket pieces. Starting exactly at the knots, close the pocket pieces from notch to waist edge on both sides. Round off stitching in corners to keep lint out.

This is called a four-point closure, because four different seams must meet with perfection at the pocket opening. This is a technique that is used many times in sewing. The tailored collar on page 231 is identical. There are sometimes three-point closures in sewing.

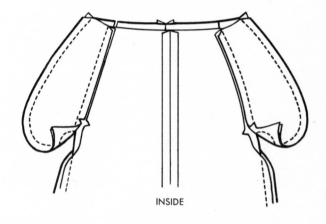

INSIDE

On both sides of skirt, trim the front side seam to ¼ inch, and understitch the edge of the front pocket piece the length of pocket opening. End the understitching 1 inch from top on left side. On the right side of the skirt, lay the pocket to the front, matching upper edges with waist edge. Baste-stitch in place.

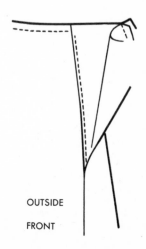

OUTSIDE

FRONT

On the left side of the skirt, part of the upper edge of the front pocket piece and the skirt must be finished to keep them free from the waistline seam and placket edge. Beginning at side seam, turn front pocket piece to outside of skirt. Stitch from side seam about halfway across width of pocket on seamline at waistline. Clip down to lockstitching. Trim seam to ¼ inch, turn, and press.

On a pleat, these raw edges may be turned into the center of the pleat, and whipstitched together.

After you learn to make the bodice, stitch the bodice and the skirt together at the waistline. Do not catch finished pocket edge in the seam; fold and pin out of the way. Insert placket zipper (p. 158).

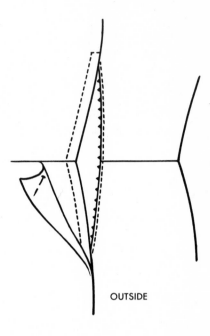

OUTSIDE

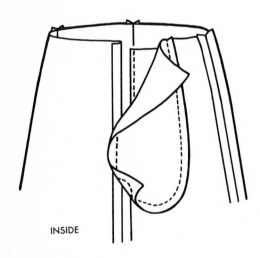

INSIDE

Finally, blind-stitch the left front pocket edge into place on waistline seam. A skirt with pleats at the placket edge is treated the same way. (See photograph, p. 158.)

Baste-stitch the remaining pocket sections and skirt together at waist edge from clip to end of pocket.

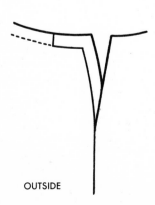

OUTSIDE

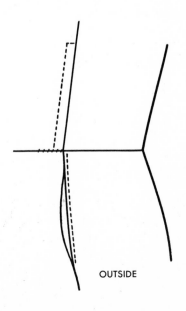

OUTSIDE

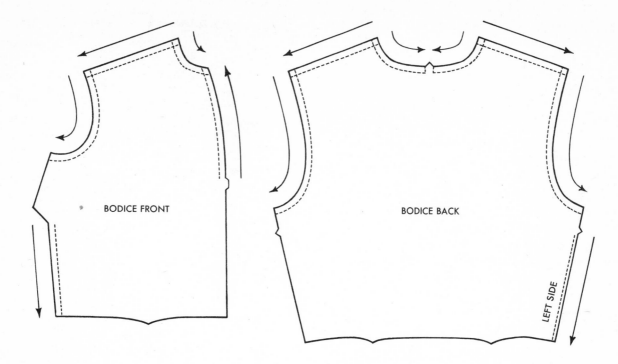

BODICE FRONT

BODICE BACK

LEFT SIDE

Bodice unit

Staystitch the neckline, front opening where it is cut off grain, shoulders, armholes, and left side of blouse front for placket opening. Staystitching is done just outside the seamline and in direction arrows indicate.

Staystitch left side of blouse back from notch down ¼ inch from edge.

Stitch the bust and bodice darts in front and back of bodice (p. 74). If permanently stitched, press to perfection (p. 136).

With right sides together, stitch shoulder and side seams in same direction in which they were staystitched. Leave left side open below notch for zipper placket. Unless you are certain of exact length of zipper placket, do not fasten threads at notch. Leave them about an inch long as was done at A. When waistline seam is sewn and correct length is determined, these threads can be tied by hand and cut off.

In stitching one of the shoulder seams, the back of the blouse will be on top; in stitching the second one, the front will be on top. It does not matter which one is on top — the correct direction for stitching is the important thing. Directional stitching is just as important for grain perfection on the finished garment as directional staystitching. So follow carefully the direction that the arrows indicate for stitching the seams.

Directional stitching eliminates many sewing and fitting problems. It holds the grain threads in position, prevents fabric from stretching, and preserves

the pattern line. You staystitch only the areas of a garment that are cut very much off grain and will have further construction detail. Yet you must hold the grain and prevent fabric from stretching at every seam of the garment by stitching in the correct direction of the grain.

If seams are permanently stitched, pink with pinking shears, and press open side seams. Shoulder seams come forward to give a yoke effect. They are pressed up.

If an individual figure has a fitting problem at the shoulders, separate front yoke on the pattern and add seam allowance at shoulders for ease in fitting shoulders.

This completes the bodice unit as far as possible at this time.

Making a dress

Collar and facing unit

Staystitch neckline, front opening where it is cut off-grain, and shoulders of front and back facings just outside seamline in direction shown.

Staystitch inside edge of front and back facings ¼ inch from edge in direction shown.

The pattern showed a round facing at the back of the neckline, but we cut it deeper and to a point. Never settle for the shape of the facing on a pattern if a different shape will give more character to a garment with a particular style, fabric, or figure (see overblouse, p. 169).

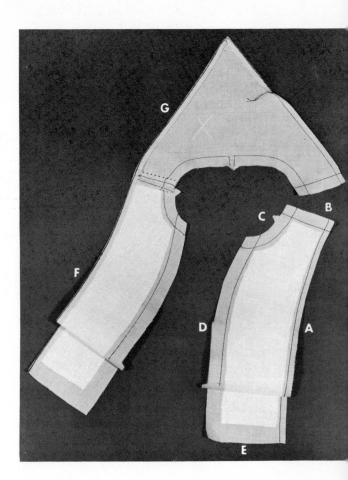

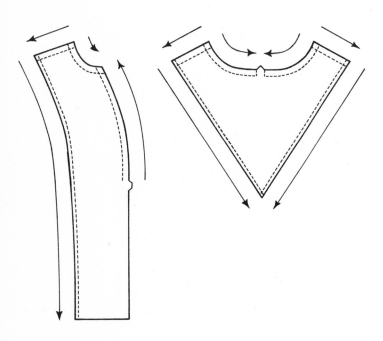

The choice of interfacing and underlining fabrics is increasing continuously in both regulation and press-on forms. A press-on interfacing is always used on the under section of the garment pieces. On these facings, instant armo dress weight was used. Here it is the front facing; next, it will be the under collar. It would have been unsatisfactory to press this on

the wrong side of the dress front, because it would show a change of texture as far over as it was used.

For handling a dress with a fold back facing, see pages 182-183.

The entire bodice front, or both front and back (see p. 169), might have been underlined with a regulation fabric that would have been staystitched with the bodice itself. For suggestions, see page 255. However, underlining a bodice completely is usually not recommended for a first dress. Neither this particular fabric nor this shirtwaist bodice design in the fabric needed more than the press-on interfacing.

At A edge, press-on is cut ⅜ inch from edge. At B, C, D, and E edges, it is cut ¾ inch from edge, so it will not be included in seamlines. After you press on the interfacing, set the piece of the garment aside for a few minutes to perfect the seal.

Join shoulder seams, press open, and trim to ¼ inch. Clean-finish outer edges of facings as you can see at F and G. To clean-finish, turn under on ¼-inch staystitching line and stitch close to folded edge.

This completes the facing unit. If you prefer to use a sew-on interfacing instead of a press-on, refer to Chapters 7, 8, and 10 in *Fashion Sewing by the Bishop Method.*

The press-on is cut ¾ inch smaller than all of the collar edges, so it will not be included in any of the seamlines. Instant armo dress weight was also used here. It was pressed on the under collar.

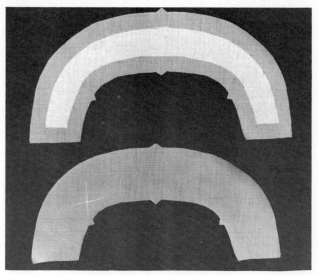

If a regulation interfacing is being used (see p. 255 for suggestions), follow these directions for stitching to under collar. Cut interfacing from same pattern piece and on same identical grain as under collar.

Staystitch to under collar on seamline in direction of grain as indicated by arrows. When the top collar is attached, the interfacing will then be stitched into the seamline. With more bulky fabrics, cut away interfacing at corners ¼ inch beyond seamline to eliminate bulk. Proceed with following techniques:

With right sides together, stitch under collar to top collar along outer curved edge. Use very small stitches at the machine, so that you may trim the seam close to ⅛ inch, and except with thick, firm fabric, it will not be necessary to trim out notches illustrated at A.

On a deeply curved collar, it is helpful to trim collar seam to ⅜ inch before stitching together outer edges (not the neckline). It is easier to handle a narrow seam when stitching to perfection on a deep curve.

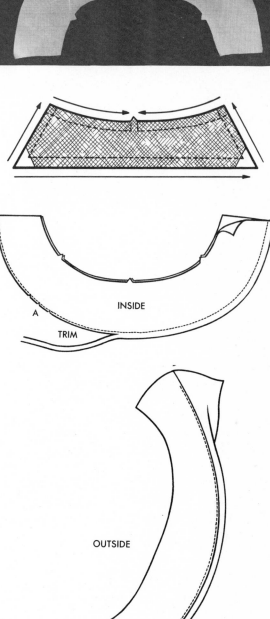

Understitch the under collar, beginning and ending one inch from the edge. (This is necessary so that ends of collar will lie flat when they are stitched together later.) Understitching is a row of machine stitching along the edge of the under collar that secures the two trimmed seams to the under collar. More information on understitching can be found on pages 88-89.

With right sides together, stitch both ends of collar, using very small stitches for ½ inch at A and A. This small stitching will make secure corners when fabric is trimmed close and corners are turned right side out. Press the seams open on point presser. Trim seams to ⅛ inch and round off seam allowance at corner to within a few threads of stitching line.

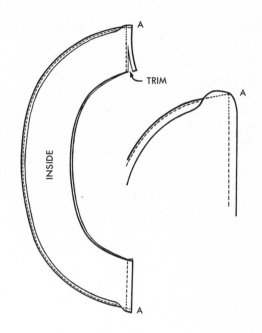

In some angles, and in some fabrics, a corner will turn easily without being trimmed close as illustrated above. Try one; if it doesn't turn satisfactorily, you can always turn it wrong side out again and trim it.

The seam allowance at A and B edges are trimmed down to ⅛ or ¼ inch as needed for entire collar. Then, turn down seam allowance at A; turn back seam allowance at B. Hold both seam allowances in place with finger or thumb, and turn corner over finger or thumb.

If edges need staggering as is done on a tailored garment, trimmed edges should be toward you, so you will have the long one to turn in and hold with your finger or thumb.

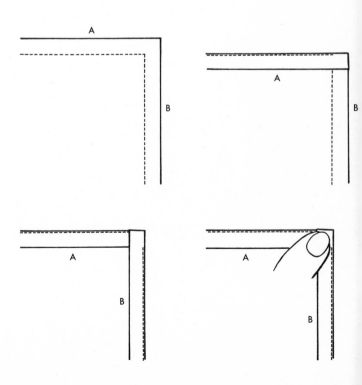

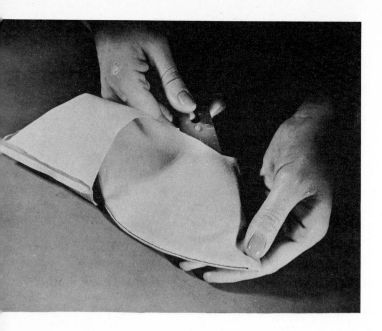

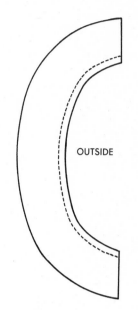

OUTSIDE

Turn collar right side out; work corners out until the stitching shows all the way to the corner. Any help you need to turn the corners can only be placed at the line of stitching. Press first with under collar up; then, press with top collar up. Press collar with grain of fabric.

If a fabric does not lie in place easily and to perfection, it will be helpful to stitch together the neck edges just outside the seamline.

Place and pin collar on dress with under collar to right side of dress. Clip the neck edge of collar and dress to give a straight line for stitching. There should be at least one clip on each side of the shoulder seam close to the seam. With the garment side on top, and with ⅝-inch seam allowance, stitch collar to neck edge from one edge of collar to the other.

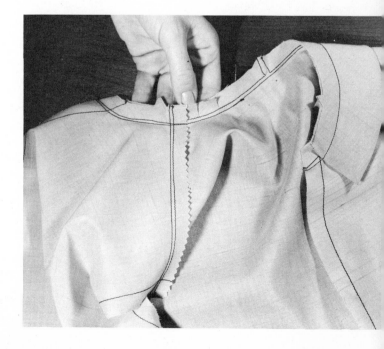

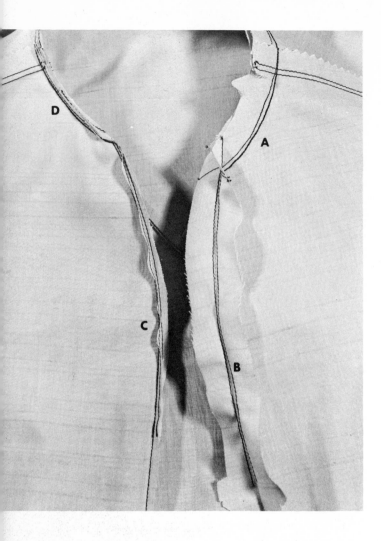

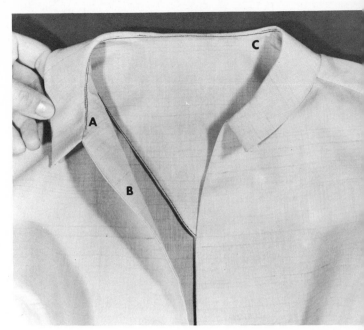

Place the facings on dress, right sides together; collar will be between them. Key centers, shoulder seams, etc., and clip neck edge of facing to give a straight line for stitching. Again, with garment side up, stitch facings to dress, stitching through same line of stitching that sewed collar to dress (A). Use edge presser to press open seams on front of dress (B) before trimming to ¼ inch (C). At neckline, trim entire seam to ¼ inch (D). Where edges curve sharply, further clip seam allowance to seamline. With heavier fabrics, you may reach in with the scissors and trim the collar to ⅛ inch to stagger width of this bulky seam.

Understitch neck edge of facing; on this style of dress, it will have to begin about one inch from corner (A). Understitching is a row of machine stitching along the neck edge of the facing that secures the trimmed seams to the facing. It is helpful in keeping the facing in place. However, it is not used on a front facing (B) because it would show on the completed garment. Turn facings to inside of dress and press in place. Use a cushion to mold them at neckline and shoulders (C). Have collar hanging free over edge of cushion while pressing facing in place up to collar. Hand tack at yoke seams. This completes the collar unit.

Sleeve unit

Staystitch ¼ inch from lower edge (A). Using hem gauge, press up hem. Then, depending upon fabric, either finish hem with rayon seam tape (see p. 172) or clean-finish. As you can see in the following photograph, this dress was clean-finished. To do so, turn under on ¼-inch staystitching line and stitch close to folded edge.

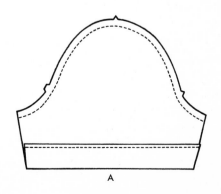

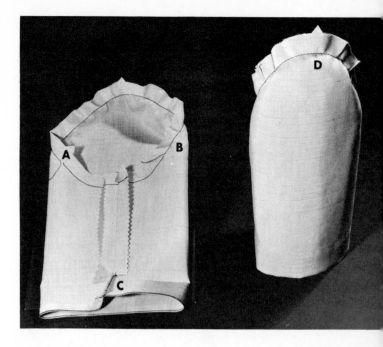

Staystitch entire sleeve cap with about ten stitches per inch in the length of the machine stitch.

Then, clip bobbin thread at front and back notches (A and B in photograph) and pull up ease. This is known as the "ease line" method.

Stitch sleeve seam from armhole down. If permanently stitched, pink seam, and press open. Trim seam in hem (C) to ¼ inch, and press up hem again at seamline to restore it.

Adjust ease to fit armhole of dress, and press cap to perfection (D) as you have learned on page 138. It is important that you manipulate the ease to have a perfect, rounded cap. Make certain that the cap (D) is grain perfect from one side to the other.

Hem sleeve with one of two methods (p. 62).

With right sides together, pin sleeve into armhole with two pins, one pin matching the underarm seam of sleeve and dress, and the other pin matching extra notch at top of sleeve with shoulder line.

You should never stretch the armhole; nor should you let it pucker. Then, in addition to the proper ease on the sleeve, there should be a graceful amount of ease all around the sleeve as it is stitched into the armhole, even underarm. This graceful ease would eliminate a sleeve's having a tendency to push out underarm.

When sewing in a sleeve, make sure it is always on top and the garment below. Begin stitching underarm and continue all the way around the circle, sewing one thread inside the ease line. You may reinforce the underarm seam by beginning the stitching at the back notch, and sewing the armhole again from the back notch to the front one, after you have completed the first circle.

Finish seam as desired, and press armhole as shown on page 138. If the fabric ravels easily, you may hold the seam allowances together and make a second row of stitching ¼ inch from the first row. Then, pink the edges.

There should not be any gathers or pleats at the seamline. One of the important aspects of sewing is learning to do a well-set sleeve for a finished appearance in a garment. Another technique is shown on page 235.

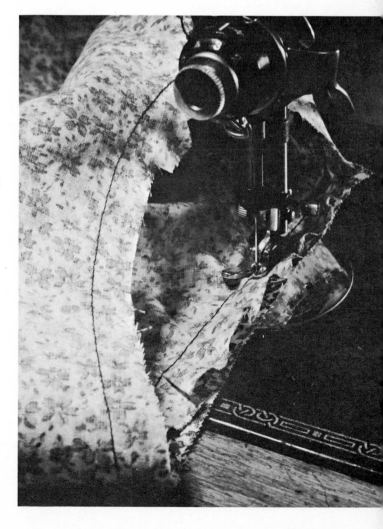

Making a dress

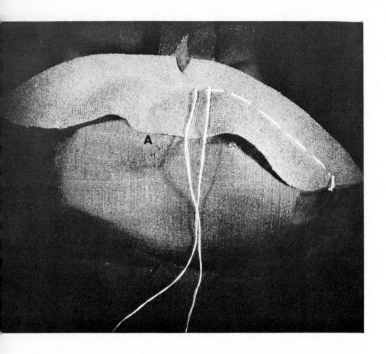

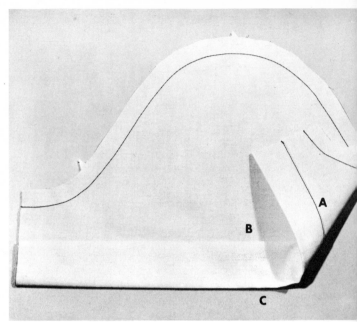

Some fabrics need more attention to achieve and maintain a rounded look at the top of the sleeve, and to keep the seam allowance from showing. You do not want a head on your sleeve, but do want the standards described above.

If further work is needed, cut a strip of true bias approximately 6 inches long, and 1½ inches wide, or use the sleeve pattern to cut bias strip the same shape as top of sleeve. This is placed only over the cap of the sleeve, and does not extend from notch to notch. Its own fabric is used, unless it is too firm or too fine, in which case a substitute like flannelette is preferred. Sometimes, as with cotton fabrics, the strip is used double and is cut with a fold at A.

Begin with the bias strip where you have the greatest ease, and pull or work it into place. Match edge (or two edges if used double) of bias strip to sleeve seam edge. Stitch by hand as close as possible to the sleeve line of stitching. The armhole seam always turns into the sleeve.

Do not use this bias strip on sleeves with dropped shoulders.

One of the principles of the Bishop method is to complete as much as possible of the lower edge of a sleeve before the sleeve seam is sewn. An exception to this would be a sleeve with a cuff; then, the seam would be sewn first, and the cuff applied to the closed circle.

You learned how to do the sleeve with a hem on pages 154-155. If the sleeve has a self-turned cuff, however, before stitching the seam of the sleeve, clean-finish the lower edge (A). Then, with sleeve out flat, press to inside on fold line (B) indicated on pattern. Next, press to outside on fold line as also indicated on pattern to form cuff (C). Stitch seam of sleeve from top down, finish seam if necessary, and press open. Re-press folds of cuff at seamline and hem sleeve in desired manner. This is much easier than trying to press the folds in a closed circle.

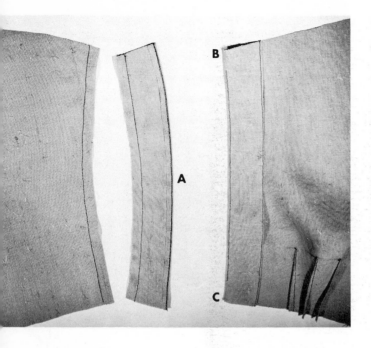 

If a sleeve has a fitted facing, the facing is cut with identical grain to lower edge of sleeve. Staystitch lower edge of sleeve and facing just outside seamline. Clean-finish upper edge of facing (A) or apply seam tape as discussed on page 172.

With right sides together, and with sleeve side up, stitch the facing to the sleeve on seamline. Trim seam to ¼ inch, and understitch edge of the facing (p. 88), beginning and ending understitching one inch from edges (B and C). Press facing in place. Stitch seam of sleeve and facing from top down. Finish seam, if necessary, and press open. Trim seam of facing to ¼ inch. Press facing again at seamline to restore edge. Hem sleeve with either of two methods described on page 62.

An interesting effect, known as a simulated cuff, can be achieved with just one row of stitching.

Staystitch lower edge of sleeve ¼ inch from edge, and turn up and press hem as discussed on page 154. Then, turn under and press raw edge of hem on ¼-inch staystitching line. After the sleeve seam has been sewn, finished, and pressed, turn hem to outside of sleeve at top of hem. Stitch close to edge of crease at top of hem, catching top of hem in stitching line also. Turn hem down in place. This gives the effect of a cuff.

OUTSIDE

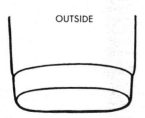

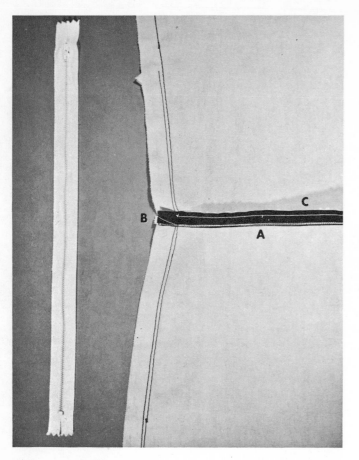

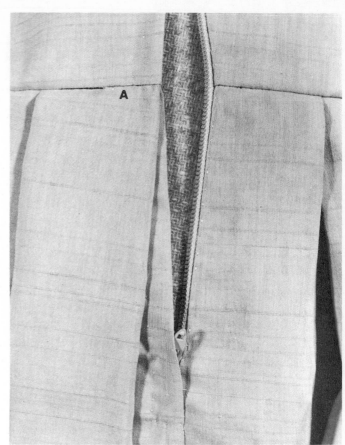

Complete dress unit

Joining skirt to bodice. Lap right front of bodice over left front, matching centers, and stitch lower edge together from end of one facing to the other.

Join bodice to skirt, matching center fronts, center backs, side seams, and placket edges. With skirt side up, stitch again along lower edge of tape (A). At both edges of placket opening, decrease waistline seam back ⅝ inch; this eliminates a pucker on front placket edge (B). Press up waistline seam (p. 136). Pink the edges, and with fabrics that ravel easily, stitch both seam edges along the upper edge of the tape (C). There is no outside stitching at the waistline.

Dress placket zipper. Insert the zipper in the dress by the same series of steps that were used for inserting the zipper in the skirt (p. 66). The only difference is that the last stitching extends across both ends of the opening. Lastly, slipstitch edge of pleat that has been cut down to make insertion of zipper easier (A).

There are many fabrics whose texture and weight make a hand-sewn placket more suitable, attractive, and quality-looking. Spongy, napped, and pile fabrics such as knits, velveteen, and corduroy, and hard-

surfaced or soft, delicate fabrics as Alaskine, chiffons, and crepes are all enhanced by a hand-sewn zipper application (see photographs, pp. 173 and 244).

Baste-stitch last row of stitching on front edge as a guide for hand-picking. Then, baste-stitching can be removed when hand-picking is completed.

Do hand-picking from topside of dress. Use buttonhole twist thread or double mercerized thread in needle. Draw thread through a beeswax holder. Bring needle to topside of fabric. Take stitch backward when putting needle to underside of fabric. Bring needle to topside of fabric ¼ inch from first stitching. Continue hand-picking placket opening for a fine custom look. Remove baste-stitching.

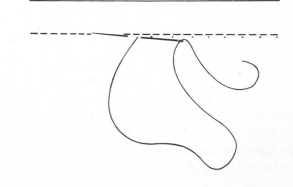

Hem. Hem the dress with one of the methods shown with the skirts on page 62, with hem tape on page 172, or with another finish on raw edge, page 243. On those pages, the appropriate finish for different fabrics is discussed.

Sewing on buttons. Make machine buttonholes in right front of dress. To mark with perfection for button placement, lay dress so that the outside of the two front edges meet exactly. If necessary, use a few pins to hold in place. Then, place a pin through the front edge of the buttonhole at the center line; this is the correct place to sew on the button.

To sew on a button, use a double thread with a secure knot at the end. However, if your needle has a large enough eye, and you use two strands double to make four for sewing, you will only need to take half as many stitches.

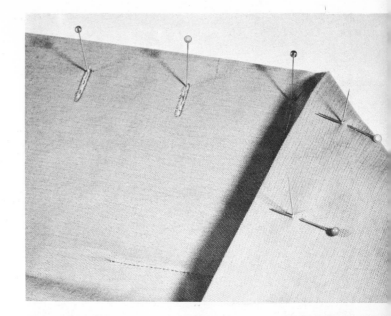

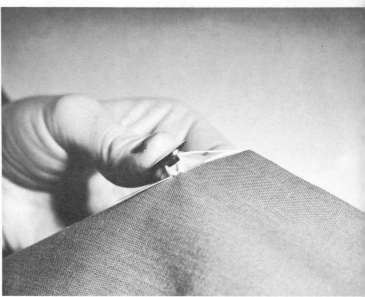

After bringing up thread in fabric, take a small stitch to secure thread and knot in fabric. Then, with the thumb on top and the forefinger under the button, and the other fingers under the fabric, sew through button and fabric the necessary number of times to hold the button securely. The forefinger holds the button up from the fabric the required amount to make shank for the thickness of the buttonhole.

Next, bring the needle out between the button and the garment, and wind the thread several times to make a firm shank. Take needle and thread to inside of garment and secure thread with several back stitches. Cut off remaining thread.

The shank is always necessary when a buttonhole lies between the button and garment, but not when a button is sewn on for decorative purposes. Buttons with cloth shanks need thread shanks also, but not those with their own metal shanks.

Final-pressing. Your dress will be final-pressed, following the suggestions on pages 140-141. When you place it on a hanger, make certain that the shoulders, sleeves, and all parts are hanging on grain perfection. Close the top button. Close the zipper.

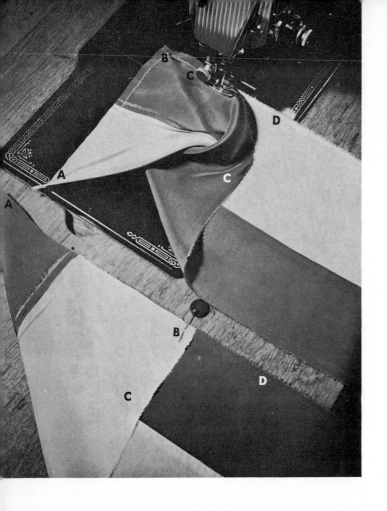

Making various belts

Suggestions for making belts and sashes follow. The width and the way you wear a belt will be determined by your figure and style of dress.

Bias sash. One of the most popular belts is this Bishop sash. This one is in two colors and can be worn many ways. More ideas can be found in the next photograph. There is no pattern. The belt can be made any desired length or width. When stitching is completed, the belt will be approximately two-thirds as wide and two-thirds as long as the original piece. Use either crosswise or lengthwise strips of fabric. Try one from scraps of fabric to determine the best size for you, and the best way to wear it.

Stitch from A to B. Place needle down in fabric exactly where pin is placed; remove pin; lift presser foot; and bring C edge to D edge. Put down presser foot and stitch to bottom of strip, continuing to bring C to D all the way. Press open seam on edge presser, and turn belt to other side; close end.

The straight strips lie on a bias when the belt is complete.

A belt on page 160 is worn with B belt. They are two colors of the same print, and are twisted and worn in several ways.

C belt shows the effect of stitching vertical strips in this sash treatment.

D is made of straight strips of black and white pique.

E is made of one-half red and white polka dot, and one-half navy and white polka dot. The two colors were joined at center front before the sash was stitched.

There are many ways to wear a bias sash. This one may be used as a cummerbund without any ends hanging, as can those shown on page 160.

This first one is tied in a knot. A bias belt adjusts itself well to the waistline.

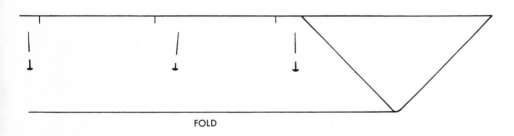

FOLD

Second bias sash. If you would like a bias belt or sash without any seams within, as in the above one, then you will have to begin with a piece of fabric cut on the bias (p. 259).

Fold the fabric in half and make nicks with the scissors about every six inches. Then, match the nicks as you stitch this bias seam. The sash will be kept from rolling.

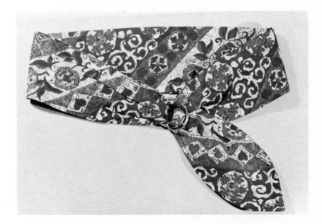

This second one has two metal rings sewn at one end. The other end of the sash goes through both rings, and then back through just one ring to keep it from slipping.

Tailored belts. Many attractive bandings are available in stores. Washable belting (A) can be purchased the same desired width of banding. Edge-stitch banding to belting at both sides (B and C). A tailored bow may be made at the front closing (D), and a large hook and eye used to fasten the belt underneath (p. 70).

You may prefer a belt of matching fabric for your dress (E). With right sides together, fold lengthwise strip of fabric over belt (F). The fabric strip should be cut with approximately ¼-inch seam allowance. Use zipper foot and stitch seam close to belting.

Remove belting and press open seam on wooden dowel (G). Other sizes of wooden dowels that you may purchase are shown at H in photograph. If the size is right, you may also use a yardstick or a pencil. Not only are dowels used to press belts, but they are also used to press open seams of bias shown many places in the last chapter.

If a belt is to be completed with a buckle or a button and buttonhole, then one end should be pointed. Place seam in center and draw point on belt from point cut on belting (I). This should never be too sharp a point. Stitch point with small stitches (J).

Turn belt right side out. Slide over belting and press. Topstitch as desired (E) and press again.

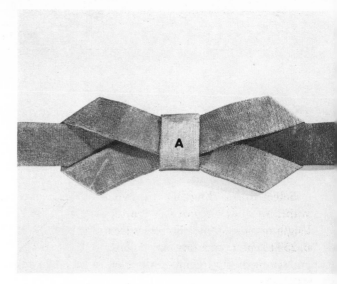

This belt fastens at the side seam with hooks and eyes. A second piece of the finished belting is folded to form the tailored bow at center front. The ends are concealed under the center of the bow (A).

Corded bias tubing. Bias tubing is versatile for belts. Note how two pieces in two colors are used for a belt in the top of the photograph (p. 163). The one in this photograph is long enough to wrap around the waistline twice, and tie in a knot if desired.

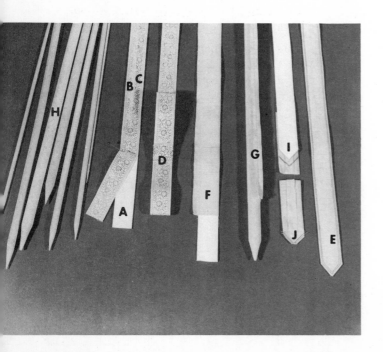

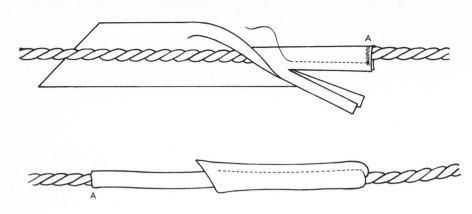

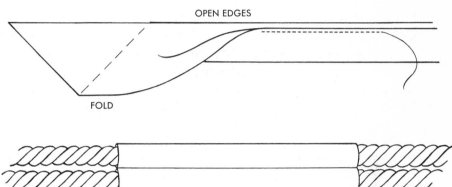

Select the cording thickness you want, and cut the cord twice the length of needed bias. Fold bias (see p. 259 to cut it) over one end of cord, and sew with zipper foot. Use a short stitch at machine, and stretch bias as you sew. At the end of the bias (A), sew bias to cord. Trim seam. Turn bias right side out (beginning at A) over other end of cord. Cut away other half of cording.

Double corded bias tubing. The top belt is described on page 162. The lower one is a double corded belt and is made with one row of stitching.

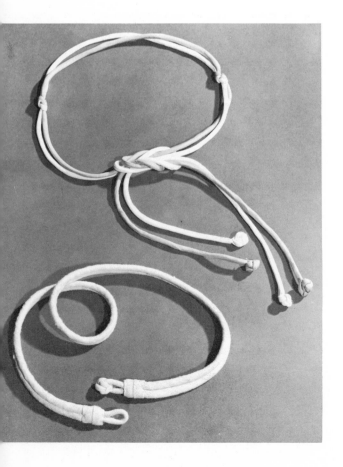

Cut true bias (p. 259). The width will depend on weight of fabric and size of cord. Fold lengthwise and press. Fold lengthwise once more, allowing raw edges to extend ⅛ inch beyond pressed fold. Stitch near fold; this forms a double tubing. Attach bobby pin or other turner to inner tube. Turn bias right side out by pulling it through inner and outer tube. This forms two connected tubes. Insert cord into tubes, if desired.

Summary of directional staystitching

As a teacher, student, or dressmaker, you will learn much from this summary of directional staystitching and of directional stitching of seams. It will summarize and illustrate the story for you in relation to grain on cut edges for all of your sewing.

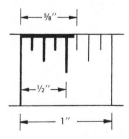

Staystitching is your first step in garment construction. It is a line of regulation machine stitching with matching thread, through a single thickness of fabric, placed just outside the seamline, unless stated another width. It is not secured at the ends with lockstitching. Staystitching is important because it holds the grain threads in position, prevents fabric from stretching, and preserves the pattern line. It eliminates many self-caused sewing and fitting problems. The correct direction for staystitching is necessary to hold the grain in place. This is done in the

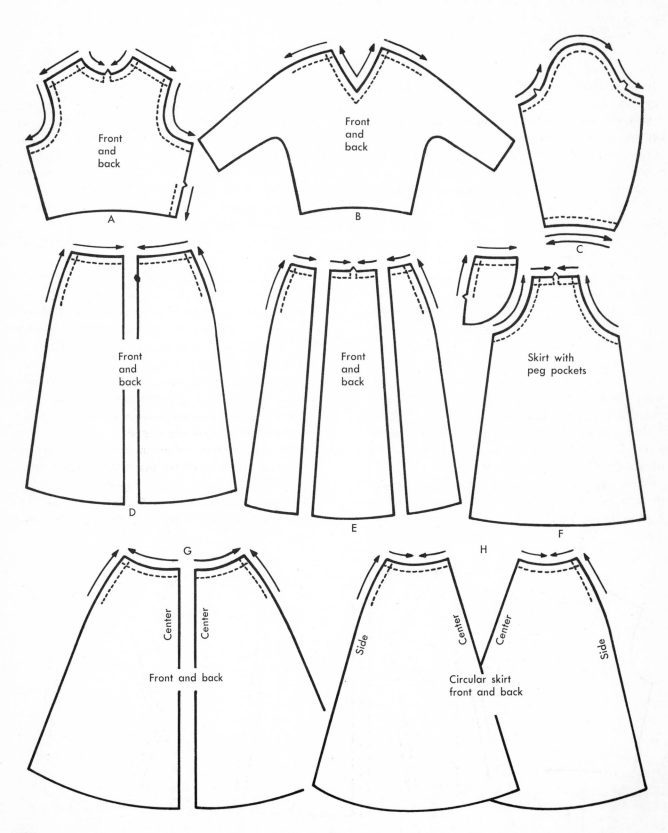

direction the threads lie in their natural position or in which the greater length of the area lies correctly. The arrows on the sketches on page 164 also indicate the correct direction and the places staystitching is needed on the lines of a garment.

The pointed neck in sketch B is staystitched in opposite direction of round neck in sketch A.

Raglan sleeve, as in sketch B, is staystitched only the width of regulation shoulder.

The placket opening in sketch A is staystitched on left side of front and back bodice for length of opening only.

Sketch B has a placket opening in center back, so left side is not staystitched.

Lower edge of sleeve (sketch C) is staystitched for facing or cuff application. The top of the sleeve is staystitched below the notches at the same time the sleeve cap is being prepared with an ease line or off-grain stitching.

Any area in the style of a garment that is to have further construction detail is staystitched, such as edge for peg pockets in sketch F.

The top of a skirt is always staystitched (sketches D, E, F, G, and H), unless on straight of grain. However, the lower edge of the bodice is not staystitched. Note that direction of staystitching changes at the top of the skirt with various styles of skirts.

Both side seams of front and back of skirt are always staystitched from notch up (sketches D, E, G, and H), unless on straight of grain.

Edges of a garment to be clean-finished are also staystitched, as are edges to have a rolled hem. This staystitching is ⅛ to ¼ inch from edge.

Sheer fabrics require a layer of tissue paper under them to prevent puckering for staystitching, or stitching together two pieces of fabric.

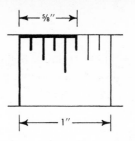

Summary of directional stitching of seams

Directional stitching is as important for grain perfection on the finished garment as directional staystitching, so carefully follow the direction the arrows indicate for stitching seams. In stitching one of the shoulder seams, for example, the back of the bodice will be on top; in stitching the second one, the front will be on top. It does not matter which one is on top — the correct direction for stitching is the important thing.

Directional stitching eliminates many self-caused sewing and fitting problems. It holds the grain threads in position, prevents fabric from stretching, and preserves the pattern line. You staystitch only the areas of a garment that are cut very much off grain and will have further construction detail. Yet, at every seam of the garment, you must hold the grain and prevent fabric from stretching by stitching in the correct direction of the grain. Sketch C shows that skirt seams are always stitched from bottom up (seam 1). The exception is when they are straight of grain and can be stitched in either direction (seam 2).

On a fitted garment (sketch D), the seams are stitched down to the waistline from the armhole. Stop there and stitch up to the waistline from lower edge for correct direction of grain.

The arrows on this chart indicate the correct direction for stitching on the majority of pattern lines. However, there may be some exceptions with unusual pattern lines, such as a peg-top skirt. Then the side seams are stitched from top to bottom of skirt.

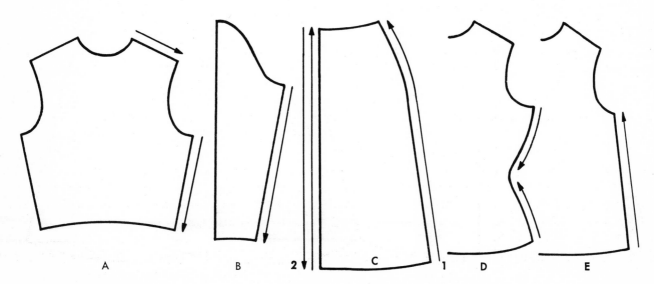

A   B   2   C   1   D   E

Chapter 11

Making a three-piece ensemble

There is quite a difference between making a torn project and an ensemble. This progress should be very encouraging.

Yet, as you develop the art of sewing, you will be repeatedly using your basic learnings while you develop new techniques. There is much you will learn on these three garments, that you will be able to use on many others. You will be making a straight skirt with a drum, fitting a straight one, using underlining in the overblouse, doing your first lining in a jacket, and placing a separating zipper in a box pleat of an overblouse.

Moreover, you will be working with more of a luxury fabric, such as linen, wool, or silk linen. It is a pleasure to work with these fabrics.

This chapter covers much material. Remember to follow all your previous learnings in Chapters 4 and 5 on preparing fabrics, cutting and marking. In making your first straight skirt, you will need to study

necessary cutting-to-fit alterations from Chapter 8, or make a master pattern (page 93) for a straight skirt and underwaist before you cut out your ensemble.

The overblouse

Cutting overblouse. After you have made the more simple blouses, skirts, and dresses without underlinings, with just an interfacing as needed, you are ready to use an underlining. Except for a few styles and fabrics, there is little of the advanced sewing done without complete underlinings in garments, as you will see in this chapter and in Chapters 12 and 13.

The underlining is cut precisely like the front and back of the overblouse, and on the same identical grain. Construction markings for darts, etc. are marked on underlining only. Crisp Si Bonne was used in this overblouse.

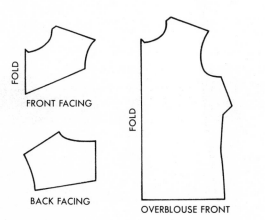

FRONT FACING

BACK FACING

OVERBLOUSE FRONT

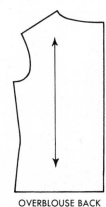

OVERBLOUSE BACK

No matter what the pattern has for a closing in the back, you may add 2 inches beyond center back marking for box pleat construction. Cut with A edge on selvage, if possible. Cut overblouse desired length for individual plus ⅝-inch seam at neckline (A in photograph, page 169) and 1½-inch hem (B) at lower edge. In planning the length, remember that separating zippers are available in 16-, 18-, 20-, and 22-inch lengths. To cut two strips for zipper application, see page 172.

If the pattern has sleeves, and you would like to make the overblouse sleeveless and bind the armholes, as we did with this one, the ⅝-inch seam should be cut off around armholes. You will be binding the finished size of armhole.

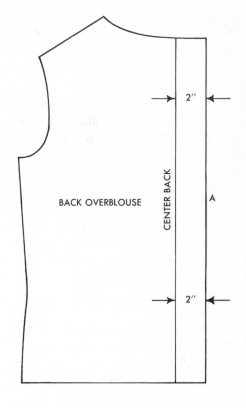

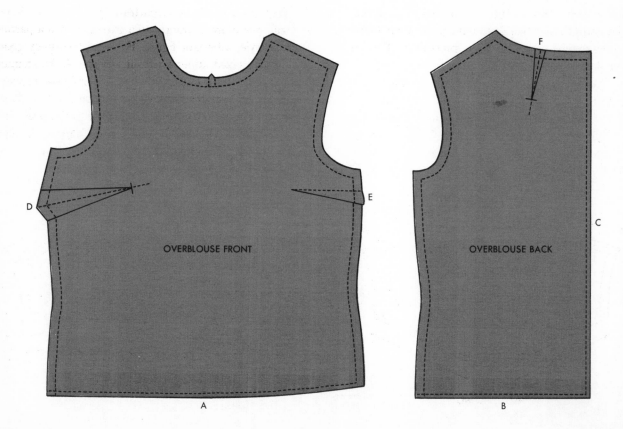

Applying underlining.   Place underlining to wrong side of fabric. Press to adhere in place, and to free any wrinkles in both fabrics. Pin in place with a few pins back from stitching line. Up to this garment, staystitching has been done in correct direction of grain. However, when you begin to work with underlining, you will be staystitching to include it, and you will have greater control when you staystitch with the firm underlining on top. This is done even though you may be sewing against the grain on some of the edges. The photograph on page 190 illustrates this point.

In all of your sewing, when one edge has more control than another, sew with the firm one or the one having greater control on top. For that reason, there are no arrows for staystitching. When you start at one edge of front or back overblouse, just continue sewing all around. Staystitch ¼ inch from edge at A and B for hem, and at C for edge of back opening. Staystitching at armholes will be ⅝ inch wide, if you are using the bias binding, and would like it that wide with your fabric. All other edges are staystitched just outside seamline.

The basting through the center of the darts at D and F will eliminate shifting of the two sections during construction. When darts have been sewn, bastestitching can be removed. Then, press darts (E). (See lower sketches, p. 168.)

Facing unit.   Baste-stitch center back opening 2 inches from edge and press open. Remove bastestitching (C). Right sides together, stitch shoulder seams in correct direction of grain from neckline out to armhole. Finish seams with pinking shears, and press open (page 134). The imprint of seams in pressing is rarely a problem with underlining. A and B are discussed on page 168.

As learned in Chapter 10, we do not settle for the shape of a facing on a pattern, if a different shape will give more character to a garment with a particular style, fabric, or figure. Facings are usually good cut to a point at center front. To give more character to the shoulders of this boxy overblouse, facings were also cut deeper and out to the armhole line.

If further help is needed to give body, press instant armo to underlining (page 226) or facings (page 150).

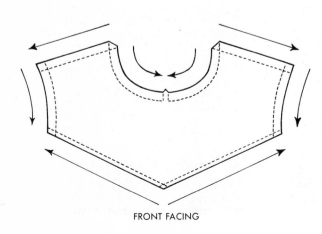

FRONT FACING

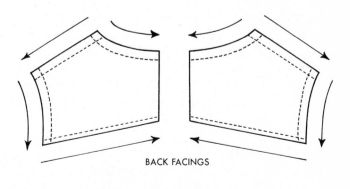

BACK FACINGS

Staystitch neckline, shoulders, and armholes of front and back facings just outside seamline in direction shown. Staystitch lower edges ¼ inch from edge in direction shown on page 169.

Right sides together, join shoulder seams of front and back facings. Press open and trim to ¼ inch. Clean-finish outer edges of front and back facings. To clean-finish, turn under on ¼-inch staystitching line, and stitch close to folded edge.

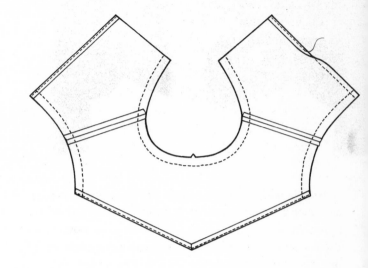

Turn 2 inches extra at center back of overblouse to right side on folded, pressed line. Place facing on top of this extension; it only needs to overlap ½ inch at A. If it was cut to extend farther, it may now be trimmed away. In heavy fabric, it may be seamed to B edge of extension.

With right sides together, and with garment side up, stitch facings to neckline, matching shoulder seams and notches at center front. Use short stitches for added strength. Trim seam to ⅛ inch; if it is heavier fabric, you can now be introduced to staggering edges, and trim as shown on page 225.

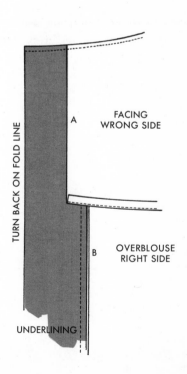

TURN BACK ON FOLD LINE

A

FACING
WRONG SIDE

B

OVERBLOUSE
RIGHT SIDE

UNDERLINING

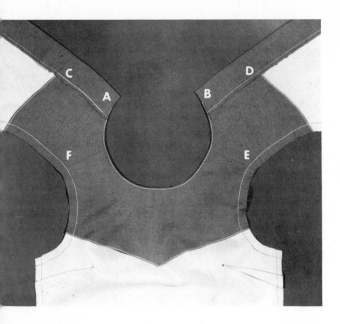

Turn facing to underside of garment. Beginning one inch from center back at A, understitch facing to within one inch of center back at B. Understitching is a row of machine stitching along the edge of the facing that secures the two trimmed seams to the facing.

Press facing in place as you learned on page 139. Stitch facings to extension at C and D through staystitching ¼ inch from edge on extension. Staystitch facings in place at armholes (E and F).

If your style of overblouse has sleeves, you could still cut the facings to extend to the armholes.

Right sides together, stitch side seams in correct direction of grain. The grain of this pattern required stitching from armhole down. Pink seams with pinking shears and press open.

Bias binding at armholes. Cut true bias four times as wide as desired finished width (see page 259). Mold it carefully around the armhole to determine size needed before it can be seamed to form a circle (see page 259). With garment side up (control side as we learned on page 169), stitch in place (A) through staystitching on seamline. Press bias flat at B, as it is turned under at C, and as it is molded to perfection around armhole.

Stitching at D is done from garment side through well of seamline at B. This gives a built-in, attractive finish in heavy fabrics. For lighter-weight fabrics, raw edge can be turned under at D, or cut double originally with fold of fabric at E.

It is not recommended to use a piece of bias as a facing instead of a binding. A shaped facing is a finer, quality finish (page 88). The facing may be cut from the pattern of the front and back bodice, and on the same grain line. If you had preferred facings, they could have been cut in one with the neckline facing (page 84).

The trim at the neckline (F) is a piece of turned bias (page 259) that is sewn in place with invisible hand stitches (page 274). Ends are sewn in shoulder seams. Ends of second piece (G) are slipped under the first piece.

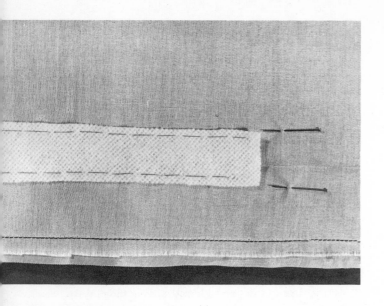

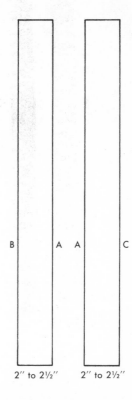

Hem unit. Hems are not too sharply defined in today's fashion. So, when hem is turned up 1½ inches, it may not be pressed at lower edge. In fact, in soft, fine fabrics such as silk linen, a piece of 1-inch wide bias flannelette or other spongy fabric may be sewn by hand to underlining. Place ⅝ inch toward garment from hemline, and ⅜ inch toward hem. This gives the hem a rolled look. Inform your cleaner.

2″ to 2½″   2″ to 2½″

Sew on hem tape to staystitching ¼ inch from edge. Hem to underlining as shown on page 243.

B edges may be finished with hem tape if not cut on selvage. They will be hand sewn to hem as shown in sketch on page 173. A edges are not fastened to overblouse, except when zipper is hand-picked in place.

Box pleat zipper application. The zipper will be sewn into two lengthwise strips of fabric. They should be 2 to 2½ inches wide with one edge (B and C) on selvage if possible. In length (see next photograph), make them the length of finished overblouse (or zipper) plus 1½-inch hem allowance at top and bottom edges.

If B and C edges could not be selvage, staystitch ⅜ inch from edge and pink with pinking shears. If fabric frays easily, seam tape may be applied at D and E edges. In this fabric, they were just staystitched and pinked.

Turn in A edges (shown above) ¼ inch and topstitch strips close to zipper (bottom photograph, next page). Hand sew D and E edges in place as well as along zipper tape at F and G.

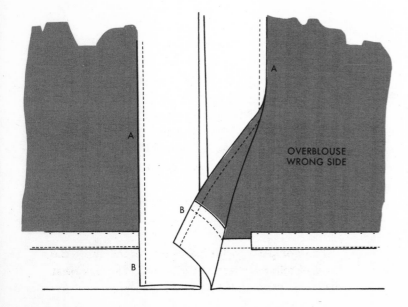

OVERBLOUSE
WRONG SIDE

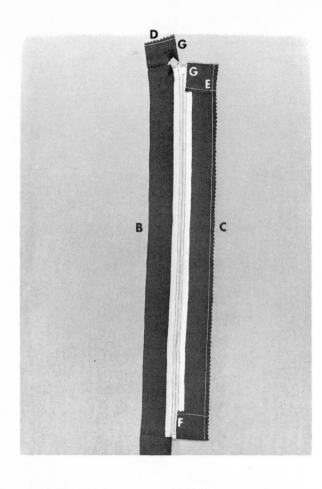

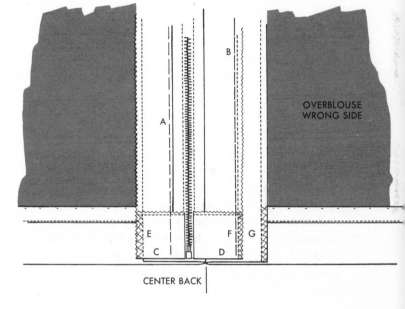

When the foregoing unit is completed and pressed, place under back of overblouse. Move zipper ¾ inch off center so it will be concealed. Pin in place. Hand-pick (page 158) strips to overblouse 1¼ inches from center back. This may be wider, if desired, when strips are cut more than 2 inches wide. Hold center back edges together at neckline with a hook and eye, and at lower edge, if desired.

A and B show where hand-picking falls on underside. In heavier fabric, it could be done through zipper tape on A side, and this strip of fabric eliminated altogether. However, in bulky fabric, you may prefer to apply the separating zipper in a seam in center back of overblouse exactly as shown on pages 80-82. The separating lightweight jacket zipper of metal is presently the only one available for this technique.

Slipstitch C and D edges at top and bottom of overblouse. Whipstitch E, F, and G in place as shown.

This box-pleat technique is also excellent on the front of tailored dresses, robes, etc. The box pleat makes an interesting detail on a garment.

Making a three-piece ensemble

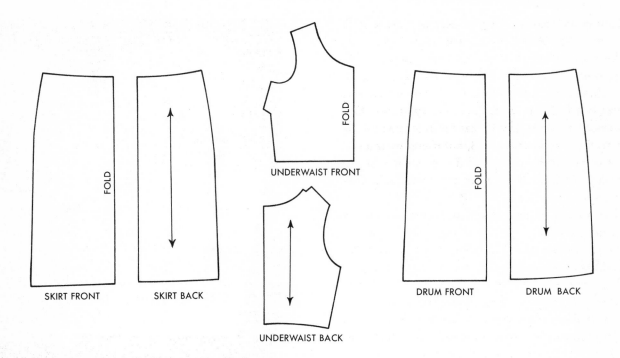

SKIRT FRONT   SKIRT BACK   UNDERWAIST FRONT   UNDERWAIST BACK   DRUM FRONT   DRUM BACK

The skirt with drum and underwaist

Cutting skirt and drum.   As you learned on the overblouse, you are now far enough advanced in your sewing that you can cut a desired technique into the line of your pattern, no matter what the pattern may show.

A drum in a skirt is going to be made in this chapter. It will give body to the skirt, help it to keep its shape, and will be your half-slip sewn right in your skirt. Many people have wondered about making one separate drum to wear with all of their straight skirts. It would never be as satisfactory as the technique shown here.

The drum is often called a lining. However, the name drum is preferred. Underlining skirts is discussed in Chapter 13. We feel that these two words, drum and underlining, best serve to describe their purposes.

The drum in this skirt is made of Earl-Glo twill. A rayon twill is a good choice, as is soft Si Bonne for warm-weather skirts. The drum should be a firm, but slippery fabric that falls into place. Many sheath linings do not have enough body for a drum. The drum is cut precisely like the skirt. Both require a seam at center back for zipper application.

An opening at lower edge for walking room has not been needed in short skirts. However, if you want one, read directions on pages 44-45, *Fashion Sewing by the Bishop Method*, before cutting skirt.

Cutting underwaist. A skirt may be finished with a band (pages 68-70), bias finish (page 244), or an underwaist, which has become very popular. An underwaist is smooth and comfortable at the waistline. Then, since the skirt has a drum which also serves as a half-slip, with the underwaist, no other slip would be necessary. A bias finish is used on the skirt to the suit in Chapter 13, but if you wear a suit as a two-piece ensemble, and do not wear a blouse to tuck in a skirt, suit skirts are made with an underwaist, also.

If you stopped along the way to make a master pattern of a bodice (page 93), you can use that to cut your underwaist. Otherwise, it can be cut from a suitable dress bodice pattern. A seam allowance will be required at center back for zipper application.

If you cut armholes ½ or ¾ inch larger (A and B), they will always be more comfortable. Neckline at C and D must always be cut lower than neckline of overblouse or jacket to be worn with it. Use crisp or soft Si Bonne or cotton sheath underlining for underwaist. Lace has been used for them in some of the best ready-to-wear. A trim of lace by the yard is also attractive (see photograph, page 179).

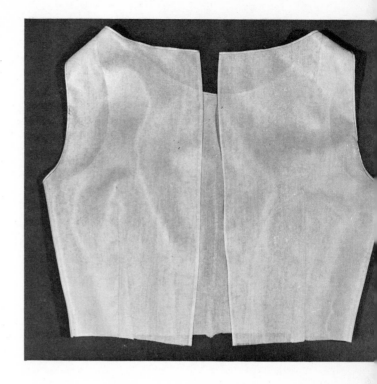

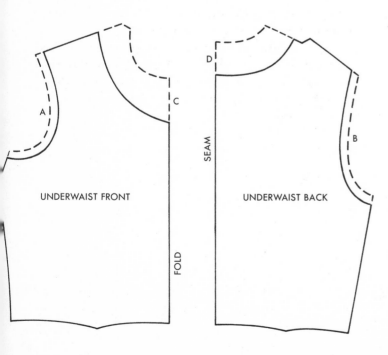

UNDERWAIST FRONT

UNDERWAIST BACK

SEAM

FOLD

Underwaist unit. Staystitch neckline and armholes ⅛ inch from edge in direction shown on page 149. Stitch and press darts. Stitch, pink, and press shoulder and side seams in direction learned on page 149.

If you would prefer the zipper placket at side of skirt instead of center back, leave left side seam open.

The neckline and armholes on this garment are finished with a ⅛-inch rolled hem at machine, because the lace trim (page 179) covered the machine hem.

However, if no lace trim is being used, you may prefer to make a rolled hem by hand for a finer, quality look. If so, turn fabric over needle twice to conceal raw edges and form ⅛-inch hem. Use a fine needle and single thread to slipstitch by hand. Run needle in fold of fabric ¼ inch, go down and prick at garment, and bring needle out under hem. Put needle in hem again at same place, and continue slipstitching around hem.

Press underwaist to complete this unit.

Making a three-piece ensemble

Skirt unit. Staystitch skirt front across top in direction shown ⅜ inch from edge. Sides are not staystitched because zipper placket is in center back. If skirt front has tucks, do not fold and stitch them. They will be made simultaneously through skirt and drum.

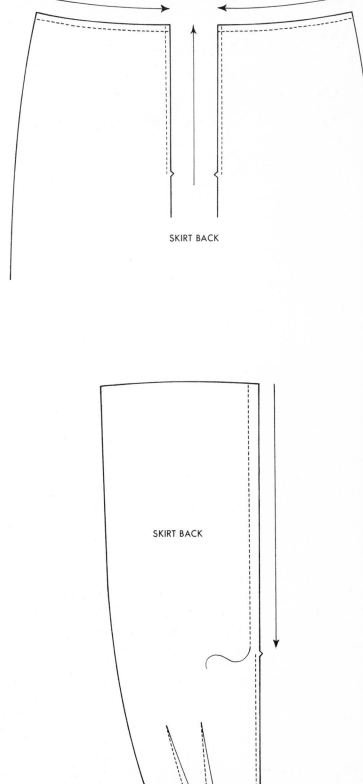

SKIRT BACK

SKIRT FRONT

Staystitch skirt back across top in direction shown ⅜ inch from edge. Staystitch center back from notch up ¼ inch from edge. The wider width would show on finished zipper placket. Staystitching at top of skirt is ⅜ inch from edge, because seam tape to be used in waistline seam is ½ inch wide.

Stitch darts in skirt back and press toward center back (see page 74). Right sides together, stitch center back seam in direction shown. Unless you can be certain of exact length of zipper placket, do not fasten threads at notch. Leave them at least one inch long. When correct length for placket is determined, after waistline seam is sewn, these threads can be tied by hand and cut off. Then, with right sides together, sew back skirt unit to front skirt unit at side seams in same direction center back seam is sewn. Pink seams with pinking shears and press open. This is the first time you have pressed a side seam on a straight skirt, so follow directions carefully on page 135.

SKIRT BACK

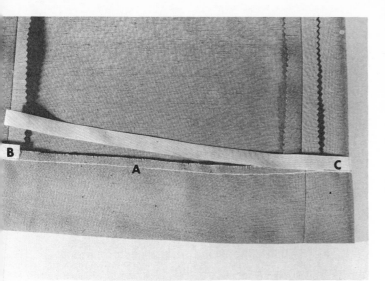

If you have made a master pattern of a straight skirt (page 93), pressing would be easier, and the skirt would be handled less, if you press up the hem with the hem gauge on skirt front unit and skirt back unit, before side seams are sewn. The standard width hem on a straight skirt is 2½ inches. However, do not attempt to press up the bottom of any garment in separate units until you have learned to cut-to-fit your figure. You may have to wait to turn up the hem after waistline seam is completed, and skirt can be tried on.

Trim width of seams in hem to ¼ inch, going a little beyond fold of hem (see page 232).

On linen, silk, or fine woolens, the top of the hem is finished with rayon seam tape. For heavier fabrics, use finish described on page 243. A perfectly straight skirt may need staystitching only ¼ inch from edge to hold crosswise grain in place (A). However, if the skirt is cut with any fullness, staystitch plus will be needed to eliminate fullness at the top of the hem. This is shown in the next photograph.

The tape is fitted at the top of the hem to be the exact width of the skirt. Run fingers along lower edge of tape from one seam to the other to measure amount needed on skirt. Pin in place at each seam-line. Overlap tape on raw edge of hem one-half the width of the tape, and stitch on lower edge of tape (B and C). Press skirt on grain from bottom up. This blocks tape to lay to perfection before doing hand stitching.

If staystitching plus is needed at top of hem to eliminate fullness before seam tape is applied, press the index finger of the right hand firmly against the back of the presser foot. The fabric will pile up against the finger, while stitching for several inches with a permanent stitch. Release the fabric, and repeat until entire edge has been stitched.

One of the hand stitches that can be used to finish the hem is a variation of the blanket stitch used in embroidery. Hold the hem forward with garment laid away from you. Fasten the thread in the garment and hem; lay the thread forward, and place your left thumb over it. Take a stitch forward, picking up a thread of the garment and small amount of tape. Pull the thread forward and place thumb over it. Continue around entire hem, taking stitches ½ inch apart. If a thread breaks, this stitch will not pull out, but will lock itself. Final-press from topside.

Another hand stitch that you can use with the hem tape is shown on page 62.

This stitching hides the thread, so it will not break or snag during wearing.

This completes the skirt unit as far as possible at this time.

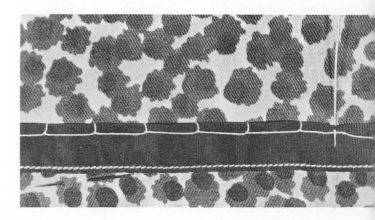

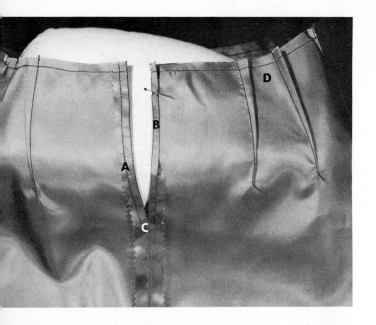

Drum unit. The drum is made exactly like the skirt except for three changes.

The staystitching at the center back opening is done on the seamline, and then a second row is done ¼ inch out from that (A). Press opening on staystitching on seamline; turn under raw edges on second line of staystitching (B), and topstitch opening on folded edge. When you cross over at C to do second half of opening, stitch back and forth across bottom of opening for reinforcement. This is shown in photograph on top of next page.

The second change is that the back darts are pressed toward the side of the skirt, instead of toward the center back (D).

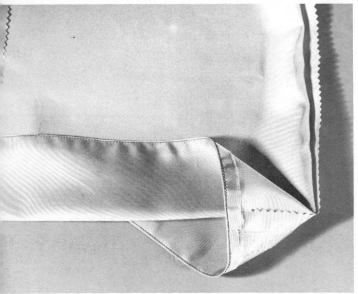

The third difference is the hem. The skirt hem is pressed up 2½ inches. However, if the raw edges of the drum are staystitched ⅜ inch from edge and turned under on staystitching line to do staystitching plus (page 71) and then the hem is pressed up 2½ inches, the drum will automatically be ⅜ inch shorter than the skirt. Therefore, it will not show at the bottom while being worn. The drum should be hemmed with one of two techniques described on page 62.

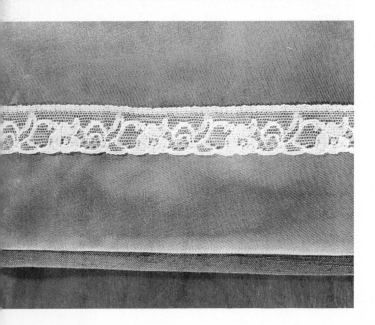

This photograph shows the drum ⅜ inch shorter than the skirt. You may choose to sew on lace, peasant braid, or other banding (page 243) at hemline for a custom look.

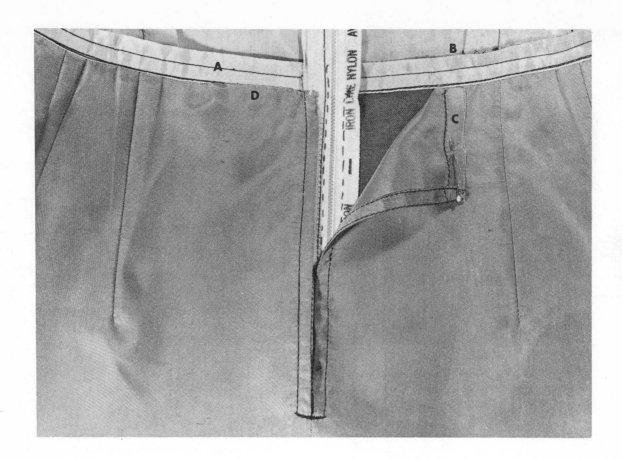

Complete skirt, drum, and underwaist unit. Place wrong side of skirt to wrong side of drum. At A and B, about 1½ inches from center back of drum, snip for ½ inch and pin top edge of drum away from waistline seam. Stitch skirt and drum together ⅜ inch from edge; then, proceed to put on seam tape at waistline as you learned on page 146. If skirt front has tucks, fold and stitch them through both skirt and drum at this time.

Then, as zipper is being sewn into center back seam (page 67), the skirt drum will not interfere at center back.

Last, turn under raw edges of drum (C), and whipstitch in place at waistline (D).

Be guided by the depth of the neckline on underwaist in selecting length of zipper for back opening. It should not be so far down in the skirt that you sit on the zipper. This is not attractive and the strain when you sit on the zipper will distort the shape of the skirt. About 6 or 7 inches can serve as a guide for zipper to extend into skirt.

This photograph shows the completed underwaist on the skirt, and the use of lace on the underwaist.

Final-press where necessary. However, you will usually find it easier to final-press skirt and drum before they are attached at waistline, or to the underwaist.

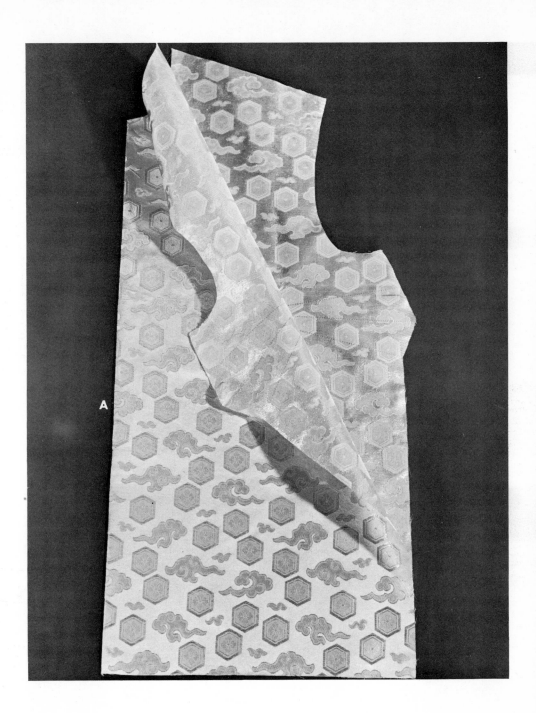

The jacket

Behind this simple, lined jacket technique, there are really five purposes.

First, if you want to make a cotton, dacron, or linen jacket to wear over a sheath dress, for example, you may choose to make the front lining only over to the side seams. The back lining could be eliminated. The front lining covers the unfinished look of a jacket at facings, interfacings, hems, etc.

Second, if you do not plan to use another color for accent (see page 184), or a print lining (page 185), it is easy to cut the entire jacket front double with a fold at A. The lining front and facing are being cut as one, and you will eliminate those steps in construction where they are attached.

Third, adding a second color is an ingenious way to make a sleeveless reversible jacket simply.

Fourth, it is not a too advanced or time-consuming technique for a lining, because you will usually not be lining the sleeves. You may choose to go beyond the first suggestion of lining only the front, and make the lining in both front and back for body and finish. However, the sleeves are not usually lined (page 185).

Last, besides making a Chanel type jacket with this simple technique, you could also make a straight-lined coat of linen, brocade, or similar fabric to wear over a dress. These identical techniques would then be used.

Cutting jacket and lining. This sketch shows the pieces of pattern for the jacket described in this chapter. For the second and fourth suggestions, back neck facings are eliminated.

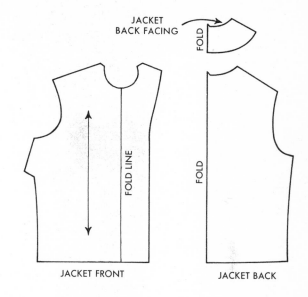

JACKET FRONT

JACKET BACK

To cut lining front, on tissue for jacket front, fold back tissue on fold line for facing. A is edge of facing tissue. Measure 1¼ inches toward front edge and mark pattern (B). This is the width to cut lining for front of jacket.

To cut lining back, place back facing pattern on back jacket pattern. A is edge of facing tissue. Measure 1¼ inches toward neck edge and mark pattern (B). This is the height to cut lining for back of jacket.

For the second and fourth suggestions, where back neck facing is not used, lining back is cut precisely like jacket back.

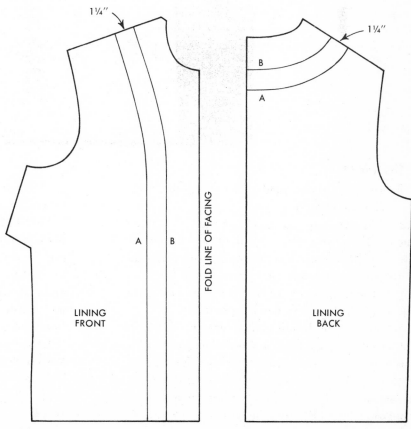

LINING FRONT

LINING BACK

Jacket unit. To press facing in place, on underside, mark one layer of fabric only with tracing paper and tracing wheel. Through both layers, place 3 or 4 pins in marking line (A). Turn back and press top layer lightly on pin line (B). Remove pins and re-press to remove pin marks. Then, turn fabric to have under layer on top. Fold back top layer to meet under fold and press second side (C).

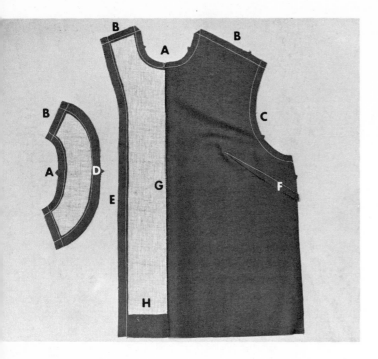

Staystitch neckline (A), shoulders (B), armholes (C), and outer edge of back facing (D) just outside seamline. Staystitch edge of facing (E) on seamline. See page 164 for correct direction of grain line.

Stitch darts, press, and pink wide edge to a ½-inch seam (F).

Instant armo (fino weight) was used as interfacing in the facings of this jacket for added support. If you are not using the back neck facing, the back interfacing can be pressed on back lining. The press-on interfacing was cut within ⅛ inch of fold line for facing (G), 1⅝ inches from lower edge (H) to remove it from hem to be 1½ inches deep, and ¾ inch from all other edges to eliminate it from seamline. See suggestions on page 150 for pressing in place.

Staystitch neckline, shoulders, and armholes of jacket back exactly as you did on jacket front. Stitch back neck darts and press toward center back.

With right sides together, stitch jacket fronts to jacket back at shoulder and side seams. Pink with pinking shears and press open. If you do not know the correct direction to stitch and press these seams, refer to page 165.

With right sides together, stitch front facings to back facing at shoulder line. Press open seams and trim to ¼ inch (A). In heavier fabric, topstitch seams (page 227), and trim away seam up to topstitching.

Then, right sides together, and garment side up at neckline, as always, facing will be sewn to jacket. Follow all of the techniques you learned on the over-blouse (page 171), including understitching beginning and ending one inch from edge, as shown at B and C. If you are making a reversible jacket, you may eliminate this step, unless you choose to do the understitching by hand (see page 89). It would be less conspicuous, and would be an attractive finish on the one side.

Finally, using hem gauge, press up jacket hem 1½ inches.

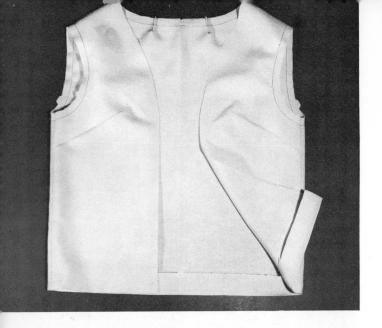

Lining unit. Staystitch neckline ⅝ inch from edge, and shoulders and armholes just outside seamline in same direction you did the front. Stitch, pink, and press bust darts as you did on jacket fronts.

If you are using a facing at the back to have a contrasting band of color on reversible jacket, only these small back neck darts remain when back lining is cut. They were stitched for the photograph to show you how small they would be, but, instead of making them, use staystitching plus (page 177) to eliminate this small amount of fullness.

With right sides together, stitch lining fronts to lining back at shoulder and side seams in same direction you did the jacket. Pink with pinking shears and press open.

Finally, using hem gauge, press up lining hem 1½ inches.

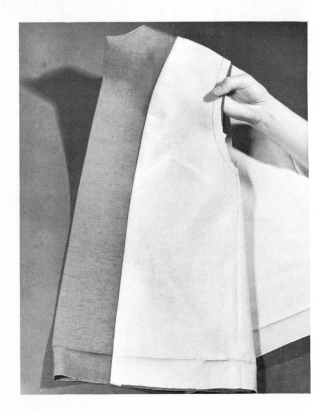

Complete jacket unit. With right sides together, at edge of front and back facings, join lining to jacket in a ⅝-inch seam. At front facings, keep facing side up, and sew through staystitching on seamline. At back facing, turn and have lining side up, and sew through staystitching on seamline.

Press seam toward lining. If it does not lie smoothly, trim away half of seam toward lining. Without trimming one edge, ⅝ can seldom be faced with ⅝.

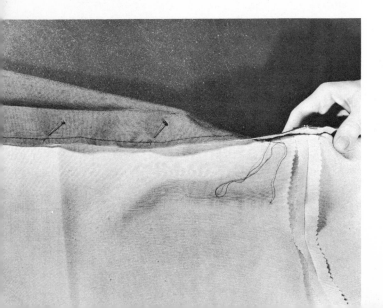

After pressing, turn jacket to wrong side again and stitch tops of hem together in a ¼-inch seam at machine. If this crosswise grain is difficult to handle, staystitch each hem edge first.

Then, hem to lining side only, using stitch learned on page 62. The hem is not sewn at all to jacket. Finished hem is shown in photograph on page 185.

Turn jacket right side out through one of the arm-holes. Then, turn back and sew one side of shoulder seam of lining to one side of shoulder seam of jacket with a running stitch by hand. This serves as an anchor at shoulders for the lining and jacket.

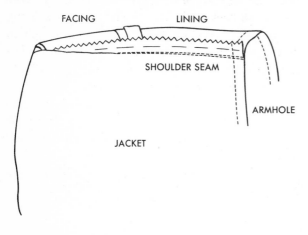

If sleeves are to be sewn in jacket, staystitch arm-holes together, and proceed to put in sleeves (page 155). Sleeves are usually not lined. If you did want to line them, use a soft lining, and follow techniques on page 240. To finish armhole seams, you may bind them (page 101, *Fashion Sewing by the Bishop Method*), or make a second row of stitching ¼ inch from first row, and pink seam up to second stitching (see photograph).

As shown in the photograph, also, print lining extends all the way to the back neckline. No back facing was used.

See photograph of front of this jacket on page 260.

If jacket is sleeveless or reversible, stitch armholes together and bind them as learned on page 171. The only difference is that D edge in that photograph must be turned in, so that the binding is finished on both sides.

Final-press jacket.

The pin placed in the hem in the photograph is only there to show you the appearance of the finished hem.

This technique is simple to do. In a short time, you have a lined jacket. From the five suggestions for use on page 180, there should be many ways you can adapt these techniques for more garments in your wardrobe.

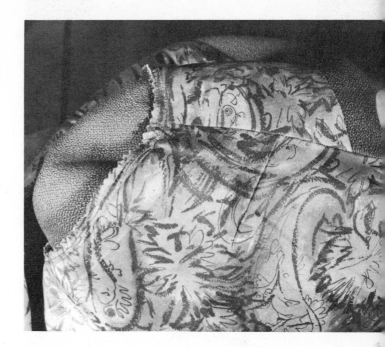

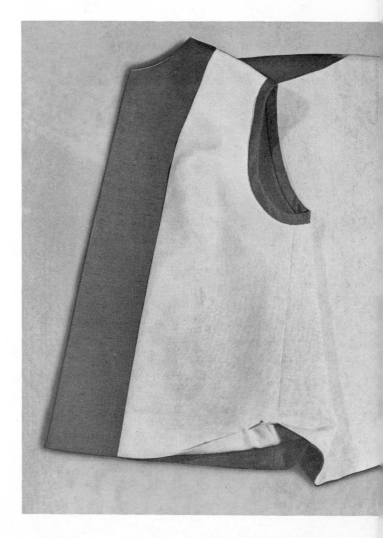

FOLD

BACK
FACING

COAT BACK
AND SLEEVE

POCKET

COAT
SIDE FRONT

SLEEVE FRONT

COAT FRONT

Chapter 12

Tailoring a coat

Tailoring is an advanced skill, but it is not difficult or time-consuming in the Bishop method. You will be using the techniques you already know as well as learning some new ones.

This first chapter on tailoring discusses the techniques used in making a coat. This style was chosen to show the techniques for underlining and lining a tailored garment with a cut-on or raglan sleeve. It could be either a coat or a jacket. It also shows the cut-on facing down the front of a garment that is especially recommended for heavy fabrics. This chapter also presents one of the several tailored buttonholes shown in this text, the techniques for a gusset, and a pocket in the seam of a coat. This type of pocket is always popular whether it is in a gore seam or side seam of a coat.

However, the coat you are making may have set-in sleeves, a collar, separate front facings, or similar features. Those variations will be found in the next chapter on tailoring.

Begin tailoring by making a simple coat or suit with few pieces to the pattern, and from a fabric that tailors and presses easily. If this is the first time you have worked with wool, you will find that no other fiber is as satisfactory to work with. Hard-finished woolens are more difficult to mold and press, but a medium weight woolen with a spongy texture and an unfinished surface such as tweed will help you to attain your goal of making a professional-looking coat. On your first tailored garments, you should concentrate on learning to tailor, and not on trying to master a difficult piece of fabric.

Since much time and effort will be put into making a tailored garment, the fabric should be of as good quality as you can afford.

Since tailoring requires that you spend quite a bit of money for fabric, underlining, lining, and notions, you may choose to pretest a coat pattern for size, style, and fit (see p. 93). You may cut it out of an old sheet, or you may prefer to use pillow ticking, cotton poplin, corduroy, or other cotton fabric. Then, the try-on could be completed for a brunch coat or short robe.

It is best to cut underlining first from the tissue pattern. The extra margin will then fall away at the same time the underlining is cut. To cut through the fabric and tissue at the same time is recommended only for firm, thinner fabrics such as underlining and cottons. To cut heavier woolens, always cut along the edge of the tissue.

If coat fabric is heavy and thick, it sometimes tears the tissue when it is pinned on the fabric and the coat is cut out. This is another reason for cutting underlining first from fresh unused tissue before cutting the coat.

Be certain your underlining is grain perfect as you learned in Chapter 4. If it needs to be steam pressed to restore it to grain perfection, it will be easier if you cut the fabric and work with lengths needed for the front and back of the coat, etc., rather than with one long piece (see p. 53). Many suggestions for underlinings in a coat are given on pages 254-255.

The press-on underlinings are recommended for small areas only, as shown on page 226.

Very few women have but one coat. A coat wardrobe is becoming as common as a dress, suit, or skirt wardrobe. You will know how to expand your coat wardrobe more appropriately after working with this chapter.

Tailoring a coat

Cutting underlining

As shown in the photograph, the underlining is cut precisely like the tissue for the entire garment, with but one exception. When working with heavier fabric, the underlining extends one inch beyond the fold line (shown with a pencil laid in top of photograph) of the facing. This edge of underlining is marked A in photograph. With lightweight fabric, the underlining may extend all the way to the edge of the facing (B). Do not have A edge selvage of underlining, because the selvage may show a mark on the completed garment.

Firm underlining extends all the way out to edge of cut-on sleeves. A set-in sleeve may or may not be underlined with a soft underlining as discussed on page 235.

Underlining is cut on the same grain as the garment.

Buttonholes, center front lines, gusset line, and the dart-seam — labeled with B, C, D, and E, respectively, on the photograph — are marked with tracing paper and tracing wheel on the underlining only. The small back dart at F will be marked on both underlining and coat fabrics. The fold line of the facing (G) is marked only on the coat.

Underlining a tailored garment helps to build the line and body into the garment, and to keep them there through wearings and cleanings. Acro was chosen as the underlining for the spongy woolen coat fabric in these photographs. Other suggestions are given on pages 254-255.

With loosely woven fabric you may need to underline a tailored garment with a matching colored underlining such as Si Bonne to enhance the color, and then use the heavier underlining below that. The colored underlining is baste-stitched to regular underlining, and the two are then staystitched to garment fabric.

You underline for character or shape in a garment, and line it for appearance. If you are making a coat from a heavy or firm fabric, and only want to interface neckline, front edges, shoulders, and armholes, instead of underlining entire garment, refer to Chapter 13, *Fashion Sewing by the Bishop Method.*

Cutting coat

If the pattern you have chosen for your coat has a separate front facing, as this sketch illustrates, you may key or superimpose the seamline of the front facing and coat front to meet, and pin the tissue together as shown. Then cut the facing all in one with the front. This is especially desirable in heavy fabrics, but cannot be done if the pattern calls for a shaped lapel, unless the line is straightened.

If you would like a wider lap on the front of your coat, especially if you want to use very large buttons, you can bring A cutting line to meet B cutting line. It would then be cut as one, but with the ⅝-inch seam allowance remaining.

Make certain your coat fabric meets all of the requirements on page 43. If not, it must be processed before cutting (pp. 45-46). After the underlining is cut and marked, remove the tissue pattern and place it on coat fabric to cut and mark coat fabric. Special techniques for marking heavy fabric are given on page 56. Then remove the tissue from coat fabric, and place sections of coat and underlining in units of work.

Even though you may never have the same lines in a coat as this pattern, study the chapter thoroughly to learn the tailoring techniques.

Unless you have pretested coat pattern for fit, do not cut lining until coat has been fitted. To cut the lining, see pages 201-202.

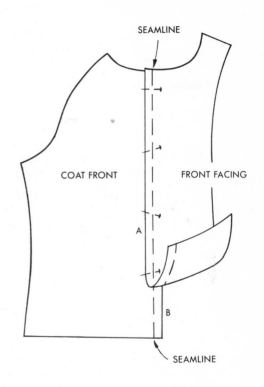

Coat front unit

With a running stitch by hand, mark the fold line of the facing to show on the right side of the fabric (A). Staystitch B edge of facing ⅝ inch from edge. In lighter-weight fabrics, when underlining is cut to extend all the way to the edge as described on page 188, this edge will be staystitched together later with the underlining.

Then, place underlining on underside of coat front and pin in place, keeping pins back from the stitching line. Turn coat right side up and stitch underlining in place at fold line with just a pick stitch on top and a ¼-inch running stitch below. The hand stitch should be invisible on the right side.

Even though you will sometimes be sewing against the grain line, staystitch underlining to coat fabric with underlining side up all around. It is easier to manage with the firm underlining on top. This is the control side, as you learned on page 169. The neck edge (A) is staystitched ⅝ inch from the edge. Hem edge (B) is staystitched one inch from the edge. On a 2-inch hem, underlining will turn up in hem one-half the width of hem. All other edges are staystitched just outside the seamline.

In this photograph, the grain threads are pushed way out of line. It's an example of what you must not let happen. It is contrary to the learnings discussed earlier about staystitching with the firm or control side on top. You should be able to control every edge and not let grain threads move ahead of your work.

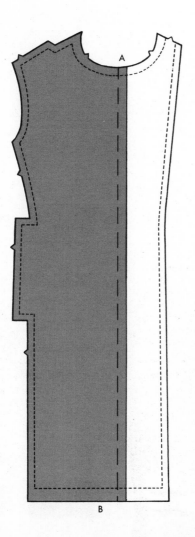

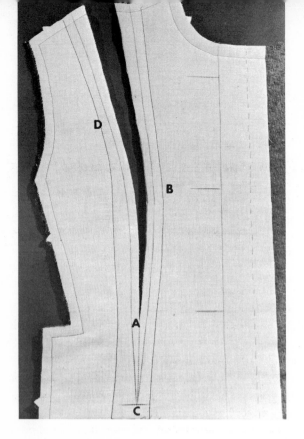

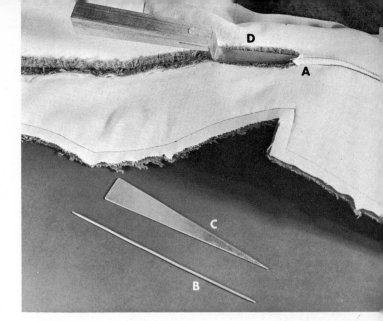

at least baste-stitch the coat together and try it on for a fitting, to check buttonhole locations. This will not be necessary if you have pretested your coat pattern. A and B are discussed on page 201.

Since this dart-seam is quite curved, it will have to be slashed as far down as it is a ½-inch seam (A). To hold underlining and coat fabrics together, first baste-stitch outside dart-seamline (B to C to D). If dart or dart-seam did not need to be slashed before stitching, one row of baste-stitching in the center of the dart would be sufficient.

Then, slash dart-seam as far down as it is a ½-inch seam (A). You must remember this technique for other style areas in patterns that will require slashing for stitching.

Pin and stitch dart-seam. At end of slash, cut into dart at an angle (A) halfway to stitching line (see p. 197). Remove baste-stitching.

Press seam open. Below seam, use a metal knitting needle (B) to divide dart (p. 197), or a piece of metal cut to a point (C or D). Press on each side of stitching line all the way to the point.

Beginning 1¼ inches from shoulder edge, trim seam away diagonally to ⅛ inch to eliminate bulk at seamline. You may see this same thing at neckline of back of coat (p. 197).

Your next step is to press back the front facings on the fold line. They should lie in place with absolute grain perfection, not only at the front of the coat, but at neckline, shoulder, and hem edges as well.

You are now ready to make the tailored buttonholes. It is much easier to make them in just one unit of the coat than to hold the entire coat at the machine. However, you may have to wait until you

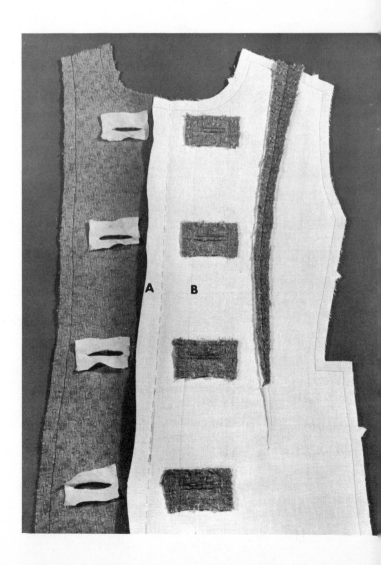

Tailored buttonholes

There are several tailored buttonhole methods given in this text (pp. 219-224). However, the first one presented here, known as the trade-method, is the most popular one taught in the Bishop method, and the most widely used. A beginner may want to try the buttonholes described on pages 222 to 224 first.

Even after you have learned to make buttonholes, you should try a sample buttonhole on a scrap of fabric to be certain you have the correct feel for a fabric you may never have handled before, and to make sure your judgment of size is correct.

With fabrics or underlinings that ravel easily, press on a small patch of instant armo in a suitable weight on underlining before marking and baste-stitching location lines.

First, baste-stitch crosswise lines (A) for button-hole locations from underlining through to outside of garment. Then, baste-stitch center front line (B) in a continuous line of stitching the length of all the buttonholes. Determine the finished buttonhole length, and baste-stitch a second line (C) parallel to the center front line. Buttonhole length should be at least the diameter of the button plus its thickness. Another thing you can do is cut a slash in a scrap of fabric until button slides through easily. Then, measure the slash for the size of your buttonhole. But-tonholes are not made less than one inch, except in a fine fabric like satin. In a heavy coat, buttonholes would be made 1¼ to 1½ inches long even if the button being used is just ¾ to 1 inch in diameter, and without height.

On fragile fabrics such as velveteen, use hand basting.

From B to D (fold line or seamline of garment) the distance must be a minimum of half the width of a button plus ¼ inch, or plus ½ inch for larger buttons.

To prepare the finishing strip, tear or cut on grain a lengthwise strip about 1½ inches wide. In length, each strip should be an inch longer than the button-hole is to be, but it is better to make a longer strip, and cut it up as needed. For checks, plaids, stripes, and ribbed fabrics, use a true bias strip. With wrong sides together, fold the finishing strip in half and

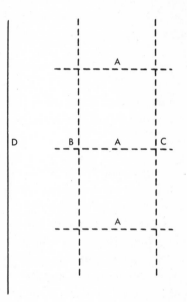

press. Stitch a tuck ⅛ inch wide on the folded edge of finishing strip. It may help you to use a slightly contrasting thread for this stitching. The presser foot can serve as a guide for straight stitching. Trim down one of the raw edges to be the exact width of the tuck on the other side.

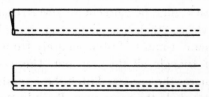

Place this short raw edge on guideline A on outside of garment, with finishing strip extending ½ inch beyond each size line. The long raw edge will then lie over the short raw edge. Stitch from one size line to the other through the line of stitching that previously made the tuck. Use a short machine stitch, and lockstitch beginning and end of stitching. If it is difficult for you to do the lockstitching perfectly and precisely at the size lines, leave the threads and pull them to the underside to tie by hand. Cut off strip ½ inch beyond stitching line; this leaves ½ inch extra at each end of buttonhole. Sew on second strip for buttonhole. Repeat for all buttonholes.

If buttonhole is made of a bias strip, or of lightweight fabric such as silk or linen, insert yarn or thin cord with a needlepoint needle through both tucks on finishing strips. Remove all baste-stitching from garment. The tuck stitching from the first step will actually be in the strips at A and B areas. It was left off sketches, so that these steps would show clearly.

On inside of garment, starting at center, clip through underlining and fabric and diagonally to corners, having triangles ¼ to ⅜ inch long at ends of buttonhole. Hold tuck strips out of way of cutting with finger inserted under them on right side.

Turn finishing strips to inside. Do not handle triangles, but carefully pull ends of strips to square the corners of buttonhole. The folded edges now meet in the center of the buttonhole.

Place garment right side up on sewing machine. Turn back edge of garment to reveal triangle and end of strips. Stitch triangle to strip, going back and forth many times to fasten securely from knots at base of triangle all the way out. This connecting line squares the corners. Stitch the opposite end of the buttonhole the same way. Press buttonhole in direction of the strip.

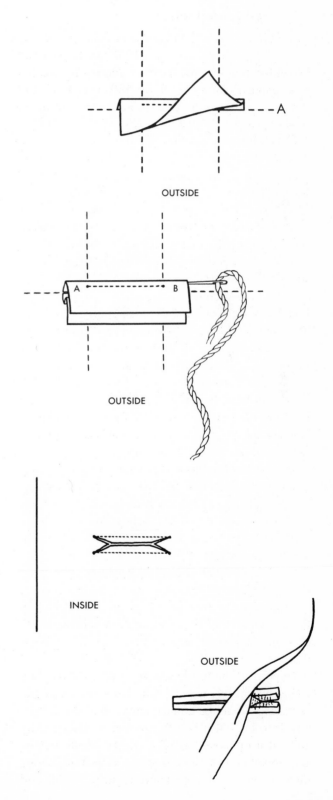

OUTSIDE

OUTSIDE

INSIDE

OUTSIDE

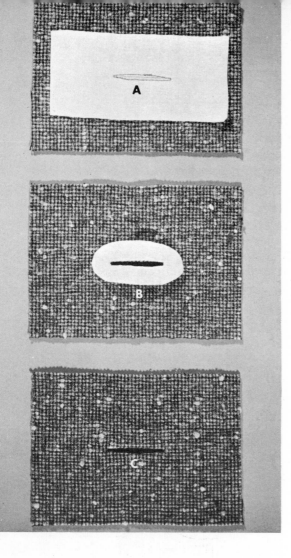

After the front facings are stitched on and pressed in place, the buttonholes will be finished through the facing. Place a pin through each end of buttonhole to determine where the facing is slashed under the buttonhole, or you may mark a location line through buttonholes with tracing paper and tracing wheel.

Then, stitch a bias strip of Si Bonne, organdy, or other fine, firm fabric over slash line on the right side of facing (A).

Use shortest stitch at the machine, and stitch a few threads from slash line on each side of it.

Slash facing and Si Bonne on the slash line, turn Si Bonne to inside and press, and trim away all but ½ inch around opening (B). The finished edge (C) will be whipped to the back of the buttonhole.

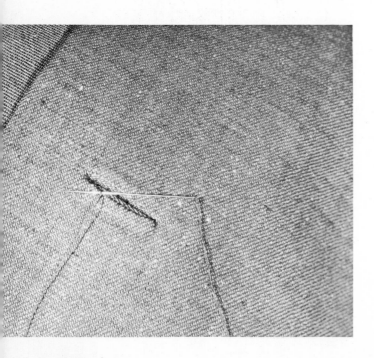

Whipstitch to back of buttonhole with a single thread run through beeswax holder. This is easier to do and more durable than just cutting and turning in raw edges of the facing. This step will not be done, however, until you have completed all the handwork on facings, page 201.

Pocket unit

With right sides together, and coat side up, stitch pocket (made of lining fabric) to side extension edges of coat front. Press seam toward pocket and understitch (p. 89). Trim seam to ¼ inch.

You can see it would be easy to add this style of pocket to a coat at a gore or side seam, even if the pattern did not call for it. Simply add an inch extension to each seam of the garment at the height you want pocket placed. Second seam edge is shown in next sketch.

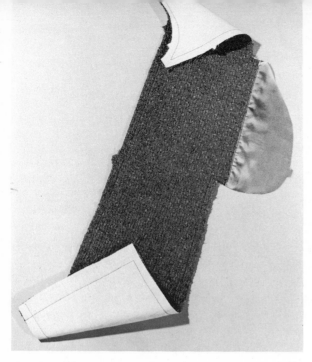

Coat side front is prepared precisely like coat front. With underlining side up, all edges will be staystitched ½ inch from edge, except hem edge, which will be one inch. With right sides together, and coat side up, stitch pocket (again cut of lining) to side extension edge. Press seam toward pocket, understitch, and trim seam to ¼ inch.

With right sides together and stitching in direction of arrows on sketch, stitch coat front to side front. Stitch ⅝ inch beyond edge of pocket and lockstitch threads securely at pocket opening (A and B). Then, beginning at lockstitching, stitch pocket sections together from A to B. Clip coat side front seam at lockstitching and press open coat seam. Press pocket toward coat front. At C, beginning 1¼ inches from edge, trim seam away diagonally to remove bulk. Final-press pocket on right side of coat, and pound with pounding block. This pocket is preferred over the slash pocket.

You may prefer another type of pocket for your coat pattern. Pockets are shown on pages 206 to 213 at the end of this chapter.

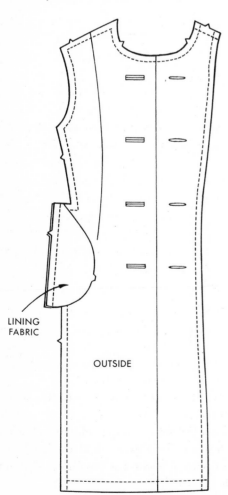

LINING FABRIC

OUTSIDE

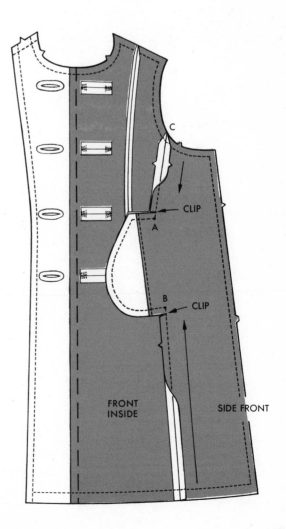

C

CLIP

A

B

CLIP

FRONT INSIDE

SIDE FRONT

Cut-on sleeve unit

Underlining is staystitched to sleeve front outside the seamline at all edges except hem edge (A). For a two-inch hem at A, staystitch one inch from the edge.

There is not enough ease on this cut-on sleeve to require an ease-line on the cap. Sew to coat front with sleeve side up, easing in fullness with your fingers as you sew. Press seam toward sleeve and trim upper seam to one-half its width to eliminate bulk.

If you have pretested your coat pattern, then you will know how much to turn up the hem. In that case, it will be easier to do it now with separate coat front and coat back units before they are joined together. It also requires less handling of the entire garment, and keeps the fabric looking better. Press up hem (p. 139). A coat should not carry a hem deeper than 2½ inches, or less than 1½ inches.

Coat back unit

When a seam in the back of a coat or suit is cut on the straight of grain, or almost on the straight of grain, the garment and the underlining should be seamed separately. Otherwise, the seam may easily have an oversewn look. An exception would be a lightweight suit, such as a silk one; then the garment and underlining may be sewn as one.

You may wonder if this seam could be eliminated, and the garment cut on a fold, when the edge is perfect straight of grain. This is permissible and desirable when working with checks, plaids, or a problem fabric in stitching and pressing. Otherwise, the seam is desirable because it improves the line of the coat. Stitch seam in correct direction of grain, from bottom of coat to top of coat.

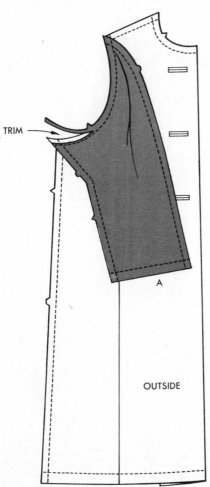

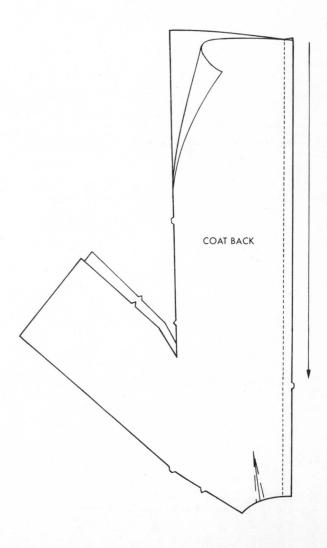

Press open seam in same direction in which it was stitched. At hem, trim center back seam to one-half its width a little beyond depth of hem. Stitch neck darts and press as shown in a close-up in the next sketch. Depending upon the weight of the coat fabric, these darts may be stitched together with underlining (see p. 191).

After the dart is stitched, slash for a depth of 1¼ inches at fold of dart. At end of slash, cut into dart at an angle (A) halfway back to stitching line. Press darts like the photograph on page 191 and trim seam of dart diagonally to eliminate bulk at seamline.

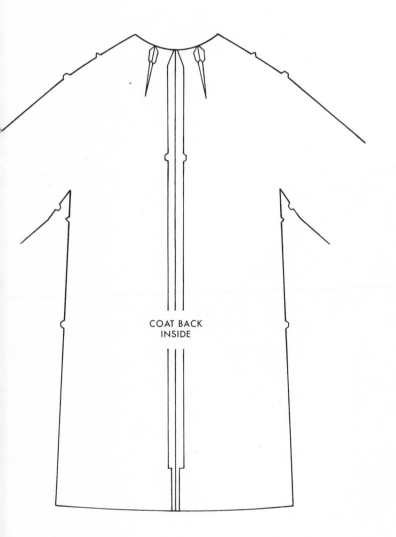

COAT BACK
INSIDE

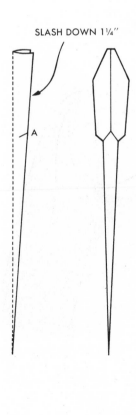

SLASH DOWN 1¼″

A

Stitch center back seam of underlining from bottom to top of coat, and press open in same direction. Stitch darts and press toward side of coat. At hem, trim center back seam to one-half its width a little beyond depth of hem.

Place right side of underlining to wrong side of coat. This is a very large piece to handle, so you should lay it perfectly flat to make certain the two pieces fit and mold together with absolute perfection. You may even press to adhere the underlining. Place pins back from stitching line.

Staystitch underlining and coat back together keeping underlining on top all the way around. At neck edge (A), staystitch ⅝ inch from edge; at coat hem edge (D) and sleeve hem edges (B and C), one inch from edge; and at all other edges, just outside seamline.

Staystitching and understitching are not enough support for this heavy fabric at the neckline. Fold a piece of ½-inch seam tape in half or use ¼-inch cotton tape, and staystitch on underlining side of coat to prevent curved neckline from pulling out of shape (see it at A in left photograph on p. 199). Remember this technique to give support at other places in your sewing.

At gusset area, reinforce underarm with machine stitching along seamlines, using very short stitches for ½ inch on both sides of corner of gusset, and taking one or two short stitches straight across at point of gusset. Now, or later when sewing gusset, clip up to corner but do not cut staystitching.

If you have pretested your coat pattern, then you will know how much to turn up the hem. In that case, press up the coat back unit before it is joined to front units as you learned on page 196.

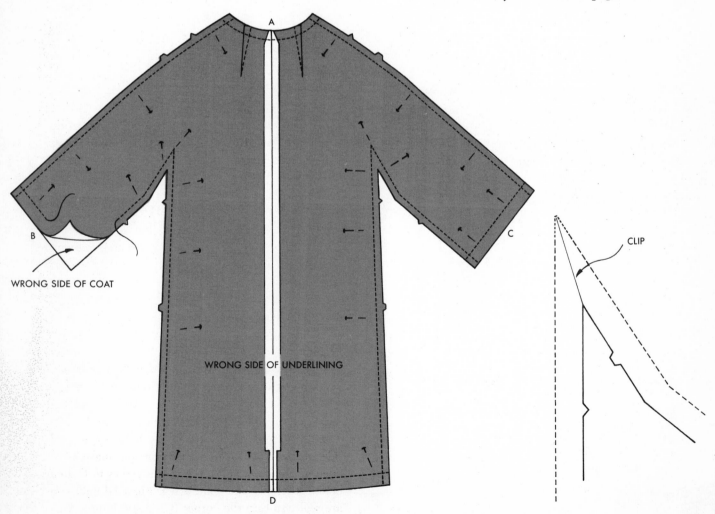

WRONG SIDE OF COAT

WRONG SIDE OF UNDERLINING

CLIP

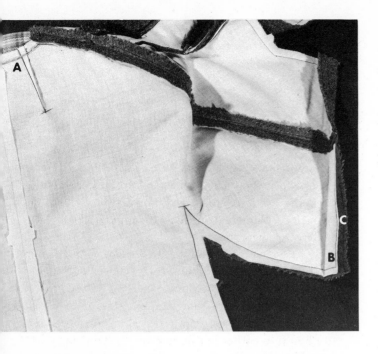

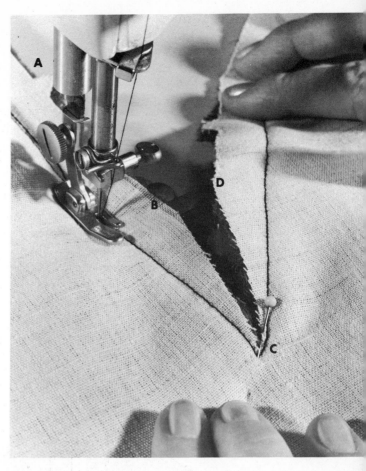

Complete coat unit

With right sides together, stitch shoulder and upper sleeve seams from neckline to bottom of sleeves. In stitching one of the seams, the back of the coat will be on top. In stitching the second one, the front will be on top. It does not matter which one is on top; the correct direction for stitching is what is important.

Press seam open on cushion. Turn up hem 2 inches, and press with hem gauge (p. 139). Trim away underlining in sleeve hem to staystitching one inch from edge (B). Staystitch sleeve hem ¼ inch from edge (C). A is described in a previous paragraph.

Finishing a hem as much as possible before sleeve seams are sewn is the same principle as you have been learning all the way through this text.

Open out sleeve hem to stitch side and underarm seams with right sides together. Begin at bottom of coat and continue to sew to bottom of sleeve. On other side of coat, sew from bottom of coat up to notch (A). Then, turn and sew from bottom of sleeve to meet stitching at notch. You should be able to have the slashed side of gusset toward you.

The gusset was staystitched according to directions on page 198. Take a full ⅝-inch seam on both the garment and gusset section (cut in one with coat front on this pattern) when you begin at B and end at D. The seam will always remain ⅝ inch on gusset underneath (see next photograph), but it slopes to nothing at C at end of slash on garment side. You can understand how important the short stitches in staystitching would be for reinforcement at this fragile corner (C).

When sewing in the gusset, always sew one thread inside staystitching. Use short stitches again for ½ inch on either side of the point (C). Always have the needle in the fabric at the point of the gusset when you lift the presser foot to turn fabric to sew second side of gusset. A mistake many people make is to open up the point and pin pieces together to D area before stitching. The point is never opened until you are ready to turn the corner (C) in stitching.

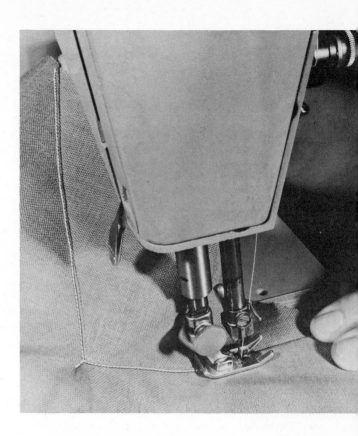

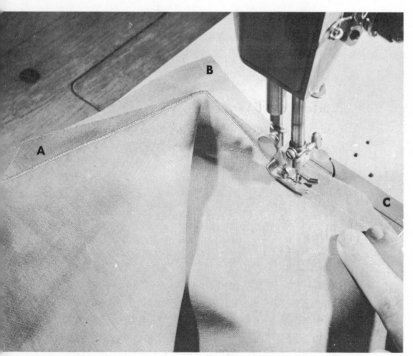

These photographs show a separate gusset section. (They are not of the coat but of a dress.) A, B, and C show that the seam is a full ⅝ inch on the gusset as you sew the pieces together. On the garment side, the seam slopes to nothing at end of slash, as you just learned on the coat.

On this coat, because of the way the gusset was designed, the entire seam of coat and sleeve was pressed open, and gusset was not topstitched. However, in most gussets, the seams are pressed together away from the gusset. On blouses and similar garments, topstitch on edge of garment, close to gusset seam. At the point, stitch out and back on fabric grain a distance of 3 stitches for reinforcement. Then continue to topstitch the second side.

Restore hemlines in sleeves and bottom of coat at seamlines, if hem had been pressed up in individual units. If it had not been pressed up, then do so at this time.

As shown in the photograph on page 232, the seams in sleeve and coat hems are trimmed to a width of ¼ inch going a little beyond the fold of the hem. Trim underlining to staystitching one inch from edge. Staystitch plus hem (p. 177) ¼ inch from edge. Press hem again from lower edge to upper edge to mold to coat with perfection. If lower edge of coat does not seem too stable, press on a bias piece of instant armo as shown on page 232.

To hem sleeves by hand, fold hem to outside of garment, and work from underside of hem, holding hem edge away from you, and garment toward you. With a single thread, hem with a loose pick stitch ½ inch apart (see p. 243). In one pick stitch, catch underlining in sleeve; in the next pick stitch, catch stitching in sleeve ¼ inch from edge. Final-press and block bottom of sleeve from topside (see p. 141).

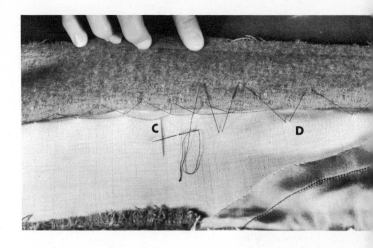

Staystitch neck facing of back facing just outside seamline and lower edge precisely on seamline. At shoulders, join back facing to front facings on seamline (see photograph, p. 227). Press open seams; topstitch each side of seam and trim away seam allowance to topstitching. This technique can be used any time you want to eliminate bulk at any seamline of a facing in heavier fabric.

With right sides of coat and facings together, and with garment side up, sew facings to neckline through staystitching on seamline. Use very small stitches for ½ inch at each corner. Grade seam; the one toward the top of the coat is made ¼ inch, and the one toward the facing ⅛ inch (see photograph, p. 225). When grading is done, the seam allowance which is to rest against the outside of the garment is usually the one that should stay the wider of the two. Turn facing right side out, and bring out corners to seamline.

Understitch the neckline facing. Stitch on right side of fabric. Start as close as possible to one corner of the facing and stitch to the other, catching the trimmed seams to the facing. To underpress and toppress an edge with understitching, refer to photographs on page 139.

Refer to top right photograph on page 233. Turn back facings, and with a running stitch by hand, stitch hem of facings to hem of coat ½ inch from edge (A). Grade under seam to ¼ inch. In softer woolens, you may also tack facing to hem halfway down width of hem (B). The stitching should be invisible on right side of the facing.

Turn facings to inside again. At edge C in the photograph, machine stitch two raw edges together for reinforcement, and whipstitch facing to hem. Stitch through hem only, and do not catch underlining or coat. In heavier fabric, use double thread for this whipstitch. Leave bottom of facing open at D. This will allow the facing to shape to the figure and form the lapel, if the pattern has one, without pull or strain.

The facing and underlining need to be hand tacked in place to hold the front edges securely, starting several inches below the neckline, and ending several inches above the facings. The first row of stitching could not be shown in a photograph. It was to tack A edge of underlining to B underlining (shown on p. 191) with a running stitch. This is not needed with an underlining like formite that creases easily, but is necessary with one like acro or hair canvas that is wiry and resists being pressed back on itself.

About one inch apart, and with loose hand stitches as shown, next tack wool facing to underlining. Two rows of stitching (C and D) should accommodate the width of this facing. This is especially needed with the softer woolens, such as mohair and fleece. Tack back neck facing to underlining in this same manner.

The finished backs of the buttonholes (p. 194) may be whipstitched in place at this time, and the buttons sewn on (p. 159). However, the hem is not sewn to coat by hand until later when the hem of the lining is completed.

Cutting the lining

There is a large selection of lining fabrics on the market. The weight and texture can be chosen in relation to what the lining can accomplish for your garment. Choose a rayon twill, rayon crepe, satin, or even a crisp silk. It may be plain or a gay stripe. Moreover, the color of the lining can contrast and add much interest to your garment.

Pages 213-215 show how to interline a coat for added warmth.

If any cutting-to-fit alterations were necessary in cutting out the coat, cut the lining with the same alterations.

If the garment has much cut-up detail, such as yokes and applied seams, the separate lining tissue that is included with many patterns should be used. Then the lining will be easier to manage. However, the original pattern used for cutting the garment is normally preferred for cutting lining. The cutting and fitting alterations are more easily made, and if the special directions below for cutting are carried out, the lining will fit the garment with perfection.

Sleeves are cut as the coat was cut, except in length. On a set-in sleeve for a jacket, lining may be cut to finished length of sleeve, but for this cut-on style, the lining should be cut to finished length of sleeve plus one inch extra. For example, with a 2-inch hem in sleeves, turn up tissue one inch to cut lining.

In length, the front and back of the lining are cut to the finished length of the coat plus one inch extra for ease. If the coat is turned up 2 inches in hemming, turn up tissue pattern one inch, and cut lining. With a firm lining, the one-inch ease may be eliminated, if the firmness of the lining fights the easing, and the lining is cut the finished length of the coat.

One inch extra width is added at center back of lining for a pleat, to give necessary ease. On a coat with a full back, the pleat in lining is not necessary.

Chalkmark, on the coat front tissue pattern, the width front facing will extend on it (line A). Measure 1¼ inches (2 seam widths) from line A toward front of coat, and chalkmark (line B). Fold under tissue pattern on line B to cut lining for coat front. This same technique is used to cut lining correctly at back neck facing.

Mark all darts with tracing paper and tracing wheel.

If you are making a jacket, or any garment with set-in sleeves, before cutting the lining, see page 234.

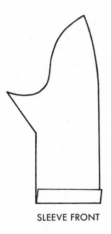

SLEEVE FRONT

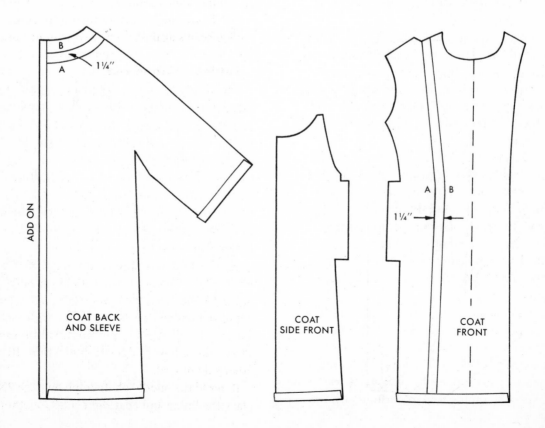

ADD ON

B
A   1¼"

COAT BACK
AND SLEEVE

COAT
SIDE FRONT

A   B
1¼"

COAT
FRONT

Sewing lining unit

Except for the neckline on the coat back, no staystitching is done on linings because the cut edges need to be easy to mold. Staystitch the neckline of coat on ⅝-inch seamline, so that this edge can be clipped later, where necessary, up to the staystitching. Then, the edge will be turned under on the seamline, and whipstitched by hand to the coat.

Stitch center seam of back lining section (A). Then stitch pleat one inch from seamline, stitching permanently up 1½ inches (B). Lockstitch threads; baste-stitch remainder of pleat to 1½ inches from top of coat (C). Lockstitch threads, and stitch permanently the final 1½ inches at upper edge (D). Then clip first baste-stitch at E and F for easy removal later.

On fragile fabrics, hand baste pleat. Press pleat to right side, and stitch in position along the neck and lower edges.

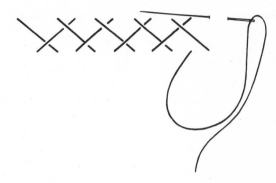

Catch-stitch across pleat at end of permanent stitching (E and F) on right side of fabric. Working from left to right, catch lining at the lower boundary, then at the upper boundary, in a zigzag fashion as shown.

Stitch and press all darts and all seams in the lining the same as was done for the coat. With a firm fabric like taffeta or milium, for ease, stitch the seams closer to ½ inch width than ⅝ inch. Seams are not finished in the lining or in the coat fabric. The lining will be sewn in the coat with perfection if the raw edges of both can be keyed together. Furthermore, when seams are enclosed as they are with the coat and lining, they cannot rub against the body during wear. Therefore, finishing for the purpose of protecting seams against such wear is unnecessary.

Putting lining in coat

The coat must be carefully and thoroughly final-pressed where necessary before attaching the lining, because the pressing cannot be done as well after the lining is in, and you would be hindered by it. To do the final-pressing, read pages 140 and 141 in Chapter 9. Hang the coat carefully on a wooden or padded hanger, and fasten one or more front closings to keep it on grain. This will give the coat time to become thoroughly dried from its steam pressing before you begin to insert the lining.

Refer to the top photograph on page 238. Place lower edge of lining to key with lower edge of coat. Several inches from the lower edge, place a pin in the lining and one in coat facing in line with each other. These are called guide pins and will be used later to key these lower edges to perfection. Repeat on other side of coat.

Refer to the middle photograph on page 238. Now place the lining and coat right sides together. Bring

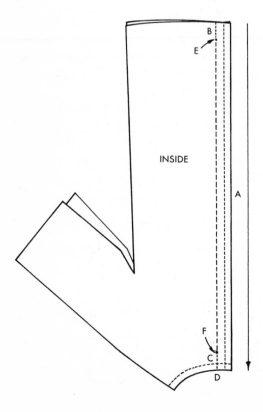

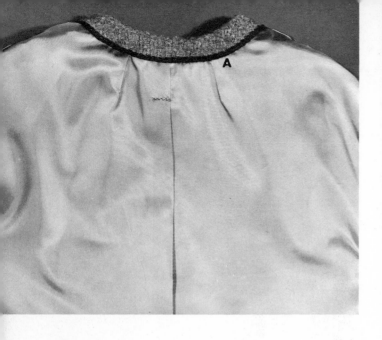

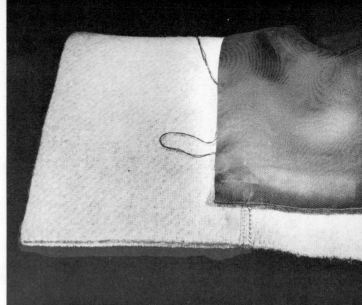

the raw edge of the lining over to meet the raw edge of the coat hem and pin to anchor at every seam. Then sew the hems with a machine basting stitch with coat side up. The raw edge of lining will extend over edge of facing for 1¼ inches.

It is much easier to do this row of stitching on lining before hem is sewn by hand to coat.

To hem by hand (see p. 243), fold hem to outside of garment, and work from underside of hem, holding hem edge away from you, and garment toward you. With a single thread, hem with a loose pick-up stitch a ½ inch apart. Continue around entire coat from one facing edge to the other.

In heavier and softer fabrics, make two rows of stitching in the hem — one halfway up the hem for extra support for the fabric, and then do the row at the top.

Refer to the bottom photograph on page 238. Key the lining at the shoulders and pin. Next, key lining to facing near lower edge by bringing two guide pins to meet and pin together. Repeat on other side of coat. Stitch the lining to the facings from guide pins to several inches below shoulder seam. Keep facing side up and stitch one thread inside staystitching on facings on seamline. Use the longest stitch at the machine unless it puckers. If it does, shorten stitch slightly, or use a small running hand stitch. As you sew, ease out the inch of lining if it was cut on extra. The neckline is left open.

Refer to the bottom photograph on page 236. Tack one side of each lining seam allowance to the corresponding coat seam. Begin and end stitching about two inches from each edge of the seam. With a single thread, make a long, easy running stitch through the middle of the seam allowance. Make several back stitches at the beginning (even with a knot in the thread) and at the end of the stitching to secure the thread in fabric. Always favor the lining. Do not attach center back seam of coat to center back pleat of lining.

The neckline opening and possibly several inches on front facing are used to turn the coat and lining to their correct positions — wrong sides together. Now close the opening at the neck. Clip the lining to the staystitching; then turn under the raw edge ⅝ inch. Overlap lining on the facing for ⅝ inch, pin and then whipstitch by hand (as in bottom photograph, p. 239). Photograph above left shows the completed lining at the neckline. The lace trim (A) was used all the way down the front facings, also.

There is an opening in the lining at the lower edge of front facings below guide pins. Press down excess lining. This is known as take-up tuck, and is necessary for longer wear on the lining. A deep take-up tuck in sleeves and hem is also an earmark of an expensive garment. Complete lower edge of front facings with slipstitching and include take-up tuck to hold in place. Press lining flat at front facings.

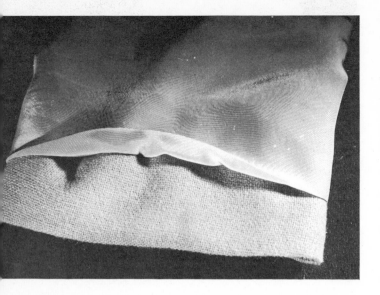

The sleeve lining, which was cut to the finished length of the sleeve plus one inch, should be turned under ¼ inch and pinned at ¼ inch from the edge of the sleeve hem. Then slipstitch by hand. Lightly press the take-up tuck.

Remove the baste-stitching in the back pleat. If the outer fabric has become wrinkled from the handling as the lining was being attached, some light final-pressing may again be necessary on the coat.

Here is the finished coat with a strip of bias coming from dart seam to act as a button loop. The loops are whipped together by hand on underside at A and B. Buttons were made of knots of bias (p. 262).

Silk-covered snaps were used under facings, in addition, to help hold coat in place.

The bias trim on sleeves was made from a folded piece of true bias.

This is another version of the same coat with a bias trim forming a bow effect. You may use a button and buttonhole or a silk-covered snap to hold the bow and coat together.

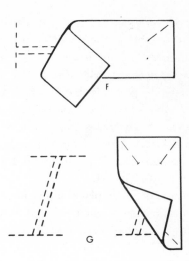

Various types of pockets

A widely used pocket is the one in a gore or side seam, shown on pages 194-195. However, you may prefer one of the following for your style of pattern.

Flap pocket. Baste-stitch location line (A) and size lines (B) through to outside of fabric. Baste-stitch another crosswise line (C) ¼ inch below location line (A). This line is a guide for placing the pocket pieces, so that the finished pocket will be in the correct location.

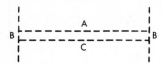

The pocket must be interfaced to reinforce the opening, and to preserve the pocket line. Use a lengthwise strip of muslin. When the pocket location is on the lengthwise or crosswise grain (sketch F), the strip of muslin will be 2 inches wide, and 2 inches longer than the pocket opening. When the pocket location is on the diagonal (sketch G, above right), a wider strip is needed, extending one inch beyond the location lines. Place the interfacing on the underside of the garment, so that it covers the location and size lines; pin in place.

The flap, the flap facing, and the interfacing are cut on identical grain. Cut away interfacing diagonally at corners ¼ inch beyond seamline to eliminate bulk in corners and to enable the flap to turn easily and to lie in perfect line (see p. 218).

Staystitch the interfacing to the flap facing ¾ inch from A and B edges, and ⅛ inch from C edge (sketch 1). Trim interfacing close to stitching at A and B edges (sketch 2). With interfacing side up, and right sides together, stitch flap to facing (sketch 3). Trim seam edges to ⅛ inch and ¼ inch, with the wider one on top, and round off the seam allowance at corners to within a few threads of the stitching line. Turn right side out, press, and pound with block. Stitch together raw edges of flap ⅛ inch from edge.

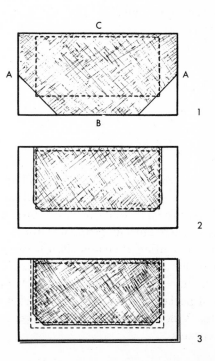

The back pocket piece is cut on identical grain of coat. In heavier fabrics, the lower ¾ of it is cut of lining to eliminate bulk and is seamed to one-fourth length of matching coat fabric. Match edge of flap to edge of back pocket piece, with ends of pocket piece extending a seam allowance beyond ends of flap. The underside of flap faces right side of pocket piece. Stitch together ⅛ inch from raw edges, easing flap to pocket piece if it is to lie on hipline or at bustline of a fitted jacket.

With flap turned down, place flap at location and size lines on right side of garment. Stitch between the size lines through pocket and flap on line of stitching that previously stitched flap to pocket piece. Shorten stitch at machine for first and last ½ inch.

Match the top pocket piece to location line, extending a seam allowance beyond each size line, with the right side of the pocket piece facing the right side of the garment. The grain of the top pocket piece is always crosswise to maintain the shape of the finished pocket opening. Stitch between size lines ⅛ inch from raw edge, again using the short stitch at the machine for the first and last ½ inch.

Check for accuracy on the inside. The stitching lines should be ¼ inch apart and should not extend beyond the size lines. Remove baste-stitching at the location and size lines in garment. On the inside of the garment, starting at center, slash between stitching lines through interfacing and garment, and diagonally to corners, leaving triangles ½ inch long at ends of pocket opening. Turn the pocket sections to inside. With care, pull ends of pocket pieces to square corners.

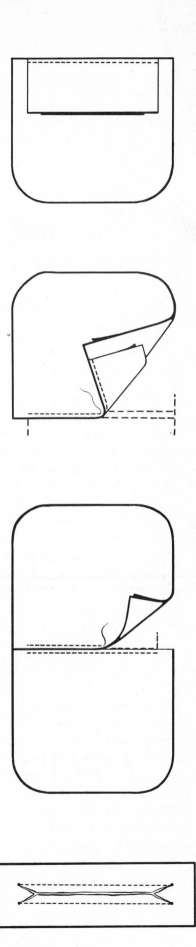

Fold top pocket piece to cover the seamline and form a narrow welt; press. Bevel ⅛-inch seam on inside on bulky fabric. With pocket open, stitch in well of seamline to hold welt in place. Press flap down to lie with perfection.

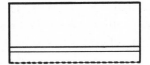

Place garment right side up on sewing machine. Turn back the edge of garment to reveal the triangle and pocket sections. Stitch the triangle to the pocket sections, going back and forth many times to fasten securely from base of triangle all the way out. This connecting line at the base of the triangle also squares the end of the pocket and makes it strong. Continue stitching around pocket sections to close the pocket, and repeat stitching at the opposite triangle. Round the lower edges of the pocket in stitching to keep out lint. Trim away interfacing to ½ inch all around pocket opening. Sometimes the flap pocket is topstitched with a row of stitching on the garment above the seamline at the upper edge of the flap (see photograph, p. 206).

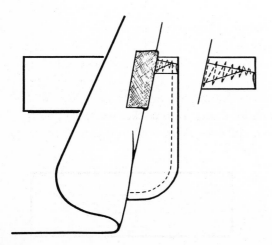

Welt pocket. The regulation welt pocket method to follow is essential for heavier fabrics. The modulated welt pocket method on pages 211-213 is preferred in tailoring for lighter-weight fabrics. Above the waistline, the regulation welt pocket is made 4 inches long; below the waistline, it is made 4 to 6 inches long.

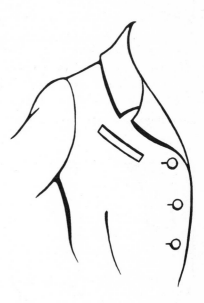

Baste-stitch the location line (A) and the size lines (B) through to the outside of fabric. The pocket must be interfaced to reinforce the opening, and to preserve the pocket line. Use a lengthwise strip of muslin, and place exactly as you learned with the flap pocket on page 206.

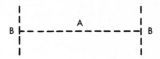

To make the welt, tear or cut on grain a lengthwise strip of fabric 1½ inches wide and 2 inches longer than the finished pocket. Fold welt lengthwise, wrong sides together; press; and stitch along the edge, allowing ¼-inch seam allowance.

Match the edge of the welt to the edge of the upper pocket piece, which can be cut of lining and is always crosswise grain; the underside of the welt faces the right side of the upper pocket piece. With welt up, stitch together on previous line of stitching.

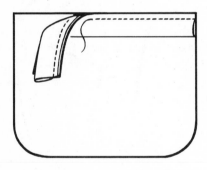

With welt turned down, place welt at location line on right side of garment. The unit of welt and pocket piece is placed below the location line, extending a seam allowance beyond the size lines. Stitch between the size lines through welt and pocket on previous line of stitching. Shorten stitch for first and last ½ inch.

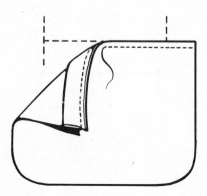

Match the under pocket piece to location line, extending a seam allowance beyond each size line, right side of the pocket piece facing the right side of garment. The grain of the under pocket piece must match the grain of the garment. Stitch between the size lines ¼ inch from raw edge, again using a short stitch at the machine for the first and last ½ inch.

Check carefully for accuracy. The width of the welt must be exactly the same as the width between the two stitching lines. If the welt is ½ inch wide, the stitching lines must be exactly ½ inch apart so the welt will fit perfectly and lie flat. The stitching lines should not extend beyond the size lines.

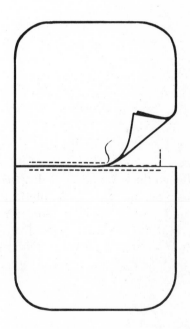

Remove baste-stitching at the location and size lines in the garment. On inside of the garment, starting at center, slash between stitching lines through interfacing and garment, and diagonally to corners, leaving triangles ½ inch long at ends of pocket opening. Turn pocket sections to inside. With care, pull ends of the welt to square the corners.

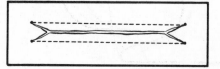

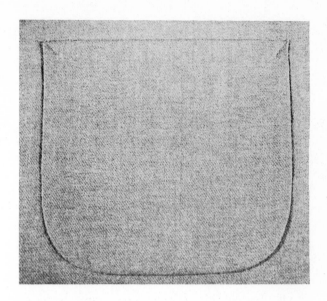

The welt automatically turns to fill the ½-inch space when the pocket is turned. Press with perfection. Understitch both pocket pieces along the top edge of the pocket pieces.

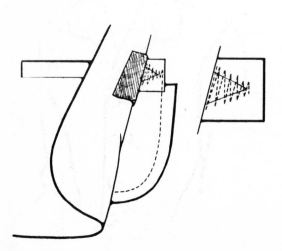

Place the garment right side up on the sewing machine. Turn back the edge of the garment to reveal the triangle and pocket sections. Stitch the triangle to the pocket sections, going back and forth many times to fasten securely from base of triangle all the way out; this connecting line at the base of the triangle also squares the end of the pocket. Continue stitching around pocket sections to close the pocket, and repeat stitching at opposite triangle. Round the lower edges of the pocket in stitching to keep out lint. Trim interfacing away to ½ inch all around pocket opening.

Patch pocket. This pocket is frequently used on blazer jackets, Chanel suits, sport coats, and men's sport jackets. It can be applied with the following method only when the lower edges are curved.

The outside pocket piece is cut one inch deeper than the lining, because it turns back to make a one-inch hem at the top of the pocket. With right sides together, stitch together pocket piece and lining on top edge with ¼-inch seam allowance. Press open seam, turn pocket right side out, and press in place one-inch hem at top.

Stitch together pocket piece and lining precisely ¼ inch from raw edges. Fold in half and snip pocket at exact center on lower edge (A). Notches of fabric should be trimmed from ¼-inch seam allowance on deepest part of curve (B and B).

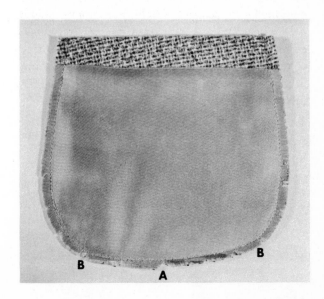

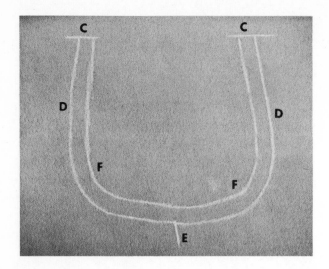

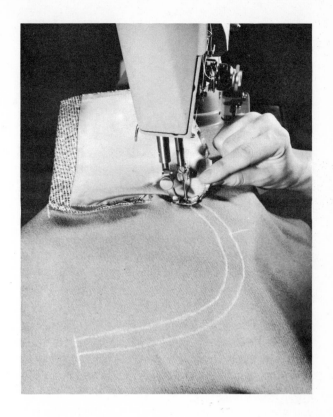

On the right side of the garment, place the pocket in position on the location line for top edges of pocket (C and C). Chalkmark (or hand baste) on garment exactly around pocket raw edges (D and D). Mark the center line of pocket on garment also (E). Remove pocket and mark a second line ½ inch from first line toward center of pocket (F and F); this is the guideline for sewing on pocket.

With the right side of the pocket facing the right side of the garment, match raw edges of pocket to inner marking line. Stitch pocket to garment through previous line of stitching exactly ¼ inch from edge. Check while stitching that the center of the pocket keys to the center marking on the garment. Pocket begins to close in on presser foot at machine, but the raw edge can still easily be keyed to the inner marking line to complete stitching around the pocket.

Press flat. Trim ¼ inch away diagonally at upper edges. Either bar-tack by stitching back and forth at machine several times for reinforcement (shown in photograph on page 210), or slipstitch by hand ¼ inch across upper edge.

Modulated welt pocket. This newly developed Bishop pocket is used in tailoring with lighter-weight fabrics. It is particularly adaptable for advanced dressmaking for silk and linen suits. It finishes ½ inch deep and can be 3 to 6 inches wide, depending upon where it is used. The higher a pocket is placed in a garment, the shorter is the length. It would be 6 inches long when used below the waistline on a coat. In general, this pocket is preferred straight across or up and down; in some fabrics, it is not good at an angle at all.

Baste-stitch location line (A) and size lines (B) through to outside of fabric. The pocket must be interfaced to reinforce the opening; always use a lengthwise strip of muslin 2 inches wide and 2 inches longer than opening. Place on underside of garment so that it covers the location and size lines; pin in place.

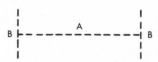

Tear a strip of fabric one inch wider than pocket opening (it must be lengthwise grain), and one inch longer than desired depth of pocket (crosswise grain). This one strip of fabric makes the welt and upper pocket piece. For the back of the pocket, tear a second strip of fabric one inch wider than the pocket opening (it must be identical grain to garment). It should be the desired depth of pocket.

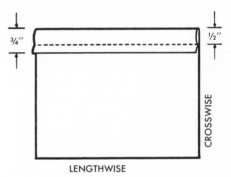

On strip of fabric for welt and upper pocket piece, with wrong sides together, fold over ¾ inch on one lengthwise edge and press. Stitch ½ inch from fold to form welt.

Place raw edge of welt to location marking line, each end extending ½ inch beyond size lines; have wrong side of pocket section to right side of garment. Stitch on top of welt between size lines over same line of stitching that formed welt.

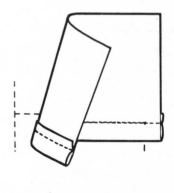

Next, place one edge of back pocket to location marking line (raw edge meets raw edge of welt) with right side of pocket section facing right side of garment. Stitch ¼ inch from raw edge between size lines. Check for accuracy on the inside. The stitching lines should be ½ inch apart and should not extend beyond the size lines.

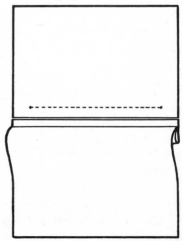

Remove baste-stitching at location and size lines in garment. On inside of garment, starting at center, slash between stitching lines through interfacing and garment and diagonally to corners, leaving triangles ½ inch long at ends of pocket opening. Turn pocket sections to inside; press open the back pocket seam in heavier-weight fabrics and press down in lighter-weight fabrics. Welt will fit with perfection in opening.

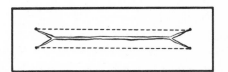

Place garment right side up on sewing machine. Turn back edge of garment to reveal triangle and pocket sections. Stitch the triangle to the pocket sections, going back and forth many times to fasten securely from base of triangle all the way out. This connecting line at base of triangle also squares the end of the pocket. Continue stitching around pocket sections to close pocket, and repeat stitching at opposite triangle. Round lower edges of pocket in stitching to keep out lint. Trim interfacing away to ½ inch all around pocket opening.

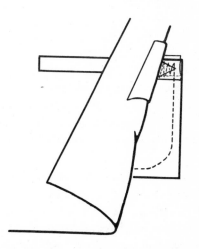

Interlining a coat

With an underlining and a lining, a coat is usually warm enough without an additional interlining.

However, if you want one, there are three choices on the market.

Milium. Milium is cut, stitched together, and put in the coat like a regular lining, as explained earlier in this chapter and in the next chapter.

Separate wool interlinings. After the regular lining is cut out, a separate wool interlining is cut exactly like the lining except for the differences noted below. Instead of buying interlining, you can cut up old woolen blankets or garments which can be used equally well.

In length, the sleeve lining is cut to the finished length of the coat sleeve (A). The interlining is cut only to the top of the hem of the coat sleeves (B).

In length, the lining for the coat is cut to the finished length of the coat plus one inch extra for ease. The interlining is again cut only to the top of the hem of the coat (like B) plus the inch extra for ease. However, it may be cut to extend only down over the hips, and need not extend all the way to the lower edge of the coat.

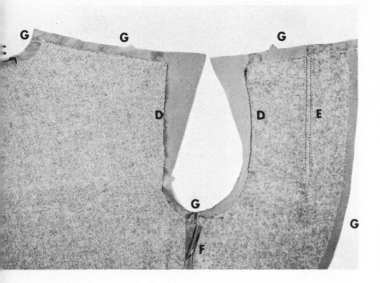

Do not cut a center back pleat in the interlining, even though the lining has one (C).

Do not cut on extra at armholes of the interlining (D and D) as you have learned to do with the lining.

Darts in interlining (E) are stitched separately, and then stitched again ¼ inch from the first stitching, so they will lie flat.

Staystitch the interlining to the lining on seamline at all edges, except armholes above notches where lining is cut wider (D and D), and lower edges of sleeves (B on p. 213) and lining for coat. Stitch seams on seamline, press open, and trim away interlining up to seamline (F).

Trim away interlining up to staystitching on all other edges that are staystitched (G). These include sleeve cap, front facing edges, shoulders, back neckline, and below notches at armholes.

Edges of coat facings would be bulky if lining and interlining were stitched as a seam to coat (p. 238). So the following technique is used to attain a flat, quality-looking edge on facings. Stitch a bias strip of lining 1½ inches wide exactly on seamline continuously around front and back neck facings, beginning and ending at bottom of coat. Trim seam to ¼ inch (A), turn bias to underside of facings without turning in raw edge (B), and press in place. Stitch at machine in well of seamline (C) or with a running stitch by hand to hold bias in place. Trim away excess width of bias (D).

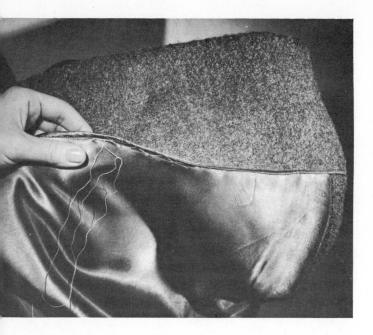

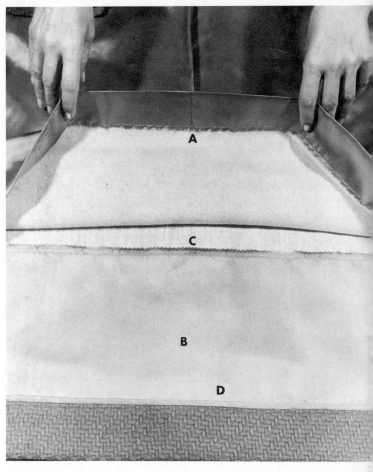

The lining and interlining are put into the coat exactly as you learned with the coat and suit earlier in this chapter and in the next chapter with one exception: the seamline of the facings is pinned on top of the lining to key exactly to the staystitching line. Slipstitch from the underside of the facing, going through machine stitching on the underside of facing and the staystitching on lining edge.

For some styles of coats, if you prefer to keep the lining (A) free at the hem, put a piece of lining (B) on top of the underlining (C) for 8 to 10 inches above hemline. This will give a more finished look to lower edge. Hemline of coat (D) should then be finished with a piece of bias, as you just learned above for facings.

Lining should finish one inch shorter than finished coat.

Catch lining to the coat with a chain stitch one inch long at each seamline.

Sunback. Sunback (lining and interlining woven together as one fabric) or a quilted lining is cut, stitched together, and put into coat precisely like the regular lining, as explained earlier in this chapter and in the next chapter with two exceptions:

1. Edges of coat facings are finished with a bias strip, and facings are laid over lining for finishing precisely as separate interlinings are done above. Sunback would be too bulky for the bias strip; use a bias strip of regular lining in a matching color.

2. The coat and lining are hemmed separately, exactly as you learned in connection with the above photograph.

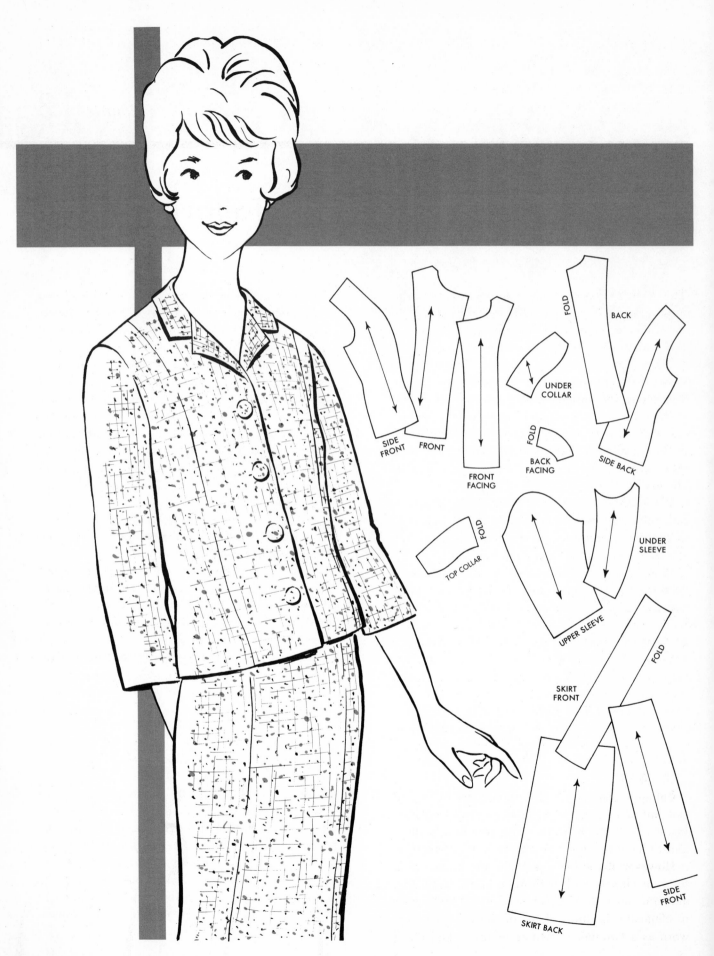

SIDE FRONT

FRONT

UNDER COLLAR

FOLD

BACK

FRONT FACING

FOLD

BACK FACING

SIDE BACK

FOLD

TOP COLLAR

UNDER SLEEVE

UPPER SLEEVE

SKIRT FRONT

FOLD

SKIRT BACK

SIDE FRONT

216

Chapter 13

Tailoring a suit

This second chapter on tailoring presents the techniques for making a suit. This style was chosen to show the techniques for underlining and lining a tailored garment with set-in sleeves. It could be either a jacket to a suit or a coat. This style also shows the techniques for a separate front facing on a garment, the notched collar, a second and third method for making tailored buttonholes, a second way to deal with a straight skirt, and the bias finish at the waistline. The suit you are making may have other features; for those learnings, refer to the coat chapter.

If you are going to tailor a suit before you have tailored a coat, be certain to read the introduction of the coat chapter (page 187) before starting the suit. Information there is not repeated here.

It is an accomplishment to be able to tailor a good-looking suit. Yet, it does not need to be a time-consuming task. To do all of the cutting of outside fabric, underlining, and lining will be the one step for which you need a longer period of worktime, so that the cutting can be done carefully. Beyond that step, when you place your suit in units of work, a unit can be completed easily in any short period of time available. The Bishop method of tailoring covers much ground swiftly, but not too fast to prevent you from turning out quality-looking suits.

The jacket

Cutting underlining.   Underlining gives a tailored garment more character than merely using interfacing would. It also helps the garment retain its shape and to have the finest quality look in appearance.

However, if you feel a jacket would be too warm for your climate with both underlining and lining, and you choose to eliminate one, it would be wiser to eliminate the lining. Most of the time, suits are worn as a two-piece costume or dress, and lining

does not show. The only exception would be if you wore a blouse and removed your jacket. You underline for character or shape in a garment, and line for appearance.

As shown in the photograph, the underlining is cut precisely as is the jacket, using the same tissue, and on the same grain as the jacket. The center front and buttonhole location lines are marked on underlining only, using tracing paper and tracing wheel. See page 228 for directions on cutting the tailored collar and its interfacing. Underlining set-in sleeves is discussed on page 235. Do not cut the lining for the jacket, if it is to be used, until fitting is completed, unless you have made the pretest discussed in the coat and fitting chapters. To cut the lining, see page 234.

Appropriate underlinings for a suit are discussed on pages 254-255. Formite was used for the suit in the photographs. It is probably the most widely used, most conforming underlining for suits of silk, linen, or wool.

There should be as much give to the underlining as to the outside fabric. Underlining must never impose itself on the outside. Formite meets all of these qualifications.

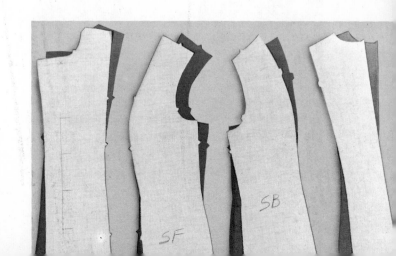

Tailoring a suit

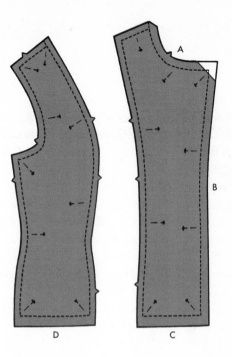

Jacket front unit. Place underlining on underside of jacket fronts and side fronts. With some fabrics, it may be helpful to press to adhere underlining to outside fabric. Pin in place, keeping pins back from the stitching line. Even though you will sometimes be sewing against the grain line, staystitch underlining to jacket fabric with underlining side up all around. It is easier to manage with the firm underlining on top, and will not push out of line under the presser foot, as the softer jacket fabric might do (see photograph, page 190).

All the staystitching is done just outside the seamline, except edges A and B, that are done on the seamline. This is where the collar and facing will be attached. It permits trimming the underlining away more easily later. Hem edges C and D are staystitched ¾ inch from the edge (on a 1½-inch hem, underlining will turn up in the hem half its width).

At the lapel, the corners of the underlining are cut away ¼ inch beyond the seamline. Any time there is a corner, this is done to reduce unnecessary bulk.

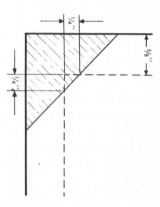

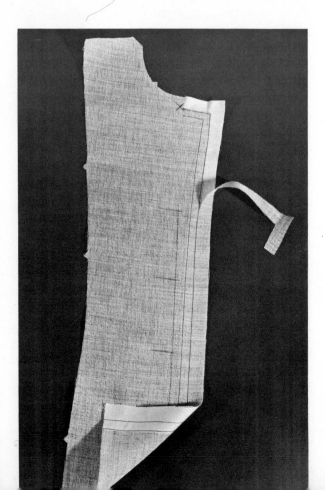

Unless you are making a walking suit from heavier fabric, it is not likely that you would be using hair canvas or acro underlining for a suit. However, you may be making a coat that has a separate front facing, as this jacket has, and may be using the heavier underlining for it. In that case, this acro or hair canvas underlining must be eliminated from the facing seamline. It is wiry and prevents a smooth, well-pressed edge. This step was not used on the suit in the photographs with formite underlining.

To do so, cut a strip of muslin on identical grain of underlining. It extends back 1¼ inches from edge of pattern. Match outer edge of muslin strip with outer edge of underlining. Stitch ⅞ inch from edge; stitch again toward inside edge of muslin for reinforcement. Press to smooth stitching line.

Trim away underlining to first row of stitching ⅞ inch from edge. Proceed with staystitching shown above.

If your jacket pattern has bustline, waistline, elbow, neckline, or shoulder darts, you will have to decide if they will be made separately in fabric and underlining (page 197), or together as one (page 191). A lightweight fabric needs the support of underlining in darts, but a heavy, bulky jacket fabric will have a smoother line on the outside if darts are made separately before staystitching is done.

Baste-stitch center front and crosswise lines for buttonhole locations from underlining through to outside of garment. Always baste-stitch crosswise lines before lengthwise ones. On fragile fabrics such as velveteen, use hand basting.

If you have pretested your jacket pattern, it will be easier to make buttonholes now in the jacket front, instead of having to handle the entire jacket, when it has been sewn together.

One buttonhole method has been shown on pages 192 to 194 in the coat chapter. A second and third method are shown here.

Tailored buttonhole. A popular buttonhole method was shown on pages 192 to 194. Another one for the beginner is given on pages 222 to 224.

The method given here is growing in popularity. When the steps are carefully learned, this method is virtually foolproof.

First, machine baste-stitch crosswise lines (A) for buttonhole location from underlining through to outside of garment. Then, baste-stitch center front line (B) in a continuous line of stitching the length of all the buttonholes. Determine the finished buttonhole length, and baste-stitch a second line (C) parallel to the center front line. Buttonhole length should be at least the diameter of the button plus its thickness. Another thing you can do is cut a slash in a scrap of fabric until button slides through easily. Then, measure the slash for the size of the buttonhole. Buttonholes are not made less than one inch, except in a fine fabric like satin. In a heavy coat, buttonholes would be made 1¼ to 1½ inches long, even if the button being used is just ¾ to 1 inch in diameter, and without height.

On fragile fabrics such as velveteen, use hand basting.

The baste-stitching should be grain perfect on both garment fabric and underlining. The distance from B to D (fold line or seamline of garment) must

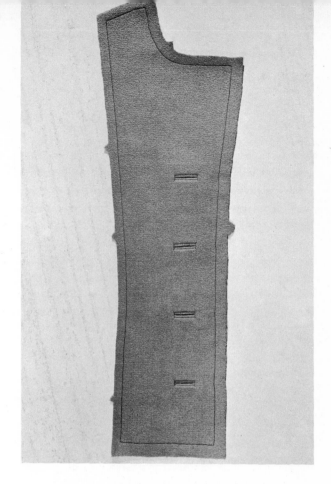

be a minimum of half the width of a button plus ¼ inch, or plus ½ inch for larger buttons.

This entire buttonhole construction will be done from the underlining side.

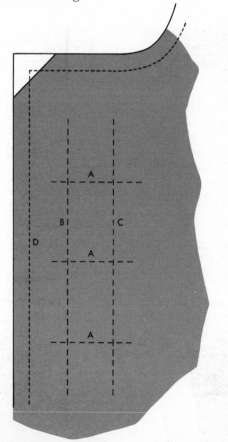

Tailoring a suit

The strip for the buttonhole will be lengthwise grain at E and E, or it may be cut on the true bias. It should be 2 inches wide from E to E, and extend ½ inch beyond size lines (B and C).

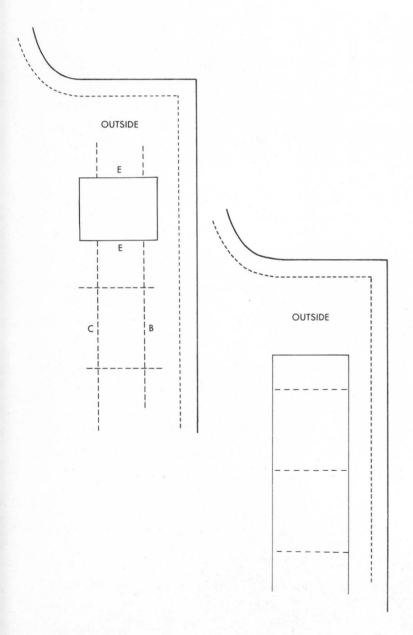

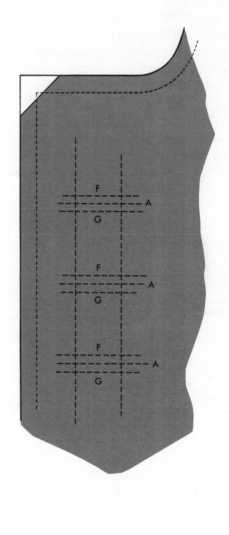

When you are making two or more buttonholes, one long strip may be used for all buttonholes.

Place right side of strip to right side of garment.

With underlining side up, make a second row of machine baste-stitching through crosswise line, A.

Then, again with underlining side up, baste-stitch lines (F and G) ¼-inch on each side of buttonhole marking line (A). You may be able to use the wide side of the presser foot as a guide for this ¼ inch stitching. In fine fabrics, such as silk, this distance may be less than ¼ inch.

At arrows, a long strip would now be cut into individual ones for each buttonhole.

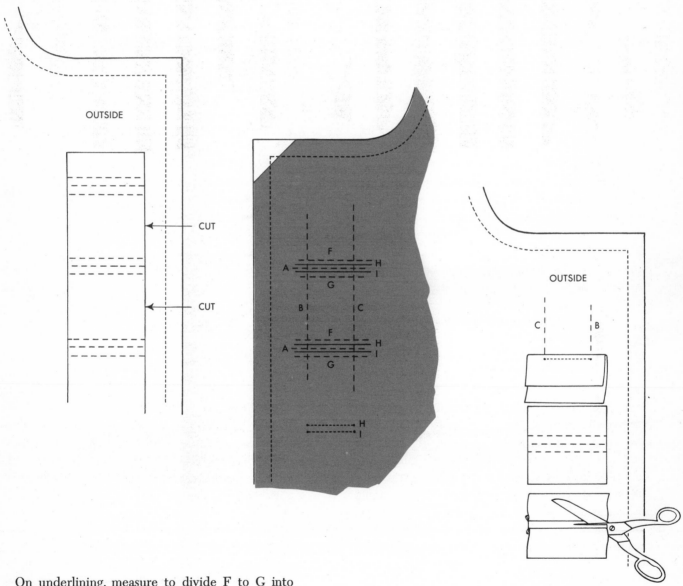

On underlining, measure to divide F to G into thirds, and mark underlining. These lines (H and I) become the stitching lines for forming the tucks of the buttonhole. Turn strip toward center line, one side at a time, and stitch on marking lines (H and I) exactly between size lines (B and C). Use a short machine stitch, and lockstitch beginning and end of stitching. If it is difficult for you to do the lockstitching precisely at the size lines, leave the threads and pull them to the underside to tie by hand.

In some fabrics, it may be easier to press strip toward center line before stitching.

Remove all baste-stitching.

Cut entire strip in two along center line. Be careful not to cut garment. In strips of true bias or in soft straight of grain fabrics, use a cording (see sketch, p. 193).

On inside of garment, starting at center, clip through underlining and fabric and diagonally to corners, having triangles ¼ to ⅜ inch long at ends of buttonhole. While cutting, hold tuck strips out of way of cutting with finger inserted under them on right side.

Turn finishing strips to inside. Do not handle triangles, but carefully pull ends of strips to square the corners of the buttonhole. The folded edges now meet in the center of the buttonhole.

Place garment right side up on sewing machine. Turn back edge of garment to reveal triangle and end of strips. Stitch triangle to strips, going back and forth many times to fasten securely from knots at base of triangle all the way out. This connecting line squares the corners. Stitch opposite end of buttonhole the same way. Press buttonhole in direction of the strip.

After the front facings are stitched on and pressed in place, the buttonholes will be finished through the facing (see p. 194).

Another tailored buttonhole. Two other tailored buttonhole methods are shown on pages 192-194, 219-222. This third one is given only for the beginner.

First, baste-stitch crosswise lines (A) for buttonhole locations from underlining through to outside of garment. Then, baste-stitch center front line (B) in a continuous line of stitching the length of all the buttonholes. Determine the finished buttonhole length, and baste-stitch a second line (C), parallel to the center front line. Buttonhole length should be at least the diameter of the button plus its thickness. Another thing you can do is cut a slash in a scrap of fabric until button slides through easily. Then, measure the slash for the size of the buttonhole. Buttonholes are never made less than one inch, except in a fine fabric like satin. In a heavy coat, buttonholes would be made 1¼ to 1½ inches long even if the button being used is just ¾ to 1 inch in diameter, and without height.

Use hand basting on fragile fabrics such as velveteen. The distance from B to D (fold line or seamline of garment) must be a minimum of half the width of a button plus ¼ inch, or plus ½ inch for larger buttons.

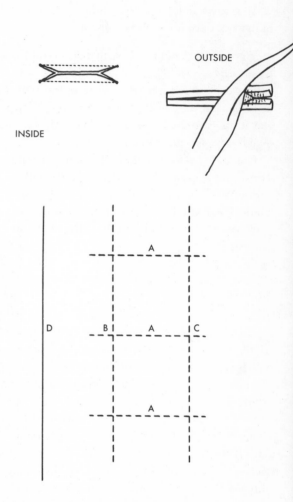

Baste-stitch another crosswise line (E) ¼ inch above buttonhole markings (A). This line is a guide for placing the finishing strip so the finished buttonhole will be in the correct location.

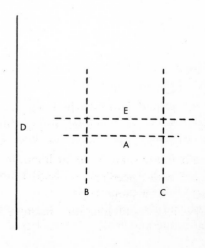

To prepare the finishing strip, tear or cut a lengthwise strip of fabric 2½ inches wide. In length, each strip should be an inch longer than the buttonhole is to be, but it is better to make a longer strip, and cut it up as needed. Use a true bias strip for checks, plaids, stripes, and ribbed fabrics.

Cut a 2½-inch strip of notebook paper with ruled lines ½ inch apart. Match edge of paper with edge of fabric. Using lines near the center of the paper as a guide, baste-stitch in contrasting thread two lines ½ inch apart for the full length of the strip. Remove the paper.

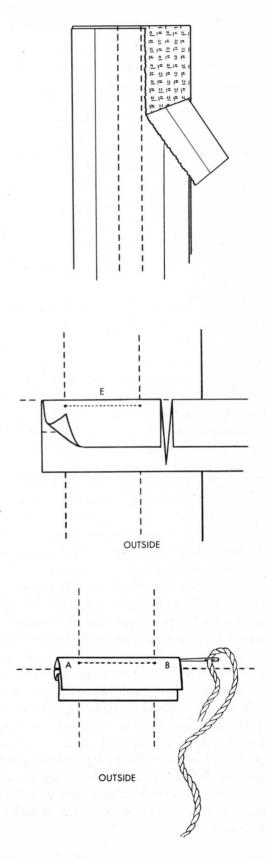

Fold the finishing strip on one baste-stitched line right side out and press flat; repeat for other baste-stitched line and press. With finishing strip extending ½ inch beyond the size line, place the fold on the guide line (E) on outside of garment. Stitch ⅛ inch from fold between the size lines with a short machine stitch. Lockstitch beginning and end of stitching. If it is difficult for you to do the lockstitching perfectly and precisely at the size lines, leave the threads and pull them to the underside to tie by hand. Cut off strip ½ inch beyond stitching line; this leaves ½ inch extra at each end of buttonhole.

Fold on second baste-stitched line and repeat stitching between the size lines. Repeat for all buttonholes. If buttonhole is made of bias strip or of lightweight fabric such as silk or linen, insert yarn or thin cord with a needlepoint needle through both folded edges of finishing strip.

Remove all baste-stitching from finishing strip and garment.

Slash the finishing strip through the center between the stitching lines. The finishing strip is now in two pieces with ⅛ inch seam allowance on each side.

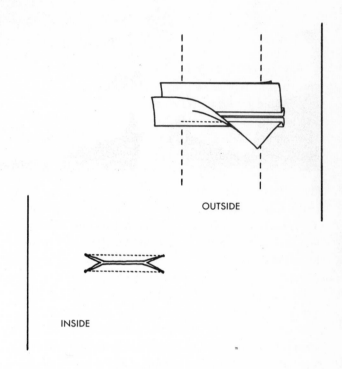

OUTSIDE

INSIDE

On inside of garment starting at center, clip through underlining and fabric and diagonally to corners, leaving triangles ¼ to ⅜ inch long at ends of buttonhole.

Turn finishing strips to inside. Do not handle triangles. Carefully pull the ends of strips to square the corners of buttonhole. The folded edges now meet in the center of the buttonhole.

Place garment right side up on sewing machine. Turn back edge of garment to reveal triangle and end of strip. Stitch triangle to strip, going back and forth many times to fasten securely from knots at base of triangle all the way out. This connecting line squares the corners. Stitch the opposite end of the buttonhole the same way. Press buttonhole in direction of the strip.

After the facings are sewn on, the buttonholes are finished through the facing as discussed on page 194. The whipstitching is not done, however, until collar and hem are completed.

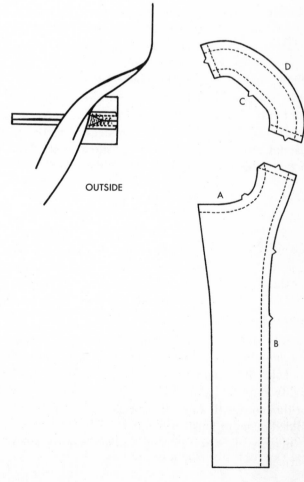

OUTSIDE

Jacket front unit, continued. Just as you found it was much easier to work with only the jacket front to make the buttonholes, the same will be true to sew on the facings. Staystitch A and B edges exactly on the seamline. At the same time, staystitch back facing at C and D exactly on seamline. If your jacket has a cut-on facing, refer to description of coat, pages 189-190.

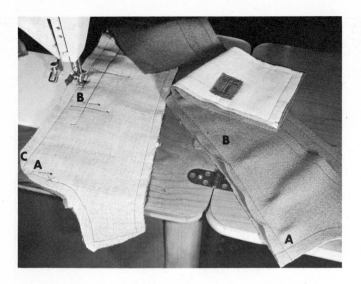

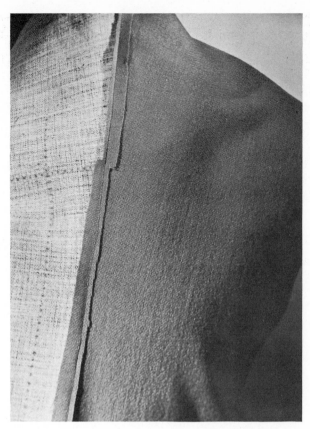

Place facings on jacket fronts, right sides together. To prevent the facing from having a tight, drawn look as it lies over jacket to form the lapel, ease facing to jacket above top buttonhole (A to B). Facing will be held firmly to jacket below top buttonhole. Sew facing to jacket with jacket side up, going through staystitching on seamline. Use short stitches at the top of the lapel (C) for one inch for greater strength in corner. Do this for greater strength in any corner. Do not sew facing to jacket beyond corner of lapel at the present time.

Press open and grade the seam. First, trim underlining close to the seamline. This is easy to do because you have made the staystitching on the seamline at these areas that have to be trimmed.

Then, from the top of the lapel to the top buttonhole, trim the jacket seam allowance to ⅛ inch, and the facing to ¼ inch. Below the top buttonhole, trim just the reverse — facing to ⅛ inch, and jacket to ¼ inch. Repeat for other half of jacket in relation to top button placement. The same principle follows here as you have learned from page 201; the seam allowance which is to rest against the outside of the garment is usually the one that should stay the wider of the two. The wider seam serves as a cushion for the more narrow one below, and prevents it from pressing through to the top.

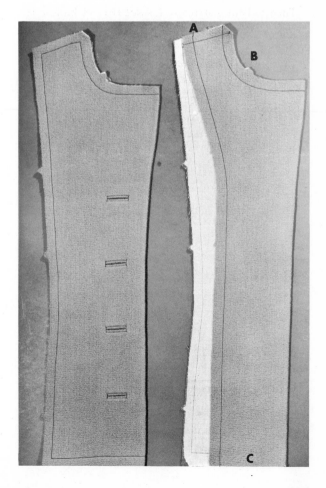

Then, turn the facing and press. Always keep the underside on top first to set this edge; then, turn to topside of jacket front to final-press. See page 139. Make certain that all edges of the garment and facing meet with perfection at A, B, and C. It would be easy to distort them in pressing.

Tailoring a suit

Stitch jacket front to jacket side front with front on top. When fullness between notches at the bustline is on the underside, it will be managed more easily in the stitching. A seam like this over the bustline, or one that curves out into the armhole, never has much character unless it is underlined. Press seam open in heavier fabrics or toward jacket front in lighter-weight fabrics. Trim seams diagonally for 1¼ inches at shoulders to reduce bulk.

If you have pretested your jacket pattern, then you will know how much to turn up the hem. In that case, it will be easier to do now with separate jacket front and jacket back units before they are joined together. There will be less handling of the entire garment, and the fabric will look better. Press up hem (p. 139); the standard width of hem in a jacket is 1½ inches.

Just as you learned to use the press-on interfacing in the dress (p. 150) and the jacket facing (p. 183), it can be used over top of underlining in tailoring where added support is needed. Here the interfacing is used at the shoulders. If sloping shoulder is a problem, the press-on interfacing may be used for just one shoulder. On some patterns it may be used for lapels; on others, for pocket openings. On page 232, it is shown being used in the hemline. We used the black dress weight, so it would show up in the photograph, but heavier tailoring weights are available (p. 255). If you do not have or do not prefer the press-on interfacing, with a catch-stitch, sew on an extra piece of underlining on the regular underlining in the garment.

Shoulder pads or shapes are not shown in this book. A more normal look at shoulders has replaced pads or shapes.

The press-on will solve any figure irregularities. This completes the front unit.

Jacket back unit. The back unit will be completed with the same learnings as the front unit. As stressed in all the chapters, working in units reduces handling the fabric, and it organizes your work to much better advantage.

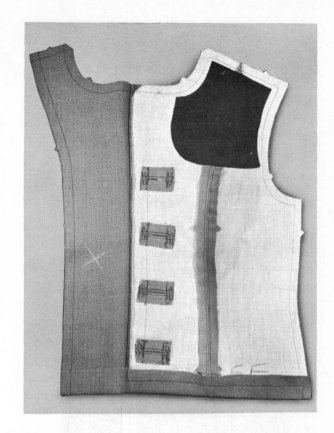

Staystitch neck edge (A) on the seamline; staystitch hem edges (B and C) ¾ inch from the edge; and staystitch all other edges just outside the seamline. As you have learned on the front unit, and in the preceeding chapter on making a coat, do all of the staystitching with the underlining on top even though you will sometimes be sewing against the grain line.

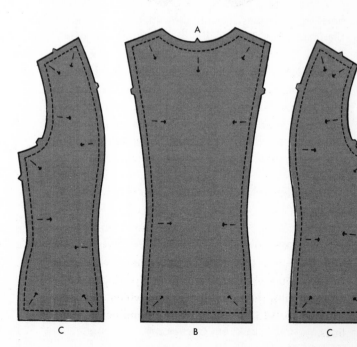

Stitch jacket back to jacket side back in direction shown with arrow. Press seams open in same direction in which they were stitched, and trim diagonally at shoulders beginning ¼ inch from edge. Do not trim out underlining from seams; it remains full width of seam for reinforcement.

Press up hem for 1½ inches, the same as you did on the front unit. This completes the back unit.

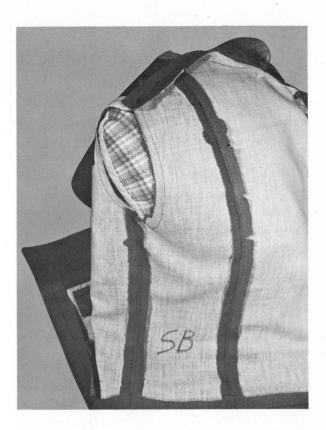

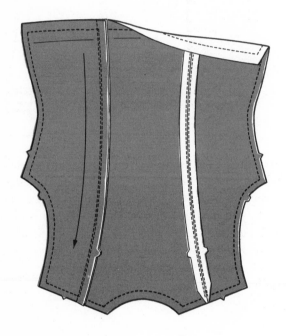

At shoulders, join back facing to front facings on seamline. Press open seams; topstitch each side of seam and trim away seam allowance to topstitching. This technique can be used anytime you want to eliminate bulk at any seamline of a facing in heavier fabric.

Complete jacket unit. With right sides together, stitch shoulder seams from neckline to armhole. In stitching one of the seams, the back of the jacket will be on top; in stitching the other one, the front will be on top. It does not matter which one is on top — the correct direction for stitching is the important part.

Stitch side seams from bottom up to armholes. In sewing this seam, it is not necessary to reverse the stitching at the waistline as was shown for a fitted garment in the sketch on page 165. This jacket is more boxy and the grain line does not reverse itself to any degree above the waistline. Press open seams on cushion in the same direction in which they were stitched (p. 135). Press to restore hemlines at seamlines.

Collar unit. The interfacing for the collar is cut from the same underlining fabric that is used in the garment. If the commercial pattern gives a separate pattern piece to cut the interfacing all in one and on the bias, eliminate this piece, and cut in two pieces from under collar pattern for best results. If the commercial pattern does not show true bias for this under collar and interfacing, redraft grain line as shown in the sketch, and cut both on true bias. All of this is important so that the collar will be easy to mold, will roll softly, and will lie uniformly at the neckline.

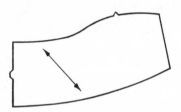

With a larger collar, or one from heavy, bulky fabric, the top collar may be cut ⅛ or ¼ inch deeper at edges A and B, tapering to nothing at C.

The only way you can determine this is to make the under collar with the steps that follow, and baste-stitch a trial top collar to under collar. Roll it over your fingers to see how it fits. When you roll a magazine, for instance, the top cover seems smaller than the under cover.

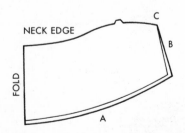

If this happens after you have the collar cut out, cut a small amount off the under collar and the interfacing. Try it together and see.

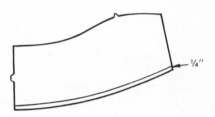

Place two sections of interfacing together for the under collar. Use two pins at A and B to hold bias interfacing in place. Using dressmaker's tracing paper and wheel, mark a stitching pattern for the under collar. This is shown in the next photograph.

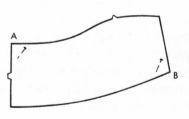

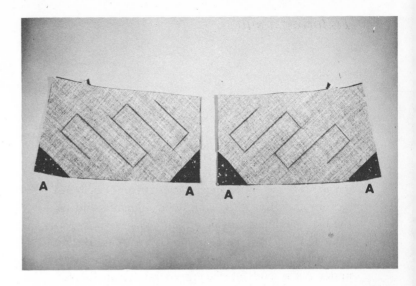

The stitching pattern can form various designs, providing lines are on crosswise and lengthwise threads of interfacing. At the four outside corners (marked with A in photograph), cut away the interfacing diagonally so that it will be out of corners ¼ inch beyond the seamline to eliminate bulk (see p. 218).

Staystitch interfacing to under collar the regulation width (between ½ and ⅝ inch) at neck edge (A) and ¾ inch from outside edges (B and C).

Stitch center back seam of under collar and interfacing. Press open. Trim away interfacing up to stitching line at center back seam. Topstitch each side of seam, beginning at neck edge and continuing down one side to ¾ inch from lower edge (D). Cross over to other side and topstitch up to neck edge. Trim away all of wool seam, except lower edge that is not topstitched (E).

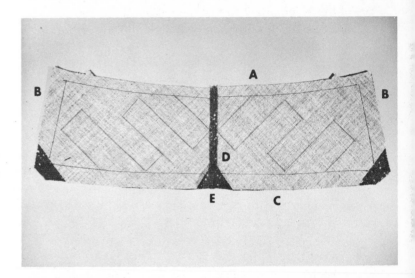

With interfacing side turned up, quilt at machine entire under collar on marking lines for stitching pattern. In crossing from one line to another, stitching must always be on grain, and must not extend beyond the staystitching around collar.

With fine fabrics, the quilting may be done by hand with a small running stitch.

Mold the under collar on a cushion to give it a curve at the neckline for a close, form fit. To do so, fold it in half at center back with interfacing side out, and pin to hold. At neckline of outer edges, fold back seam allowance, and pin to hold. Mold half of the collar at a time on the cushion. Place steam iron down on edge of collar to hold collar on cushion. With left hand, curve collar while taking iron on grain up to fold of collar. Continue to curve collar with left hand and press with iron in right hand until the under collar takes on a curved shape. The aim is not to stretch the outside edge of the collar, but to press in a breaking point for the collar at the neckline. Repeat for the other half of the collar. Remove pins to give a final shaping.

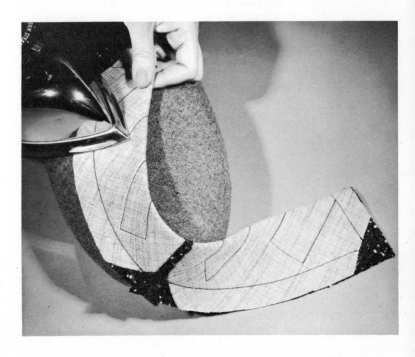

On a larger collar, instead of folding it in half at the center back, only about a third of the collar will fold back at the neckline to form the curve. If it is too large, the collar will not stay in half at the center back when the seam allowance is folded back at the neckline on the outer edges.

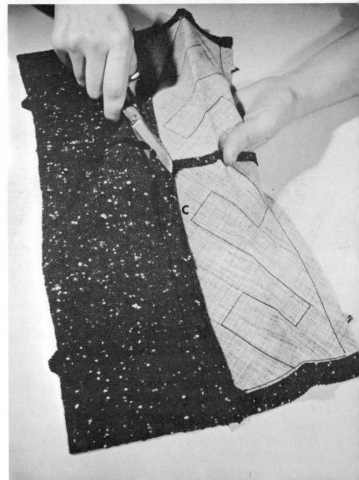

Trim away interfacing close to ¾-inch staystitching line at edges (B and C), and trim wool to point at center back seam.

At outside edge (C) stitch top collar to under collar, right sides together. (If it is a rounded collar, stitch collar together around curve and leave open at least one inch at neck edges.) Begin and end for one inch with short stitches at machine, and match with perfection center back of top collar to center back of under collar. Have under collar side turned up, and the stitching on the seamline will not include the interfacing. The staystitching will show on the underside of the completed collar.

Press seam open and stagger edges of seam allowance. The upper seam is trimmed down to ¼ inch and the under seam to ⅛ inch. In using the scissors, bevel the edges in heavy fabrics; this bias cut will not make as blunt an edge to fabric as a straight cut and will not mark outside fabric in pressing.

Staggering the edges of seam allowance is done to all faced edges in tailoring and also to garments made of heavier fabrics in dressmaking. This collar is not understitched; whenever the under collar and interfacing are bias, the collar is never understitched. The bias controls the edge of the under collar, and there is no need for understitching.

Turn collar right side out. To set the outside edge, always have under collar side up, and press along stitching line. Then, turn and have top side up to press again and pound (p. 140). Top collar will appear to be wider than under collar until it is sewn on garment.

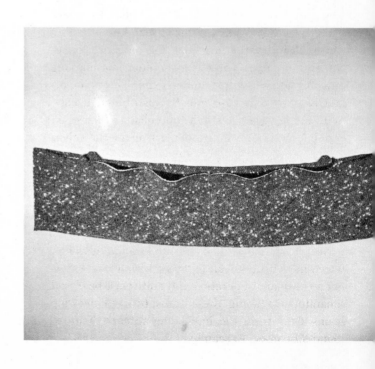

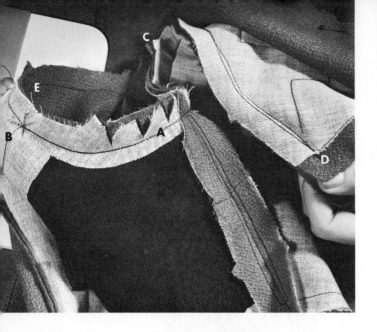

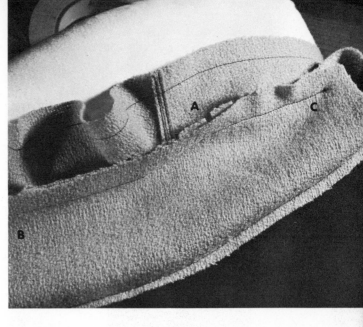

Clip neck edge of jacket at intervals almost to staystitching to give a straight line for stitching (A). Make certain marking is evident on jacket and on front facings indicating location of finished end of collar (B). Key and pin center back of under collar to center back of jacket neckline (C). Key and pin seamline of end of under collar (D) to neckline location marking; repeat for opposite end of collar (E). There is a shoulder line marking on collar to key with shoulder seam. This is important, also, so that ease will be distributed evenly. Ends of collar are still open.

With jacket side up, stitch under collar to jacket on seamline from one location marking to the other.

Clip neck edge of facings at intervals (A) almost to staystitching to give a straight line for stitching. Key and pin center back of top collar to center back of facing (B). Key and pin seamline of end of top collar to location marking (C); repeat for opposite end of collar. There is a shoulder line marking on collar to key with shoulder seam. This is important, also, so that ease will be distributed evenly. With facing side up, stitch top collar to facings on seamline from one location marking to the other.

With right sides still together, close ends of jacket lapels (A), stitching from outer edge to location markings at neckline, which have been keyed together with a pin.

Next, close ends of collar (B) to location markings, which have been keyed together with a pin. This is not a continuous operation and ends must be closed separately. In doing these steps, turn all neckline seams away from the line being stitched. Trim to round off corners to seamline.

In putting on this collar, we have sewn what is known as a four point closure — 4 seams stitched separately, but all meeting at one point. This technique will be used many times in sewing. Another illustration is the pocket in the side seam of a dress or skirt (pp. 146-148).

You may prefer to close ends of collar and lapel in one operation. To do so, first clip facing and garment seamline down to lockstitching at collar location marking line (C). Then, press open top and bottom neckline seams, and trim ends away diagonally before continuous stitching is done at end of collar and lapel. Key lockstitching on top and under collar before doing final stitching.

Using edge presser, press open seams and stagger seam allowance to ¼ inch on top and ⅛ inch on underside, as described previously.

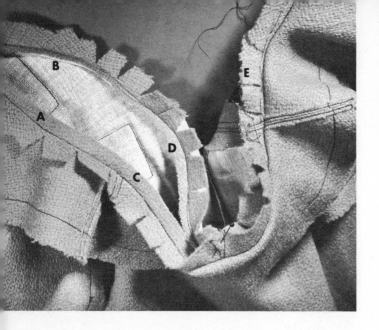

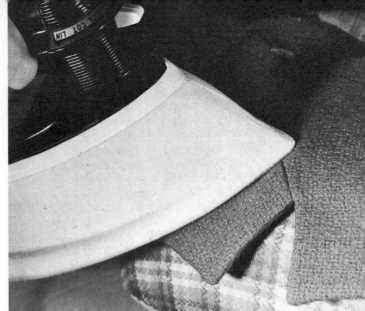

Next, using edge presser, press open top collar (A) and under collar (B) seams. To complete the collar, trim underlining to seamline and grade the top collar seam allowance to ⅜ inch (C), the under collar seam allowance to ¼ inch (D). These are the seam allowances that go upward into the collar. Turn collar right side out.

Then, sew the remaining untrimmed jacket and facing seam allowances with a single thread (E). Use a loose stitch, close to the seamline. Then grade these remaining untrimmed seam allowances, top collar ⅜ inch, under collar ¼ inch.

Final-press collar and front facings. Using a press cushion, shape and mold the collar and front facing as a well-tailored lapel unit. They will not be treated as separate collar and facing units again. Use iron directionally on fabric grain.

Whether your coat or jacket has a separate facing or a cut-on one, it is always easier to leave open the ends of the collar and the ends of the lapel until the collar is sewn to the garment.

Hem unit.   At hemline, trim seams to half their width, going a little beyond depth of hem (A). In hem, trim underlining from the seams. Next, trim underlining to staystitching ¾ inch from the edge (B). Staystitch plus (p. 177) ¼ inch from edge of hem. Press hem again in directional pressing from folded edge to top of hem; upper edge should match garment with perfection. A strip of bias press-on gives added support to hems in softer woolens and similar fabrics. It is cut to extend about an inch above the hemline (C) and to fold of hem (D). If you try a sample and feel that this makes your jacket look stiff or hard (in a silk suit, for example), an alternative is to press the bias on hem instead of jacket (E). If

you do not have or do not prefer the press-on interfacing, with a catch-stitch, sew on an extra piece of underlining on the regular underlining.

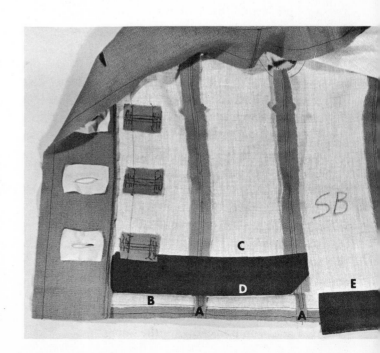

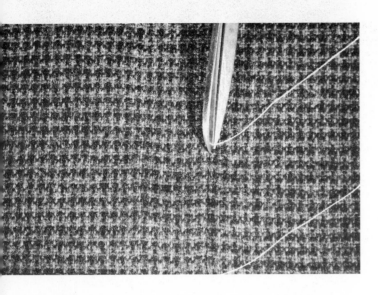

To make a good, sharp bend or fold where the facing and jacket join at the hem, trim facing seam to a scant ⅛ inch on both sides to top of hem. Pin well of seamline of jacket front to the well of the seamline on jacket hem, and stitch (by hand or at machine) from right side of jacket in the well of the seams to top of them. Stitching will not show and enables facing to roll back easily and press flat.

Turn back facings, and with a running stitch by hand, stitch hem of facings to hem of jacket (A) ½ inch from edge. Grade under seam to ¼ inch. In softer woolens, you may also tack facing to hem half-way down width of hem (B). The stitching should be invisible on right side of facing.

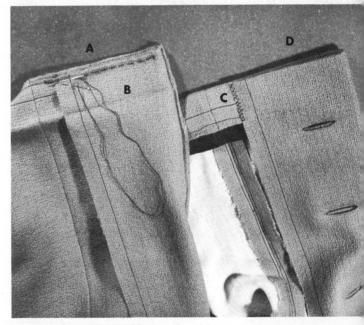

Turn facings to inside again. At edge C in the photograph, machine stitch two raw edges together for reinforcement, and whipstitch facing to hem. Stitch through hem only, and do not catch underlining or jacket.

Leave bottom of facing open at D. This will allow the facing to shape to the figure and form the lapel without pull or strain.

The finished backs of the buttonholes (p. 194) may be whipstitched in place at this time, and the buttons sewn on (p. 159). However, the hem is not sewn to the jacket by hand until later when the hem of the lining is completed.

You may carefully and thoroughly final-press the jacket where needed at this time (see pp. 140-141). The final-press cannot be done as well after lining is in, and you will be hindered by it. As you learned on page 141, the hem is always pressed on up and down grain, and never by running iron across lower edge of jacket.

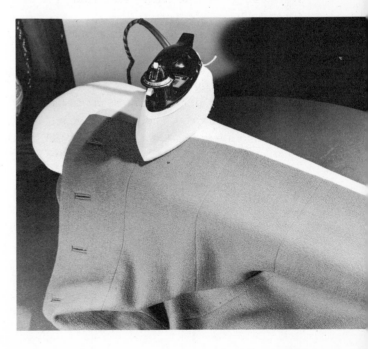

Hang the jacket carefully on a wooden or padded hanger, and fasten one or more closings to keep it on grain until you proceed with the lining.

Cutting lining.   You may wonder why the lining is being cut before the sleeves have been sewn up, or put in the jacket. If you have pretested your pattern for sleeve fit and adjusted the length for fashion and figure, it will be much easier to complete the sleeves and put the lining in them before they are sewn into the jacket. It also demonstrates one of the principles of the Bishop method — that of completing one unit before it is joined to another. If you did not pretest your patterns, the sleeves may be baste-stitched for a fitting, and then removed to complete the unit.

See page 201 for suggestions of linings to use.

If any cutting-to-fit alterations were necessary in cutting out the jacket, cut the lining with the same alterations. Then, if any fitting is necessary when the jacket is tried on, cut and stitch the lining with the same alterations.

When the garment has much cut-up detail, such as yokes and applied seams, the separate lining tissue that is included with many patterns should be used so that the lining will be easier to manage. However, the original pattern used for cutting the garment is generally preferred for cutting lining. The cutting and fitting alterations are more easily made, and if the following special directions for cutting are carried out, the lining will fit the garment with perfection.

Sleeves are cut precisely as the jacket was cut, except in length. Cut the lining to the finished length of the jacket sleeve. Turn up the tissue pattern the width of the hem before cutting the lining.

A little additional length may be needed in cutting lining if a firm lining is used without any give to it, or if a sleeve does not have 1½-inch hem allowance.

In length, the front and back of the lining are cut to the finished length of the jacket. If the jacket is turned up 1½ inches for hemming, turn up tissue pattern the same amount to cut lining. One inch extra width is added at center back of lining for a pleat, to give necessary ease.

Chalkmark, on the jacket front tissue pattern, the width front facing will extend on it (line A). Measure 1¼ inches (2 seam widths) from line A toward front of jacket, and chalkmark (line B). Fold under tissue pattern on line B to cut lining for jacket front. Repeat at neckline of jacket back.

Cut-on 1½ inches of lining at armhole front and back, tapering in a gradual line to nothing at notch. At shoulder line, add ¼ inch extra height, tapering to nothing about half-way to neckline. Cut-on ½ inch underarm, tapering to nothing gradually.

You may prefer to use another technique at armholes. It is shown on page 240.

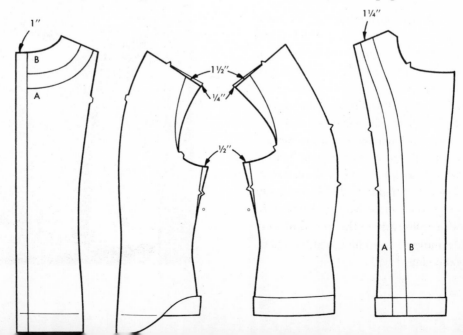

Sleeve unit. A set-in sleeve may be underlined with soft Si Bonne, super-soft Siri, lawn, or any soft fabric. The underlining would be staystitched to sleeve sections just outside seamline, and the sleeve cap would be prepared as discussed on page 155.

With right sides together, join upper sleeve to under sleeve at seam at back of sleeve, sewing directionally from top down. Press open seam in same direction in which it was stitched, and trim diagonally at upper edge for 1¼ inches. See A in photograph below.

Besides the technique for preparing sleeves to set-in an armhole discussed on page 155, there is a more advanced technique called "off-grain stitching" which will be described below. The cap, in being prepared to fit in the armhole, is stitched while the fabric is held off grain. It is easier to manage before the second sleeve seam is stitched. It would not be done to a sleeve that is underlined because you could not pull both fabrics at the same time. In that case, the method on page 155 would have to be used. Without underlining the method described here could be used. The sleeve pictured below did not have underlining because the wool had enough body.

Exactly on ⅝-inch seamline and with matching thread, stitch around entire cap with a regulation stitch. The scored plate on this machine eliminated the need for the seam guide. Below the notches it is staystitching; above the notches it is the off-grain stitching.

To do off-grain stitching, place forefingers opposite each other in front of the needle. Pull fabric off grain, and stitch 4 to 5 stitches where fabric is pulled. Stop the machine before lifting the fingers to pull next short area. When fingers are placed in front of the needle again, start the machine again. Both hands must be kept at the sleeve cap and cannot be used to operate the machine. Certain fabrics will need to be pulled more than others before stitching, because of their firm weave or finish. Once the ryhthm of off-grain stitching is developed, caps can be made to fit the armhole with perfection. If the cap does not fit the armhole the first time you use this method, remove the stitching and try again. It will not harm the cap.

MIDDLE THIRD   MIDDLE THIRD

The sleeve cap requires most of the ease where it is most off grain, and above the notches; that is, in the middle third of each half of the cap.

Turn up hem to correct finished length and press. A sleeve should not carry a hem deeper than 1½ or 2 inches. Trim width of seam in hem at B to ¼ inch, going a little beyond fold of hem.

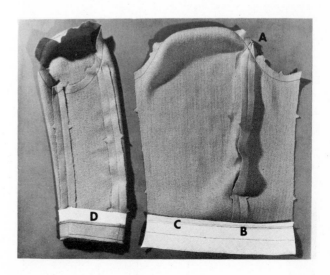

Tailoring a suit

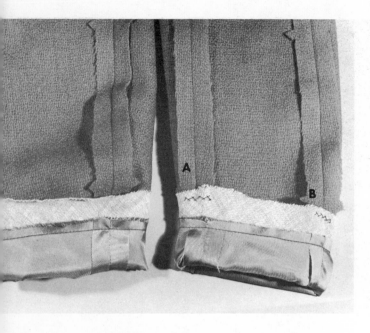

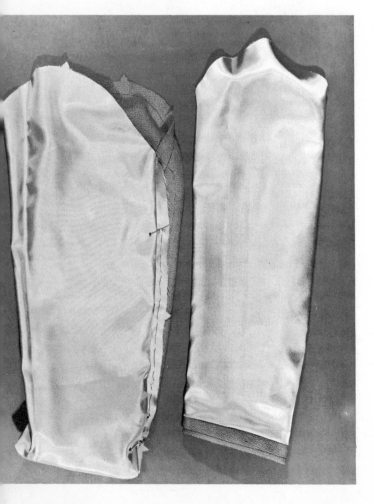

Cut a piece of true bias of same underlining used in jacket. Make it three inches wide. Place it to extend ½ inch beyond fold of hem (C). With sleeve side up, stitch bias to hem ¼ inch from raw edge of sleeve and ¼ inch from fold of hem. Bias will extend one inch above hem (D). (Photo: bottom p. 235)

Press hem again and block bias to bottom of sleeve with perfection.

Open out hem and stitch second sleeve seam from armhole down. This front seam needs to be held firmly on the lengthwise as it is being stitched; it may even need to be clipped in some fabrics.

Press open seam in same direction in which it was stitched.

Restore hemline at seamline. Trim this seam, also, to ¼ inch, going a little beyond fold of hem. Do not hand tack hem in place until directed.

Block bottom of sleeve from right side as in photograph on page 141 and final-press sleeve, including the cap as shown on page 138.

Sew the seams of the lining in the same direction as sleeves; with firm linings, sew seams a little less than ⅝ inch. Press open in same direction. Do not do any kind of stitching at cap.

Slide the lining inside the sleeve with right sides together. Draw out the bottom of the lining, and bring it up to the raw edge of the sleeve hem. Sew with a small running stitch, or a machine basting stitch. Then, catch-stitch underlining at A and B. Hem is not sewn to sleeve any other place. Next, draw the lining out of the sleeve.

Beginning about 2 inches below the armhole, attach one side of lining seam to the corresponding side of the sleeve seam with a single thread and a long, easy running stitch through the middle of the seam allowance. Fasten the thread about 2 inches above top of sleeve hem. Make several back stitches at the beginning (even with a knot in the thread) and at the end of the stitching to secure the thread in fabric. Repeat for second seam of two-piece sleeve.

Draw the sleeve inside the lining. Press the excess lining at the bottom of the sleeve to form a take-up tuck. Many expensive garments feature a deep take-up tuck in the bottom of the sleeves.

Lay lining back out of the way at the armholes, and pin sleeve in armhole with two pins, one pin matching underarm notch on sleeve with underarm seam on jacket, and the other pin matching extra notch at top of sleeve with shoulder seam. Sleeve is always on top and garment is below when being sewn. See photograph of sewing in sleeve on page 155. Press as in photograph on page 138. In some fabric, you do not need to press the armhole seam. Simply turn the seam allowances into the sleeve and mold them with your fingers. Do not trim any of the seam allowance or any interfacing from armholes until stitching in lining below.

If you need any further help in rounding out the ease, or in maintaining a true line at the top of the sleeve, see page 156.

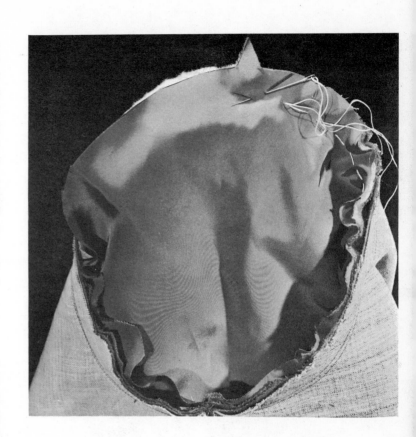

Match raw edges and key armhole of lining to armhole of sleeve at notches, underarm seam, and shoulder seam. With a loose running stitch, tack sleeve cap of lining to that of jacket, easing in lining fullness over cap. Take small running stitches close to seam below notches. Trim seam (four thicknesses) to ¼ inch from notch to notch under the arm.

For another technique at armholes, see page 240.

Lining the jacket. Except for the neckline on the jacket back, no staystitching is done on linings because the cut edges need to be easy to mold. Staystitch the neckline of jacket back on ⅝-inch seamline, so that this edge can be clipped later, where necessary, up to the staystitching.

Stitch one inch from fold at A. Then stitch pleat one inch from seamline, stitching down permanently for 1½ inches (B). Lockstitch threads; baste-stitch remainder of pleat to 1½ inches from bottom of jacket (C). Change to permanent stitch, lockstitch threads, and stitch permanently the final 1½ inches at lower edge (D). Then clip first baste-stitch at B and C for easy removal later.

Hand baste pleat on fragile fabrics. Press pleat to right side, and stitch in position along the neck and lower edges. Catch-stitch in place at lockstitching, B and C.

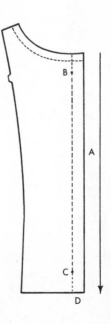

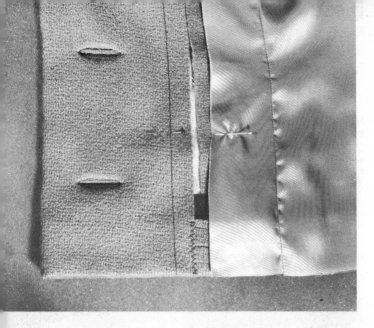

Stitch together and press lining before it is sewn into jacket. For ease, with a firm lining, stitch seams closer to ½ inch than ⅝ inch.

Stitch and press all the seams of lining, but do not stitch shoulder seams. Seams are not finished in the lining or in the jacket fabric. The lining will be sewn into the jacket with perfection if the raw edges of both can be keyed together. Furthermore, when seams are enclosed, as they are with the jacket and lining, they cannot rub against the body during wear. Therefore, finishing for the purpose of protecting seams against such wear is unnecessary.

Place lower edge of lining to key with lower edge of jacket. Several inches up from top of hem, place a pin in the lining and one in jacket facing lined up with each other. These are called guide pins and will be used later to key these lower edges to perfection. Repeat on other side of jacket.

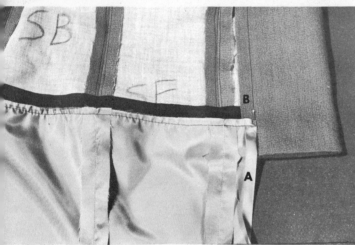

Now, place the lining and jacket right sides together. Bring the raw edge of the lining over to meet the raw edge of the jacket hem and pin to anchor at every seam. Then sew with a small running stitch, or a basting stitch at the machine. The raw edge of lining will be folded back ⅝ inch at A, and brought to staystitching on seamline at B.

At this stage, the jacket will be hemmed by hand. It is much easier to sew the lining to the hem at the machine before doing hand hemming.

To hem by hand, fold hem to outside of garment, and work from underside of hem, holding hem edge away from you, and garment toward you.

With a single thread, hem with a loose pick stitch ½ inch apart. In one pick stitch, catch underlining in jacket; in the next pick stitch, catch stitching in jacket ¼ inch from edge (see p. 243).

Key the lining at the shoulders and pin. The raw edge of lining will extend over shoulder seam of facing for ⅝ inch (A). Next, key lining to facing near lower edge by bringing two guide pins to meet and pin together (B). Repeat on other side of jacket. Stitch the lining to the facings from guide pins to shoulder seam. Keep facing side up and stitch one thread inside staystitching on facings on seamline. Use the longest stitch at the machine unless it puckers. If it does, shorten stitch slightly, or use a small running hand stitch.

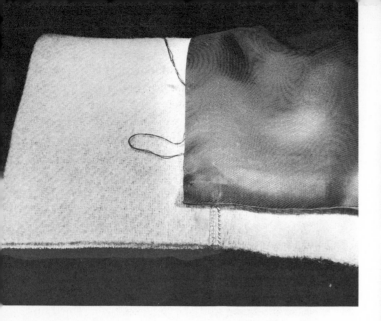

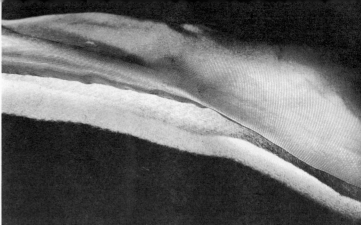

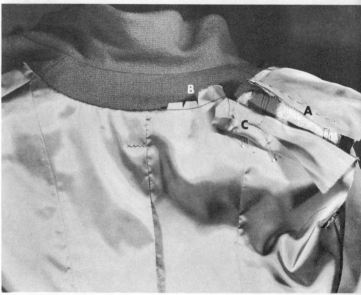

Turn jacket and lining to their correct positions — wrong sides together. There is an opening in the lining at the lower edge of front facings. Press down excess lining. This is known as a take-up tuck, and is necessary for longer wear on the lining. Complete lower edge of front facings with slipstitching and include take-up tuck to hold in place. Press lining flat at front facings.

One of the earmarks of a quality garment is a deep take-up tuck in sleeves and hems.

Now, tack one side of each lining seam allowance to the corresponding jacket seam. Begin and end stitching about two inches from each edge of the seam. With a single thread, make a long, easy running stitch through the middle of the seam allowance. Make several back stitches at the beginning (even with a knot in the thread) and at the end of the stitching to secure the thread in fabric (see p. 236).

Key raw shoulder edge of lining front to raw edge of back half of jacket shoulder seam (A). Attach with an easy running stitch. Clip the back of the neckline on lining to staystitching (B). Turn under seam allowance at back of neckline and back shoulder seams (C). At back of neckline, you may trim seam to ¼ inch.

Whipstitch in place using double thread, heavy-duty thread, or buttonhole twist. The whipstitch is a firmer stitch than the slipstitch, and is used where greater strength is needed. To whipstitch, bring the needle up through the lining fold; then, sink the point right beside that spot but into the front of the lining and back facing. Move ahead inside the garment and bring needle up again through the very edge of the lining fold. The amount of thread showing at the lining fold should be so small that stitches can scarcely be seen.

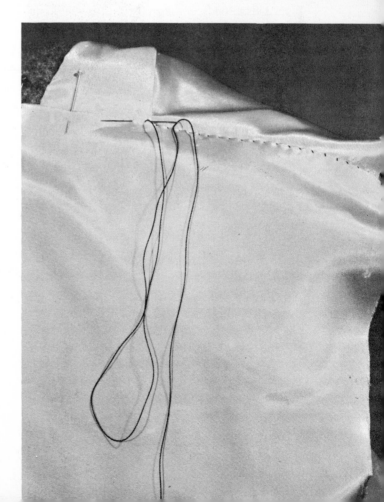

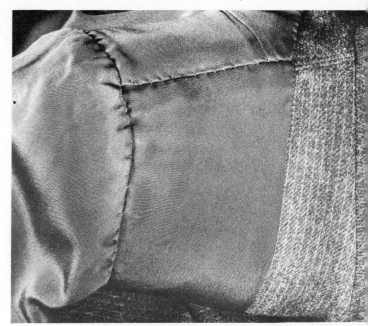

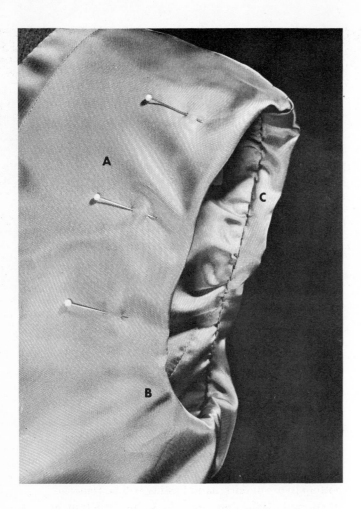

Place pins in body of the jacket (A), so you do not draw lining when pinning at armholes.

Below notches at armhole (B), turn in lining ⅛ inch (clip curve, when necessary); lap over sleeve lining ¼ inch, and pin in place. Above notches, turn in lining to fit over seam (C), after raw edge is turned under ¼ inch. If all of the 1½ inches cut on extra is not needed, cut away excess before turning under raw edge and pinning lining in place above the notches. Hold the jacket in such a way that you are turning armhole seam toward you. One of the secrets of this method is how you hold the jacket.

Whipstitch the lining around armholes, the same as you did at the shoulders and back facing.

Another method for finishing armholes is to turn the sleeve lining over the armholes. To cut the lining for this method, at armholes, add ¼ inch at shoulder seam at armhole edge (p. 234), tapering to nothing toward neckline.

Sew jacket lining to armhole with a running stitch ¼ inch from edge; underarm, stitch it near seamline. The ¼ inch added extra at shoulders gives some ease. Trim all of the seams to ¼ inch from notch to notch underarm.

Stitch an ease line on sleeve cap ¼ inch from edge. Draw up thread to take out fullness in cap. Fasten thread, and turn under raw edge on stitching line. Bring sleeve cap over armhole ¼ inch; whip-stitch in place.

Remove the baste-stitching in the back pleat. If the outer fabric has become wrinkled from the handling as the lining was being attached, some light final-pressing may again be necessary on the jacket. Do not press lining at shoulders, back neck-line, and around armholes.

The skirt

It is not inaccurate to say we are tailoring a skirt, because the highest level of accomplishment in clothing construction is to have both an underlining and a drum. The two-in-one skirt is found only on fine quality ready-to-wear.

As you learned on page 174, a drum in a skirt does many things. It gives body to the skirt, helps it maintain shape, and acts as a half-slip.

The underlining serves two different purposes. First, it helps to build character into certain style lines of skirts, such as the center panel on this skirt, an eight-gored one, or a skirt with pockets or yokes.

A second reason for an underlining is that it gives more weight, body, and firmness of weave to lightweight, spongy, or loosely woven fabrics.

Sewing underlining in seams has often been a problem to the seamstress, and to the dry cleaners. Two factors cause this: the underlining fabric used; and, the construction at side seams, which is solved on the following pages.

Either soft or crisp Si Bonne has been a very desirable choice for underlining skirts. This skirt has crisp Si Bonne.

As you learned in Chapter 11, a skirt may have merely a drum. The style and fabric in this one now needs both the drum and underlining. An eight-gored skirt, to hold its line well, would need an underlining more than a drum, and the drum may be omitted.

If you have made a master pattern of a skirt, you are ready to finish it from the start. If not, you may choose to fit the drum; then, cut the skirt.

An opening at lower edge for walking room has not been needed (with shorter skirts). However, if you want one, read directions on pages 44-45, *Fashion Sewing by the Bishop Method,* before cutting skirt.

Skirt back unit. The underlining is cut precisely like the skirt. Mark darts on underlining only. Place underlining sections on skirt sections, and press to adhere to perfection.

Three lines of machine stitching would make many fabrics pucker. Staystitching all the way down the seams of a skirt on each of two sections, plus a third of machine stitching when they are sewn

together, would make three lines of stitching, more than some fabrics can take. For such fabrics, it has proved to be more satisfactory to hand baste underlining to skirt fabric ½ inch from edge until seams are sewn. Then, hand-basting will be removed. With this technique, there will be but one row of machine stitching with four layers of fabric. See photograph, page 242. If a fabric like silk linen will take the staystitching on the entire skirt seam, it should be done ⅛ inch from edge.

As you have learned throughout this text, the skirt back is staystitched across the top in direction previously shown ⅜ inch from edge, and on the sides from notch up ¼ inch from edge.

Machine or hand baste through center of darts (A) going one inch beyond termination point. Stitch darts, remove baste-stitching, and press toward center back (B). After center seam is sewn from bottom to top of skirt, hand basting will be removed. Then, pink seam and press in same direction in which it was stitched. If you have pretested your pattern or are working from a master, press up the hem to complete this unit. However, unless you have learned to cut-to-fit, you will not press up the bottom of the skirt in separate units.

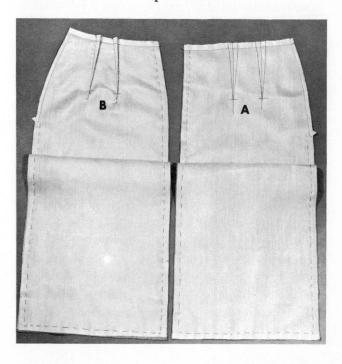

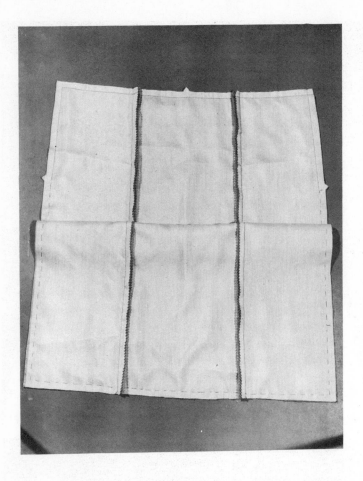

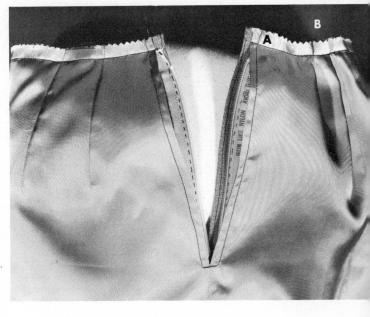

Skirt front unit. The skirt front unit is prepared exactly like skirt back unit with two exceptions.

First, the staystitching at the side edges above the notches is ½ inch from the edge.

Second, to form the paneled look on the skirt front, after hand basting is removed, the two gore seams are pressed toward the center front. In pinking these seams to finish them, pink the under one ⅛ inch narrower than the top one. You do not want to face ⅝ inch with ⅝ inch. Then, press up hem, as discussed with back unit. Open up hemlines to stitch side seams as learned on page 177.

Complete skirt and drum unit. When the zipper is applied (see directions, pp. 66-68), for a quality look, use hand-picking at both front and back of placket. See finished placket on page 244.

The drum is cut precisely like the skirt, and made exactly like the one on page 178 with but one exception. The opening that is shown in this photograph is on the left side of the skirt; but on page 178, it was in the center back. This drum is made of Earl-Glo twill.

Place drum and skirt wrong sides together, and stitch at waistline (A) ⅜ inch from edge. Tucks in skirt front are folded through both skirt and drum (B) before stitching is done.

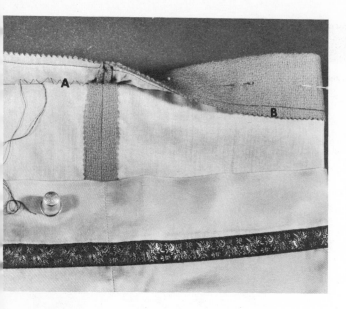

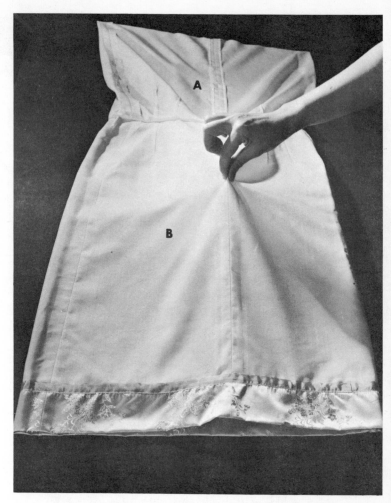

Notice the rayon banding on hemline of drum. Lace or peasant braid may also be used.

Turn the underlining up in the hem. Staystitch plus (p. 177) top of hem ⅜ inch from edge; remove hand basting (p. 241). Then, pink edges. If your fabric ravels easily, and you have a swing needle machine, you may go over staystitch-plus line with a zigzag stitch. You may even find it very easy to release the presser foot, and slightly twist hem back and forth to make a zigzag stitch with a regular machine. Press hem again from bottom up to perfect line of hem.

Do not use hem tape on heavier fabrics. Pulling the tape toward the garment in doing the hand stitching would make the hem show. Having the width of the hem show is not considered a quality look and adds no beauty to your garment. For a fabric that frays easily, bind the top of the hem with a bias strip of Si Bonne (see page 214) before hand stitching is done. This will give a quality couture finish.

The hand stitching on the hem of a skirt goes through the underlining only. With just one row of stitching at B, there is too much pull on underlining between seams, and the skirt bows at the bottom. For extra support, hem at A, halfway up the hem, and then make a second row of stitching at top of hem (B), the same way as it is being done at A.

On heavier fabrics, such as knits, this method of hemming is used even when there is no underlining.

To hem by hand, fold hem under, and work from underside of hem. With stitches ½ inch apart, and working from right to left, pick up a thread of hem. Then, pick up a thread of underlining in skirt diagonally across. Do not pull the stitches tight.

Some fabrics, however, are too much of a problem in pressing to have the underlining in the seams. In this beaded brocade, the underlining turns up in hem as you have learned; but contrary to what you have just learned above, the seams and darts of the underlining (B) are made separately, as is the placket opening of underlining (see p. 242 for drum opening made separately). If you are not sure of your fabric, try a sample first to pretest it. Though there is a regular drum (A) in the skirt, it is turned back for the photograph.

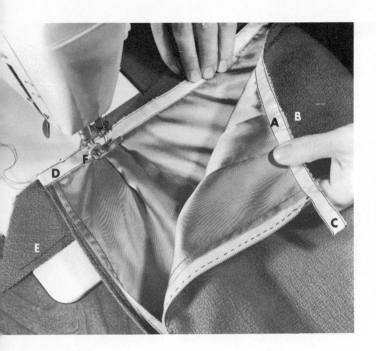

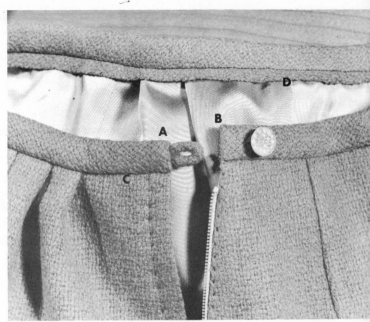

Bias finish at waistline. If you are not going to wear blouses that tuck inside your skirt, you may prefer an underwaist (p. 179) to any other finish.

The use of a lengthwise strip of fabric for a band on a cotton skirt was shown on page 68. In more advanced sewing, the bias has been widely used and accepted as a finish, not only by seamstresses but also by leading designers. It is not called a band, for it does not extend to be a band. It is a binding to cover the waistline seam. This is more comfortable than a band, looks smarter (particularly for women who have a cut-in waistline), and is easily managed in all weights of fabric.

Since the finish is bias and would give no support, hem tape must be sewn to top of skirt first for support and to ease skirt to the figure (p. 146). Hem tape is only ½ inch wide. Therefore, cut skirt, underlining and drum inside blue pattern line at the waistline (if you think of it), and you will have a ½-inch seam.

After lower edge of tape is stitched to skirt (A), according to directions on page 146, stitch at top (B), also, for reinforcement and to prevent the top edge from turning over when binding it.

Extend tape at both placket edges (C) for an inch, so it can be turned back as bias is sewn on (D) for greater strength of band at both ends.

Cut a strip of true bias 2½ inches wide. Staystitch inside edge ¼ inch from edge (E). With right sides together and skirt side up, sew band to skirt through lower edge of hem tape (F). Do not let the bias ream; hold it firmly and diagonally as you prepare to stitch each area around top of skirt.

Since A and B edges are bias, also, stitch back and forth several times for support. Enclose narrow strip of bias in front seam for button loop. This gives more of a quality look than extending bias as had been done with the lengthwise band (p. 70).

Lightly press up bias at seamline (C) and mold carefully over edge of seam. Stitch in well of seamline (C) at machine, or make a small running stitch by hand in bulky fabric.

Since D edge is bias, it will not ravel. However, on lighter-weight fabrics such as silk linen, this edge can be staystitched and clean-finished before bias is sewn on skirt.

Chapter 14

Fabrics suggest their own techniques

The fabric will tell you what to do

Many new fabrics have appeared on the market in the past few years. Manufacturers are always working on new fibers to keep up with the trend of the times. More new fabrics will doubtlessly be "discovered."

Each new fiber or new fabric will require some variances in sewing techniques. No sewing book could possibly be right up to the minute on techniques for them, because even the fabrics that are presently on the market keep improving in their qualities.

So, to be an up-to-date seamstress, you must develop a certain trained intelligence about the art of sewing. The following suggestions are an excellent way to carry this out.

If you are going to undertake working with a new or unfamiliar fiber or piece of fabric, try some samples of construction on little pieces to determine the best technique for turning out a quality look.

1. Is any special help needed to cut fabric to absolute perfection?

2. How will you mark the fabric so that construction lines will show up, but not show on, or harm right side of fabric?

3. Will an underlining or interfacing enhance the fabric and the sewing area, or will it destroy the purpose or the beauty of the fabric? Are you satisfied with the results of your sample? Is it the finest look your garment could have?

4. What must you do to have a perfect seamline in sewing this fabric, and then in pressing? What machine tension will the fabric take? Does it sew easily with all the pressure on the presser foot, or should some of the pressure be released? Try various lengths of machine stitching to determine which one gives the smoothest seamline. Does the fabric

need any special thread, or size of needle? Does it need to be held any special way to obtain a strong, secure seam? Long, lengthwise seams are most difficult to do in some fabrics. Try a sample, and if they seem to be a real problem, avoid such seams in your choice of pattern.

Study and try the techniques in the pressing chapter to decide what is best for your sample of fabric.

5. Does the fabric seem to be one that takes stitching very well, or would it be better made up with as few pieces to the pattern as possible? Does it take outside or topstitching nicely?

6. Does a seam finish really seem to be needed? Many new fabrics are woven in such a way that a seam finish is not necessary.

7. Are darts bulky looking? Do they lie well in pressing, or should they be slashed, etc., as you have learned in many places throughout this text?

8. You will also have to try the techniques for hemming to judge which one will make the most inconspicuous hem, but with the necessary give for the particular fabric.

9. Are there some design lines or details to which the fabric or fiber does not lend itself? Will it make a good tailored buttonhole? Will it make a machine-made buttonhole? — on the lengthwise grain? — on the crosswise grain?

10. If the pattern has facings, will the fabric press well, lie well, be bulky with a facing of its own, or would another fabric be a better choice for the facing?

These are the same tests any professional seamstress will make when new fabrics are developed. The fabric will always suggest its own techniques, and will tell you what to do.

Knits

The fabric itself. Knitted fabric is characterized by the yarns being looped together rather than being interwoven. It may be a single or double knit. Double knit is really two layers of knit yarns. Knits may be made of wool, cotton, silk, any of the synthetic fibers, or blends.

Knits are usually made in tubular form. They are also available opened and folded. They do not have finished edges or selvages. Knits stretch more, and in more directions, than woven fabrics do. Knits do not crease well, so they do not lend themselves as well to pressed pleats or crisp edges. Knits tend to fit easily, and are comfortable and practical. They do not wrinkle, and they offer serviceability and wearability.

The fashion interest in knits continues to grow. Knits now appear in every type of garment, from the most casual sportswear to the most formal dress.

Pattern selection. The choice of pattern will certainly be governed by the weight of the knit, as well as by the design of the fabric. Soft styling is the best choice. Straight knit skirts are form-revealing. They should be avoided if you are not very slim. Avoid having too many pieces to the pattern. A knitted fabric does not behave crosswise, so yokes and other horizontal lines should be avoided.

If they can be done well, tailored buttonholes are attractive in knits. If not, use frogs (p. 263), or make a straight jacket without any closing.

In heavier double knits, the facing at the neckline should be made of a firmer, thinner fabric because knit does not crease well. If the facing can be topstitched, however, you may use the knit.

Instead of a separate facing on the front of a jacket, a turn-back facing is used frequently. A row of machine stitching on the facing just inside the fold line helps to keep the front from sagging and to retain its shape. Another suggestion is to bind the edges with self-bias that finishes ½ or ⅝ inch wide.

Because of the nature of the fabric, it is generally true that only women with perfectly proportioned figures should wear knits.

Cutting knits. Knits have no crosswise grain. The lengthwise rib is comparable to the selvage edge of a woven fabric. Use one rib as a guide for placing pattern pieces on lengthwise grain. The rib may be folded incorrectly when the fabric is purchased, so you may need to run a hand basting line down one lengthwise rib to be able to see to fold it accurately on lengthwise grain.

If the present fold marks in the purchased fabric will not press out, refold the fabric so that the creases are in the center of the fabric, and not in the center of the garment when you lay out the pattern.

Straighten the crosswise ends of knit by drawing a chalk mark with a yardstick that is placed at right angles to lengthwise grain of fabric.

Many knits have a slight nap or texture. When this is the case, place all pattern pieces in one direction. Use the cutting layout for napped fabric.

Sewing knits. After removing the pattern pieces, staystitch necessary edges as you have learned throughout this text.

When stitching the garment, use shorter stitches and mercerized thread. Nymo or taslan thread will give greater strength. If you have a zigzag machine, you may set the stitch slightly toward zigzag. This strengthens the seamlines.

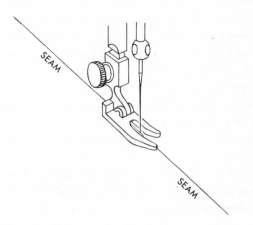

After the seams have been pressed open, on the right side, stitching in the groove of the seam prevents it from cracking. This technique would only be used at areas of strain in a garment.

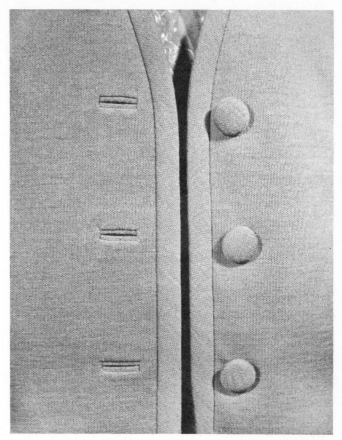

To give added elasticity, lengthwise skirt seams and shoulder seams with cut-on sleeves may be stretched slightly when stitching. This helps prevent the stitches from breaking, or the seams from pulling, when the garment is worn.

No seam finish is required on knits.

Press all knits with the lengthwise ribs to avoid stretching the fabric. Use a lowering and lifting motion; pushing the iron tends to stretch the fabric. Note the photograph on page 135 where the point of the iron is being used at the line of stitching only.

The hem of a knit is not finished with hem tape (see p. 243). Use two rows of hemming stitches as shown on that same page. Make certain the hand stitches are quite loose.

Grading is needed on double knits to eliminate bulk. Refer to the top right photograph on page 225.

Lining knits. As you learned throughout this text, you underline a garment for character or shape, and line it for appearance.

If you sew an underlining into seams or darts of a knit, you defeat the very purpose of the fabric.

A knit skirt or sheath dress will need a support lining, but it is not sewn into the body of the garment.

The skirt will have the support lining or drum put into it exactly as you learned on pages 179 and 242. The skirt and drum may be hemmed separately, as shown there, or sometimes the drum hem is turned up with the hem of the knit. It will depend upon the weight of the knit and the style of the skirt.

This sheath dress has a support lining of Si Bonne. The only places it is sewn to a knit dress are in the neckline, shoulder seams, and armholes. Bias binding was used to finish the neckline and armholes.

If you do not want to use the binding, and prefer to have the support lining act as the finish at the neckline and armholes, the dress will be finished exactly as you learned on the jerkin on pages 84 to 86. The lining will be left free in the remainder of the sheath.

A close-up was taken of this sheath so that you could see the two rows of handsewing to hold the lining in place at the completed zipper. With just one row of stitching, sometimes the lining rolls and gets caught in the zipper. So, a second row of handsewing is used ¼ inch back from the first row. A catch-stitch (p. 203) may be used instead of the two rows of handsewing.

In fabrics other than knits, this is the way a lining is usually sewn into a straight sheath dress.

When seams and darts are free, and wrong sides face each other, it is called a lining, not an underlining.

In a jacket or coat of knit, a lining may be used to give a finished appearance to the inside. This depends in part on how many seams the pattern has. However, the knit fabric is still not underlined.

Attractive finishes. This photograph shows how attractive buttonholes and self-bias binding can be on double knit.

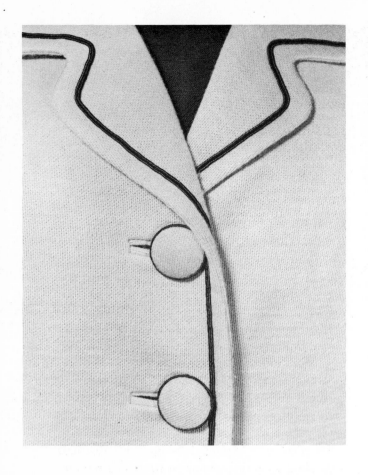

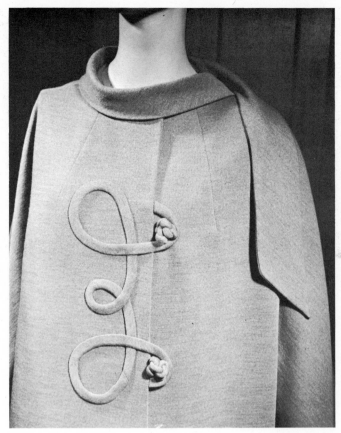

Staystitching the front facings to jacket to give support to buttons and buttonholes before binding was applied follows the same principle as staystitching the underlining to jacket front (p. 218). The technique for putting on bias, as used on page 247, is given on page 171.

This jacket has a separate front facing. Soutache braid was sewn on, not only for a trim, but to help hold edges to perfection, since knit does not stay creased very well. Topstitching can also be used. Double knit takes topstitching beautifully.

Note trim of soutache braid around buttons. Many other button ideas are given on pages 262 to 264.

This knit coat is cut with a turn-back facing, which is desirable when pattern line will allow it. Note that instead of buttonholes, bias trim forms loops to hold coat in place over buttons.

The buttons are made of knots of a narrower width of bias (p. 262).

Directions for making bias are given on page 259.

This bias tubing was made according to the directions on page 259. Knits handle very well when made up in bias tubing. Bias was handsewn in place with stitches from the underside.

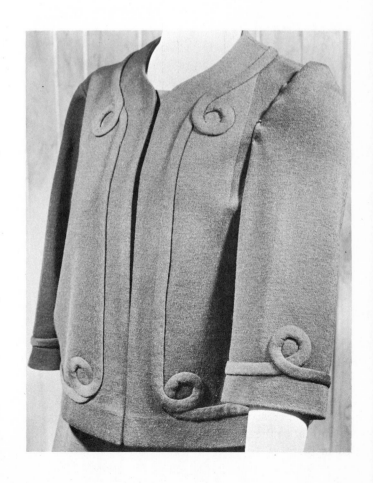

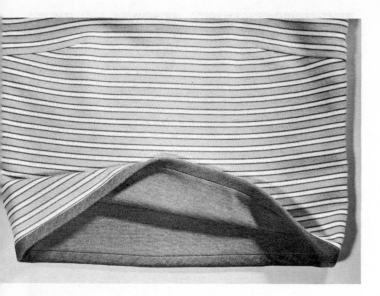

The pins were placed in the sleeve cap because we needed to bring the sleeve forward to show the trim at the lower edge in the photograph.

This overblouse is completely reversible. When bias is stitched to each side of overblouse, and seams are pressed open, the bias lies in place smoothly, and gives a flat finish. This technique can be used at other areas. It was also used at neckline and armholes of this overblouse.

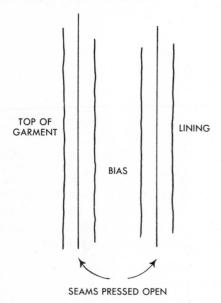

TOP OF GARMENT   LINING

BIAS

SEAMS PRESSED OPEN

Stretch fabric

The fabric itself. Stretch fabric is relatively new on the market, and has been more popular in ready-to-wear than in yard goods. It can be defined two ways: according to the direction of the stretch and the degree of stretch. Both are interrelated and are important to the performance of the fabric and the garment.

The direction of stretch falls into the three following divisions:

1. *Warp stretch.* It is a lengthwise or vertical stretch which runs parallel to the selvages of the fabric. The trade also refers to it as North and South stretch. These fabrics are used primarily for ski pants and active sportswear.

2. *Filling stretch.* It is a crosswise or horizontal stretch which runs at right angles to the selvages of the fabric. The trade also refers to it as East and West stretch. For dresses, skirts, suits, blouses, and for all types of garments, these fabrics contribute freedom of movement.

3. *Two-way stretch.* This is a combination of both warp and filling stretch. These fabrics stretch both lengthwise and crosswise and are used for bathing suits and other tight-fitting garments.

The degree of stretch falls into two divisions, depending upon the amount of stretching required for specific garments:

1. *Action stretch.* This is used for ski wear, swim wear, and other active sportswear. It is usually a warp stretch with the power to expand and also the ability to recover instantly. These action stretch fabrics were the first stretch materials.

2. *Comfort stretch.* These fabrics are used in garments for everyday wear. They are usually a filling stretch, and afford greater comfort and smoothness of fit.

Fit and comfort are synonymous with stretch. It is said that stretch is giveable and liveable. It also gives to accommodate some growth, and therefore is popular in infants' wear.

Stretch fabrics are available in many fibers and combinations of fibers. Gingham, corduroy, gabardine, poplin, and denim are popular stretch fabrics on the market.

Pattern selection. When selecting a pattern to be used with stretch fabric, purchase it according to your measurements and figure type as discussed in Chapter 3. Also, you will make your usual pattern adjustments as you learned in Chapter 8. There is no need to make special pattern adjustments for stretch fabric.

It is desirable, however, to select a pattern with simple lines and as few pattern pieces as possible.

Such a choice reduces the number of seams which must also stretch and recover.

Inasmuch as the function of stretch fabric is to provide both comfort and a smooth appearance, the maximum benefit from comfort stretch is realized in garments with slim classic styling.

Reversible garments work well in stretch.

Cutting stretch fabric. Straighten stretch fabric exactly as you learned with knit on page 246.

After it has been taken from the roll or bolt, the fabric should be completely relaxed before cutting out garment. This is particularly important for warp or lengthwise stretch. To do this, spread the fabric on the cutting table for a 24-hour period before cutting.

In laying out the pattern, be certain to place pattern pieces in the direction of the desired stretch. Lengthwise or vertical stretch is preferable in pants. They are made with straps or stirrups under the feet. Crosswise or horizontal stretch is generally used for dresses, skirts, blouses, shorts, and suits.

Place pins near edge of tissue, and at right angles to edge, so fabric will not curl in cutting.

Use sharp shears to avoid stretching or distorting the fabric, and keep fabric as flat as possible while cutting.

Before deciding which technique from page 54 to 56 to use to transfer pattern markings, try each one on a scrap of your particular fabric.

Sewing stretch fabric. Basically, there is very little difference between sewing with a stretch fabric and with any similar non-stretch fabric.

Mercerized thread can be used, but nymo or taslan thread gives added strength, because it is nylon and has a natural give to correspond with the give in stretch fabric. Nylon thread has up to 20 percent give, while mercerized thread has only 4 to 6 percent.

Make some test seams on scraps in the direction of the stretch to determine machine tension, balance, and pressure. A looser tension is needed for sewing stretch fabric, but the needle and bobbin tension must be balanced. The stitches should hold when the test seam is stretched in the direction of the stretch.

A greater number of stitches per inch produces a seam with greater stretch. Therefore, 12 to 16 stitches per inch are recommended. A fine sharp needle and light pressure are also recommended. The fabric should not be stretched while stitching.

In seams where stretch is not desired, such as across the shoulders, seam tape or ¼-inch satin ribbon is sewn into the seamline (see p. 82).

Darts should be tapered to a very fine point; otherwise, they will not press out smoothly as in regular fabric.

At crucial areas, where seams are under much strain, stitching in well of seam (see p. 246) helps further to prevent stitching from cracking.

Stretch fabric is not underlined because it would defeat the purpose of the fabric. An interfacing is used in the same sections of a stretch garment as in a non-stretch garment. The interfacing helps to stabilize fabric in areas where stretch is not desired. On a close-fitting shirt or dress collar, however, interfacing of a stretch fabric cut on the bias is desirable.

Machine-made buttonholes are preferable when done against the direction of the stretch. Tailored buttonholes can be made in either direction.

Seldom is a seam finish required on stretch fabric.

Hems are usually finished without turning in raw edges, as shown on page 243. Until stretch hem tape is available on the market, the hem tape now available will have to be eased when it is sewn to a stretch garment. A loose hand stitch is required in hemming, also.

A coat or jacket lining, unless of stretch fabric, requires a deep pleat at center back.

When pressing stretch fabrics, the temperature setting of the iron is, of course, dependent upon the fiber content of the fabric. Care must be taken to avoid stretching the fabric with the iron.

Bonded fabric

Bonded fabric has a tricot backing or underlining fastened or sealed on the underside of it. The most popular ones on the market to date are bonded jersey, knit, flannel, lace, and crepe.

If necessary, the bonded woolens can be processed according to the directions on page 45. However, if the crosswise grain is not true, it is almost impossible to straighten it. If the underlining is not applied to the outside fabric on the same grain as the outside fabric, nothing can be done to correct it.

If the fabric and underlining both give, as a bonded knit or jersey, then, the garment will need support. Depending upon the pattern used, it may be underlined; a straight skirt or one-piece sheath dress would need a support lining, as shown on pages 178 and 247.

Some of the bondeds are good for beginners who are not ready for underlining. They have also been popular for children's A-line patterns.

Try to press out the center fold before cutting garment. If it is difficult to press out the crease, refold fabric and eliminate center fold in cutting.

Use a pattern that does not have too many pieces. A turn-back facing is preferred over a separate facing (p. 189) if it can be incorporated with the pattern.

A bonded crepe is easier to handle than regular crepe, but it has lost one of its fine characteristics — drapability. This must be recognized in selecting a pattern.

With the heavier bonded fabrics, self fabric is not as suitable for neckline facings, etc., as a finer fabric would be. A rayon twill would be a good choice. The darts may also need to be slashed (p. 191) to eliminate bulk.

The top of the hem should be finished as shown on page 243 or page 177.

A seam finish is rarely necessary. Bonded fabrics press easily and nicely. They hold a pleat very well.

Plaids and stripes

Small-scale stripes or plaids are best for the petite woman, while larger-scale stripes or plaids flatter the taller woman.

A dominant vertical design will add height, while a dominant horizontal design will add width.

Stripes are easier to handle than plaids, because the design runs in only one direction, and, therefore, needs to be matched or arranged in only one direction. Plaids, however, must be considered in both crosswise and lengthwise directions.

Make certain that plaid or striped fabrics are recommended for your pattern choice by checking the back of the pattern envelope.

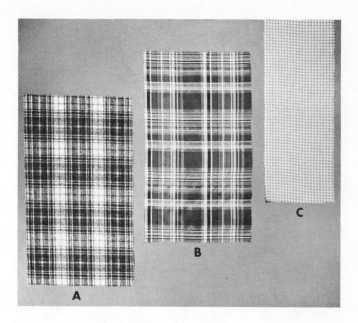

Analyzing the fabric. A balanced or formal plaid or stripe (A) has a uniform design with no definite up and down or right and left. The pattern can be cut, therefore, in either direction.

An unbalanced or informal plaid or stripe (B) does not have the same uniform design up and down or right and left. All pattern pieces must be laid out in the same direction before cutting. To make this possible, the style of garment must have a center front and center back seam, and the fabric must be exactly the same on the right and wrong sides. Each piece is cut separately. Cut one piece from a single layer of fabric; then lay the cut piece on the other side of fabric to cut the second one over corresponding plaid blocks, so that they match perfectly. All pattern pieces must be cut in opposite directions for unbalanced plaids. An exception to this rule is a garment that has unbalanced plaid used in a continuous line around the garment. The plaid does not balance at center front and center back. The choice of pattern for unbalanced plaid must be made carefully.

Sometimes it is difficult to tell whether or not a plaid or stripe is balanced. To check, fold the fabric in half across a dominant block of the plaid to see if the design and color repeat. Then fold the fabric in half up and down the dominant block and check if the design and color repeat. If so, the plaid is balanced.

If the distance from one complete design to another in a checked fabric (C) is less than ¼ inch, the checks are never matched. A straight seam should be avoided in this fabric, however, for it may bring together two light or two dark lines of the check.

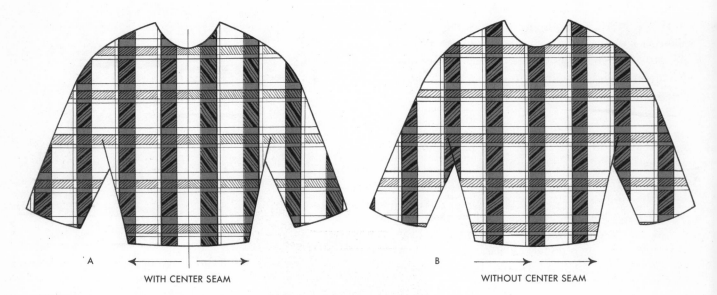

A

WITH CENTER SEAM

B

WITHOUT CENTER SEAM

This sketch shows an unbalanced plaid with a center seam (A), and how it would look without one (B). The same would apply to the skirt.

Planning the garment. When planning a plaid or striped dress, the pattern design must follow the fabric design as far as possible. For example, do not cut up a fabric with a square design (A) into a curved pattern line (B). Also, choose a pattern of simple design with a minimum number of seams.

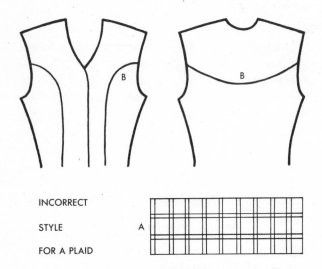

B   B

INCORRECT

STYLE   A

FOR A PLAID

Work and play with the fabric to try to find an interesting way to use it for a detail or trim on the garment. Making fringe, using bias, and developing interesting pockets and collars are examples.

For the garment that has a front or back opening with buttons and buttonholes, a fold-back facing is preferred over a stitched-on facing because the line of the design will not be absorbed by a straight facing which is stitched on and folded back. Do not use more than a six-gore skirt with plaids and stripes. In stitching these seams, they may not match perfectly in design toward the top because of the bias line (see sketch, p. 253). This is also true for the shoulders of a raglan or cut-on sleeve. Shoulder seams with regulation armholes will not always match, because of the off-grain line, ease on back shoulder, and darts. Bodice side seams can only be matched under the arm, below bust darts. The dark area of the design should fall at the bottom of the skirt and sleeves. If the dark area of the design falls at the bottom of the bodice, then for balance of design, begin the top of the skirt with a light area of the design.

Because plaid fabrics must be matched at the seams, you will need to buy more fabric. For small-scale plaids and checks, ⅛ of a yard extra is recommended. For medium-scale ones, buy an extra ¼ to ½ a yard. For extra large-scale patterns, an extra full yard is safest.

Cutting the garment. The most pronounced line of the plaid should fall across the shoulders, front and back, and in the center of the sleeve. The most pronounced line should also run down the center front and center back. On a sleeve, match merely

252

the front notch. Match the center back of the collar with the center back of garment. Before placing pattern pieces on two thicknesses of fabric, pin the fabric layers together along the plaid lines in both directions to hold the lower layer in position during cutting.

When placing tissue on the fabric, place bodice front first. From there, the bodice back, skirt front, or sleeve can be placed on fabric, and so on. Place pattern so that corresponding notches meet on similar color stripes; also, the top and the bottom of corresponding tissues should meet on similar color stripes. Small plaids are easier to match than large.

If your pattern has a yoke, cut the yoke with the lengthwise grain of the fabric running across the back.

On slacks and shorts, match the plaids or stripes at center front and center back seams and at the side seams of plaids.

A plaid or stripe design can be matched the entire length of a skirt seam or cut-on sleeve seam only when the two seamlines are identical in amount of slant or bias. The two pieces shown here cannot be matched the entire length of the seam because one slants across two stripes, while the other slants across three.

Stitching. If you do not have much skill in stitching plaids or stripes to meet with perfection, slip-baste the seams before stitching. To slip-baste, on the right side turn under one edge of a seam on seamline and press (A). Then place flat on top of the matching seamline (B), match plaid or stripe, pin in place, and slip-baste from the right side.

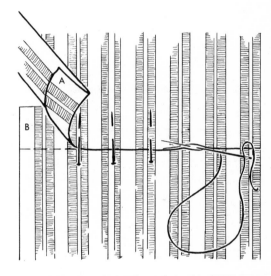

Diagonals

A diagonal fabric is one that is woven with a noticeably embedded or raised diagonal rib or bias effect in regular repeat formation. The diagonal line runs from the lower left hand corner of the fabric to the upper right hand corner. The completed garment is made up with the design lying in that same direction in the front — and in the back.

Twills or fabrics having diagonal weaves, such as denim, whipcord, silk surah, gabardine, and covert, are treated as non-diagonal fabrics and do not require matching or any special handling. The diagonal line is almost imperceptible.

The choice of a pattern for a noticeable diagonal fabric is most important. Often, the back of a pattern envelope will be marked suitable or unsuitable for diagonals.

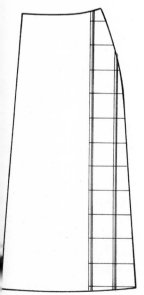

1   2

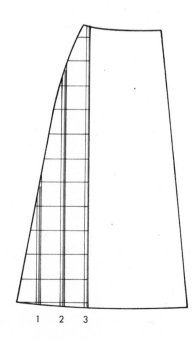

1   2   3

Unless a special cutting chart is given, this kind of fabric should be made with set-in sleeves. The bias line of raglan or kimono sleeves creates a poor design line at the top sleeve seam.

A diagonal should be made up in a slim skirt. Gored, flared, or A-line skirts will generally have bias seam edges which will force the diagonal line to run in different directions.

Generally, the pattern should have classic, simple lines. Many pattern pieces or intricate seaming details may create numerous problems in keeping the diagonal line going from lower left to upper right.

A reversible diagonal fabric is woven so that the wrong side of the fabric is exactly the same as the right side. It can be cut to create a chevron or pointed effect at the center front and center back seams.

A bias trim of diagonal gives an interesting effect of a straight-lined stripe.

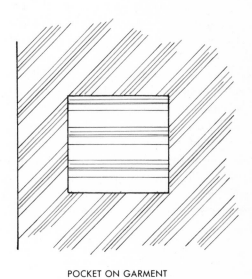

POCKET ON GARMENT

BIAS BINDING ON NECKLINE
AND DOWN FRONT

Choice of underlinings or interfacings

Throughout this text, the names of the interfacings and underlinings were given that were used in the particular garments in the photographs. However, a more complete list of those available on the market is given here (page 255).

The weight of the interfacing or underlining should be in relation to the weight of the outer fabric. If it is too stiff, it will impose itself on the outer fabric. If it is too limp, it will not provide the needed support. Try holding a piece of your fabric over the interfacing or underlining to judge how it will conform and if it will provide sufficient firmness.

Uses	Materials Available
I. To tailor coats and heavy suiting fabrics.	1. Armo-Style P-20—heavy weight hair canvas—width, 25". Color: Natural 2. Armo-Style P-17—medium weight hair canvas—width, 25". Color: Natural 3. Armo-Style P-27—lightweight hair canvas—width, 25". Color: Natural 4. Armo-Finolight—highest quality lightweight hair canvas—width, 25". Color: Sand 5. Armo-Acro—automatic wash-and-wear style, but also used in other fabrics—excellent in mohair coats—width, 25". Color: Ecru 6. Armo-Formite—automatic wash-and-wear style, but very popular in other fabrics. Use in lightweight coats—width, 25". Colors: Black, White, and Natural 7. Super Siri, firm finish—automatic wash-and-wear style—width, 45". Colors: Black and White 8. Veriform, crisp finish—washable—width, 39". Colors: Black and White 9. Stashape Tailor's Canvas—width, 27". Colors: Black, White, and Natural
II. To tailor medium or lightweight suiting fabrics of wool, silk, linen, cotton, etc. (If you may choose to launder the suit, make certain your underlining or interfacing choice is washable.)	1. Numbers 3, 4, 6, 7, 8, and 9 above can be used for these garments also. 2. Armo-Fino—highest quality lightweight hair canvas—width, 25". Color: Natural 3. Armo-Style P-26—lightweight hair canvas—width, 25". Color: Natural
III. To underline or interface dresses, two-piece dress ensembles, over-blouses, etc. (If you will launder your garment, make certain your underlining or interfacing choice is washable.)	1. Si Bonne by Armo—crisp and soft finishes—100% machine washable and pre-shrunk—width, 45". Available in 50 colors 2. Undercurrent—crisp finish—100% machine washable and preshrunk. Available in many colors 3. Super Siri, soft and super soft finishes—automatic wash-and-wear style—width, 45". Colors: Black and White 4. Veriform, medium soft and basic liner finishes—washable—width, 39". Colors: Black and White—basic liner also in Natural 5. For cotton garments, Cloth of Gold, lawn, batiste, and many wash-and-wear cotton fabrics are available.
IV. Various techniques for using iron-on interfacings are shown in Chapters 10, 11, 12, and 13. The ones available on the market are given here.	1. Instant Armo—dress weight—preshrunk for washing or dry-cleaning—width, 19" or 38". Colors: Black and White 2. Instant Armo—sheer canvas—preshrunk for washing or dry-cleaning—width, 25". Color: Natural 3. Instant Armo—red edge and fino—preshrunk for dry-cleaning—width, 25". Color: Natural 4. Staflex Iron-On Interfacing—washable—width, 18" or 36". Colors: Black and White 5. Staflex Iron-On Canvas—dry-cleanable only—width, 25". Colors: Natural and White

Fabrics suggest their own techniques

Seam finishes

Many fabrics do not require any seam finish. They will not ravel in laundering or dry cleaning. Then, too, seams that are cut very much on the bias are less likely to ravel than those that are cut straighter of grain. Thus, the straighter seams in some fabrics will require a seam finish while those cut on the bias will not. From the many suggestions which follow, choose the appropriate finish for your fabric.

Pinking. The most common seam finish is pinking with pinking shears. This is done after the seam is permanently stitched, but before it is pressed open (p. 135). In using pinking shears, pink close to the fabric edge, so that the width of the seam is retained.

Stitching with swing needle machine. Stitching the edge of a seam with a swing needle on an automatic machine makes a fine seam finish. With the growth in popularity of the swing needle machine, it is being used more and more.

Edge-stitching and pinking (A). If finishing with pinking shears will not prevent the fabric from raveling, the process of edge-stitching a seam and then pinking is often used. Each side of a seam is stitched ⅛ or ¼ inch from edge, or both can be stitched together if they are pressed to lie together (see p. 185). To prevent puckering, the machine stitch may need to be a little longer than regulation, and the stitching must be done in the correct direction of the fabric grain (see chart on p. 165). Use pinking shears after the stitching is completed.

Bound seam (B). A bound seam is recommended for fabrics that ravel very easily, and also for unlined jackets or coats. Stitch and press open the seam. Encase each edge with bias rayon tape and stitch on edge of tape in correct direction of grain (pp. 163-165). (Or the sides of the seam can be bound together if they are pressed to lie together as suggested on p. 185). Straight rayon seam tape, folded and pressed in half, can be used on straight seams.

Overcasting by hand. Overcasting raw edges is an excellent seam finish for fabrics that ravel easily. Its only disadvantage is that it is time-consuming. It is preferred over the bound seam in softer fabrics because it gives a softer finish and will not leave a press mark on the top of the garment. Stitch and press open the seam. Overcast each edge, working from right to left. Edges can be overcast together if they are pressed to lie together (p. 185). Use a single thread; take up about ⅛ inch of fabric in the stitch; and do not draw the thread tight.

Overcasting by machine (C). For most makes of machines, attachments for overcasting are available that will eliminate the time-consuming task of doing it by hand. Overcast at the machine in the correct direction of the grain (pp. 163-165). A zigzag attachment that may be used to prevent fabrics from raveling is also available.

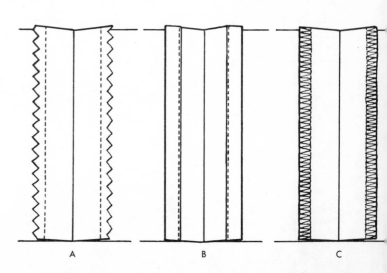

A   B   C

Flat-felled seam (A). A flat-felled seam gives a tailored look to shirts, pajamas, play clothes, and uniforms. Place together the wrong sides of the fabric; on the right side, stitch the regulation ⅝-inch seam.

Press the seam with both seam allowances turned in the same direction. Press across the seam to keep the fabric flat and to avoid pressing a pleat in the underside. Trim the lower seam allowance to ⅛ inch; staystitch the top seam allowance ¼ inch from seamline (width of left side of presser foot). Trim off seam edge to ⅛ inch of staystitching line. Clip up to staystitching line where necessary on curves; turn under raw edge on staystitching, place flat and topstitch close to folded edge. On a quality-looking garment, a flat-felled seam is always finished from the top side of the garment instead of the underside.

French seam (B). A French seam is used with lightweight and transparent fabrics where the seam would show through to the top. It is used on underwear and on infants' clothes. It will finish ⅛ or ¼ inch wide, depending upon the fabric; try a sample piece before beginning a garment.

A French seam cannot be used on a curved line. Place the wrong sides of the fabric together. Stitch the seam ⅜ or ½ inch wide on the right side, depending upon finished width on underside of sample. (The two together must total ⅝-inch seam allowance.) Trim seam to a scant ⅛ inch and press together to one side. Turn to the underside of garment, and crease on the stitching line. Stitch ¼ or ⅛ inch from crease. This amount will take up the remainder of seam allowance. In soft fabrics such as nylon and lawn, this second row of stitching is often done by hand with a short running stitch.

A mock French seam may be used on curved seams where it is impossible to make a regular French seam. It may be made in two different ways. First make a plain seam on the underside of garment. Then (1) stitch the two seam allowances together ¼ inch from the seamline and trim, leaving ⅛ or ¹⁄₁₆ inch of fabric beyond the second line of stitching. Or (2) trim the seam allowance if too wide, turn the edges in toward each other, and stitch them together close to the folded edges.

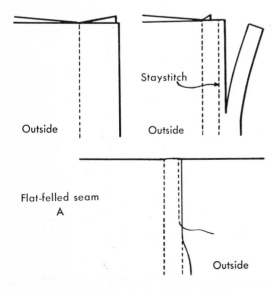

Flat-felled seam
A

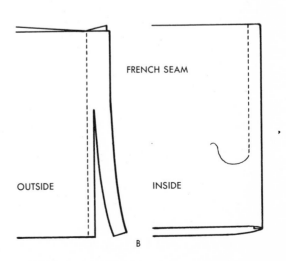

FRENCH SEAM

B

Chapter 15

Details on clothes for simple elegance in fashion

The art of selection for a quality, elegant look

For elegance in fashion, an economy of line and of trim is desired. Usually, when a garment is made from a handsome piece of fabric, or from an impressive line in a pattern, no trimming would be desirable. If you feel an ensemble seems to be too simple, it may be far better to increase its interest with smart accessories than with a trimming.

If you study fashion, you will find that fads are almost always concerned more with trimmings than with line.

Avoid a cluttered look. More than one type of trimming seldom appears in a single ensemble.

For further help in planning that total look in your clothes, the following point system for dressing smartly serves as a guide. It could certainly help you to decide whether to add any trim, or remove a button or bow that may already be there.

A well-dressed woman does not wear more than 9 points for work or daytime wear. She does not wear more than 12 points for dress or evening wear. Study the columns to learn how the points add up. It is better to have fewer rather than more points in a complete ensemble.

It has been said in the Bishop method that a trim should never be used unless it will add a quality look to a garment. The fabric itself, the line of the pattern, the mirror, scraps, and fashion magazines will help you develop what is exactly right for you. Do not be a slave to a pattern, but learn to personalize it, not only in a trim but in pattern line.

The point system for dressing smartly

Dress	One color	1 point
or	Print or two colors	2 points
Suit	Two-piece	2 points
	Contrasting collar or belt	1 point
	Any trimming, such as bows, flowers, etc.	1 point each
	Contrasting buttons	1 point
	Scarf	1 point
Jewelry	Necklace	1 point
	Bracelet	1 point
	Pin	1 point
	Earrings	1 point
Hat	Plain	1 point
	Trim	1 point extra
	Veil	1 point extra
Shoes	Plain	1 point
	Others	2 points
Gloves		1 point
Purse		1 point (2 points if elaborate)
Muff		1 point
Umbrella or Walking stick		1 point

Your own image

Before selecting patterns, fabrics, trims, and accessories, develop a sense of your own image. Stop and consider which of your clothes are most becoming. They must make the most of your good features, express your personality, and at the same time conform to your way of life. Study lines, fabrics, designs, textures, colors, and accessories in the light of your own image which should be developed from year to year. Whether your image is feminine, tailored, casual, dignified, sporty, youthful, or mature, you will choose what is best for you, for your own individuality.

The best judge of what styles suit you best will be you, yourself.

Trimming details

Bias tubing. One of the most versatile trimmings is bias tubing. It can be finished in any width and length desired.

A popular width is made by cutting true bias one inch wide, folding in half with wrong side out, and stitching through the center of the folded bias strip. Always have the fold of bias to the right when stitching it.

The seam will be as wide as the finished bias tubing. Use a short stitch at the machine (18 to 20 per inch), and hold bias firm when stitching to take all the stretch out of the fabric. The stitching should not crack when the bias is pulled.

To turn bias, insert a bodkin, and secure it with hand stitching at machine stitching on bias, or insert a bobby pin.

Depending upon the way it will be used, the bias tubing may either be pressed flat or used as a roll; the type of fabric often controls the width it will be made and how it will be used.

If the bias is to be pressed flat, the seam should be pressed open first, before turning bias right side out (see photograph, p. 162).

If you want the tubing to be soft, cut away the seam allowance close to the seamline.

For a firmer tubing, the seam may be made several times as wide as the desired tubing.

To make a firm, corded bias tubing, see sketch on page 163.

For a full but soft, round tubing, 4-ply wool yarn or lamb's wool may be drawn through finished tubing.

If it is necessary to stitch together several pieces of bias for the needed length, make a ¼-inch seam on true grain (A), press open, and trim seam to ⅛ inch before bias is stitched as a tube (B).

In some fabrics, you may find it easier to make these short seams (A) by hand with small running stitches.

Also, the pieces are often easier to handle if you join them on lengthwise instead of crosswise grain.

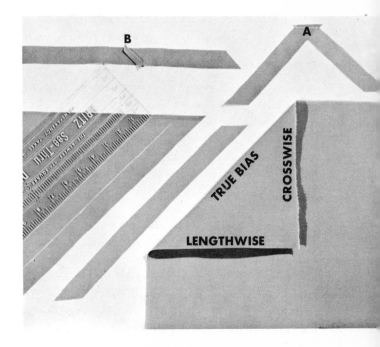

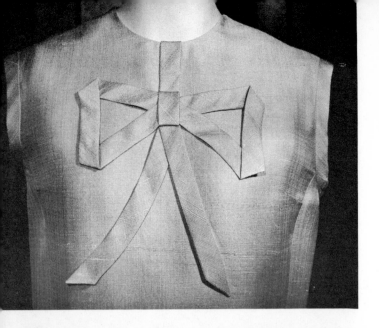

This bias bow finishes ¾ inch wide, and the seam is trimmed to ⅛ inch. The ends of the bow are pressed in reverse of the one on the belt on page 162. The bow is handsewn to overblouse with hand stitching shown on page 274. The hand sewing should be so inconspicuous that it hardly seems to exist.

This bias trim (⅜ inch wide) is used at a yoke seam on a Chanel jacket. Notice particularly the interesting manner in which the bias is laid to form the center of the bow. It, too, is handsewn to jacket on underside (see p. 274).

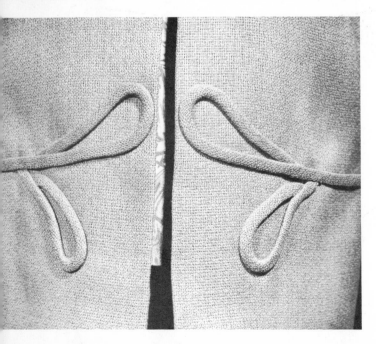

This bias trim (¼ inch wide) extends to center fronts from the side seams at waistline of a Chanel jacket. You may prefer to use this trim above the bustline. It is handsewn to jacket on underside (p. 274). The hand stitching should be so inconspicuous that it hardly seems to exist.

Another photograph of this jacket is shown on page 185.

For the trim across the neckline, the two raw edges of bias are stitched together with a long machine stitch. Then the bias is drawn up and pressed to fit curve of neckline to perfection. It is then stitched to garment, and pressed down to conceal raw edges.

The two bias scrolls were made according to the directions given for **C** on page 262.

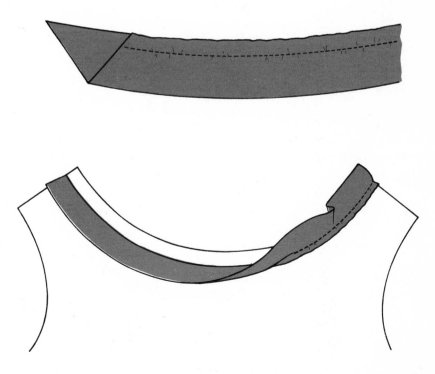

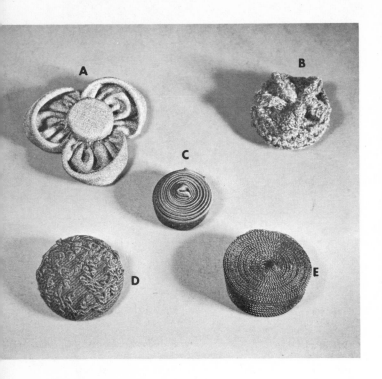

Buttons. Many times the buttons you make will complement your garment and give it more of an elegant look than some you might buy. Also, they will be far less expensive and will usually take less time than you might spend seeking the correct buttons to purchase.

A button is made exactly like the larger one used as a trim on the front of a dinner dress (p. 270).

B is the popcorn crochet stitch. The crocheted cap is made and slipped over a regular covered button.

C gives interesting effects depending upon weight of fabric used. It is a strip of bias (p. 259) rolled into a scroll, and handsewn together on underside.

D is a regular covered button. Two strands of buttonhole twist are twisted or rolled together until they form little twisted rolls. The rolls are then handsewn on covered button. They can be used closer together, or piled high, if desired.

E is made of horsehair braid that is folded in half and rolled into a scroll. It is easy to run the needle through the button from one side to the other to sew the horsehair braid in place.

F button has hand-tucks sewn in circle of fabric before button is covered. The circle in the center was drawn the size of a dime.

G is a single crochet button similar to **B**.

H and **I** are covered buttons with an added design made by crocheting or braiding threads taken from weave of fabric.

J is made by braiding threads taken from woven fabric and rolling the braid into a scroll and fastening it on top of a regular button.

K and **L** are made by knotting regular bias tubing. Ends are handsewn on underside.

M is a folded strip of fringe made into a scroll. The raw edges are handsewn together on underside. Fringe is made by pulling threads within a strip of fabric (see p. 215, *Fashion Sewing by the Bishop Method*), and then folding strip in half.

N is a scroll of fabric that is fringed on one edge only, and is handsewn on underside. Fringe may be trimmed to desired size and shape.

O is a strip of fabric with selvage on outer edge. It, too, is made into a scroll and handsewn on underside. A little twist of selvage is fastened in center of button.

P is a button covered with lining fabric and with a piece of fabric to match the garment. The fabric is a loosely woven one as you can see from the strip at the left. Some threads were pulled out in both directions to give the open effect on the button.

Q is a Chinese knot and scroll made from turned bias, page 259. Another version is shown on page 273.

R, S, and **T** are made from rubber washers for faucets.

R is red and white soutache braid intertwined through hole in the center of the washer.

S is navy and white soutache braid which is not taken through the hole in the center of the washer. The braid covers the entire washer.

T is made of two washers covered separately with circles of fabric. The two washers are then placed together, concealing the raw edges of the fabric. The edges of fabric are handsewn to hold washers in place securely.

U and **V** are covered in white linen from a purchased covered-button kit. **U** has a twist of red soutache braid sewn on outer edge of fabric.

V has two strips of red and navy braid that were applied to fabric before the button was covered. A single piece of braid to match that on suit is used around button in photograph on page 248.

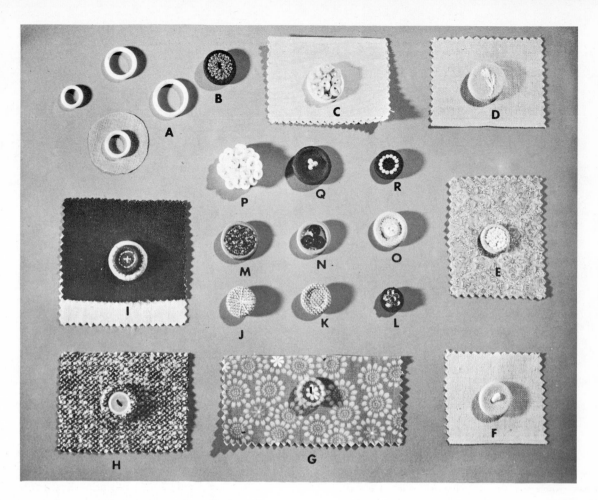

There is no limit to what one can do with buttons made from bone or plastic rings of various sizes.

A. Make a running stitch around circle of fabric and draw it up to cover ring. The circle of fabric must be cut large enough to cover the ring with perfection. In sheer fabric, the circle will need to be double.

B. Except for the center, the button is completely filled with French knots made from embroidery floss. This one was navy blue with red French knots.

C. Fill the center of a button with small pearl buttons stitched on fabric covering.

D. Fabric was embroidered to form a design in the center before button was covered. The same embroidered design may be repeated somewhere else on garment, such as on pocket flap or on corners of a collar.

E. The center of the button is completely filled with French knots made from embroidery floss to bring out a color in the print.

F. One large French knot in the center enriches this button.

G. The daisy in the print is repeated for the center of the button.

H. One button is stitched to fill the center of the covered button.

I. Bone rings in two sizes are covered with fabric and then tacked together to form a higher button. Hand stitching around the inner edge of bone ring gives the button a flat, sunken center. The cross stitch on the button is also done by hand with embroidery floss.

J. Stitching with buttonhole twist or embroidery floss forms cartwheel to trim button.

K. Hand stitching with embroidery floss or buttonhole twist around the inner edge of the bone ring gives the button a flat, sunken center.

L. A rhinestone button is made by sewing on little rhinestones.

M. The center of the button is filled with seed beads.

N. Three sequins and beads beautify the center of this button that is also stitched to have a flat center.

O. One small button is used in the center of this button that is also stitched to have a flat center.

P. The center of the button and the ring are covered with small pearl buttons stitched in place through covering.

Q. Three small pearls are sewn in this center, and the button is stitched to have a flat center.

R. Small pearls are stitched in a ring to trim and give flat center to button.

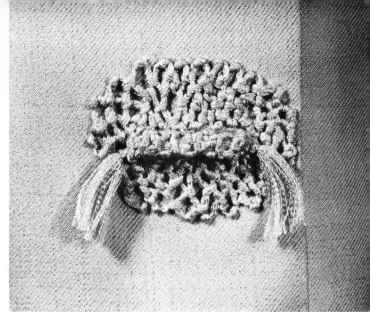

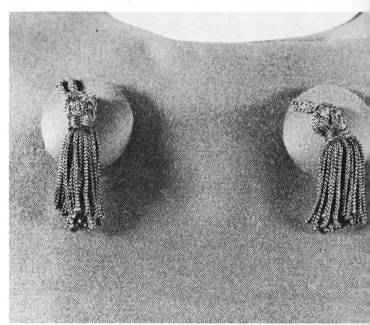

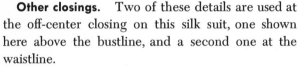

Other closings. Two of these details are used at the off-center closing on this silk suit, one shown here above the bustline, and a second one at the waistline.

Silk-covered snaps are used on the underside. The scroll is made like **C** button on page 262. Five individual pieces of bias with a knot in the center of each are handsewn under the scroll to give the effect of petals.

This hand-knotted detail is made of threads frayed from the woven fabric. Two of this trim are used on the off-center closing on a silk suit — one above the bustline, and one at the waistline. They are handsewn to garment.

Silk-covered snaps are used on the underside.

The buttons are covered in matching fabric. The tassels are then made (see p. 273) and used as a detail on the buttons. Two are used at the neckline of this double-breasted jacket, and two at the waistline.

Two of these details are used on the double-breasted line of an Alaskine suit, one at the neckline and one at the waistline. They are made of bias from dull-finished satin.

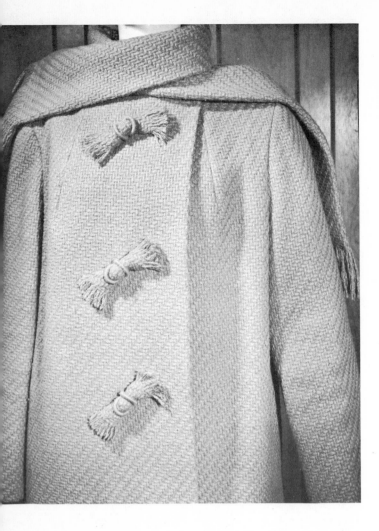

The bone rings are covered with threads taken from weave of coat fabric. Lengthwise strips of fabric are fringed at each edge, stitched into a tube, and pulled through bone rings.

Note the stole that is also made from a lengthwise strip, fringed at each edge, and stitched into a tube.

Selvage often lends itself to an interesting treatment on a garment. The buttonholes are lengthwise in this jacket, and the buttons are also sewn on.

There is a ½-inch fold of fabric in center at A. These folded edges are handsewn together on underside, and only left open as needed to reach in and fasten buttons.

A piece of turned bias is laid double and sewn together on underside. It is left open at A and B to fasten under buttons and to give this understated trim from neckline of jacket.

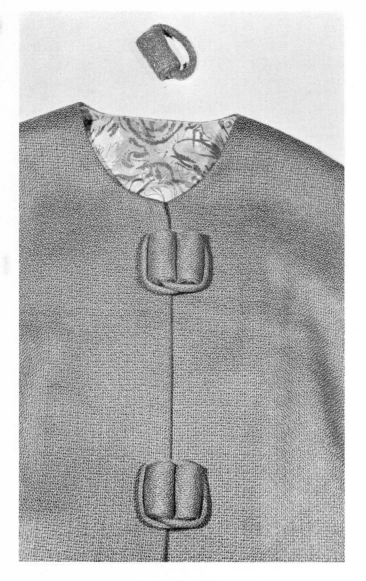

This detail is used between buttons and button-holes on a robe. It is made from a square of fabric (see sketch) that is folded, pressed, and cut into shape as shown.

Make satin stitch with zigzag machine or by hand to fasten flower to robe, and to conceal raw edges.

This trim may be used in many ways on a garment.

A roll of fabric on lengthwise grain with raw edges turned to meet in the center, and bias tubing caught in the center of the roll, makes an interesting trim open or closed on the front of a garment. It replaces buttons and buttonholes, and is handsewn to garment. It is shown open in upper part of photograph.

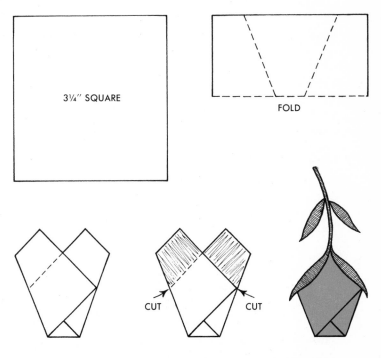

3¼" SQUARE

FOLD

CUT   CUT

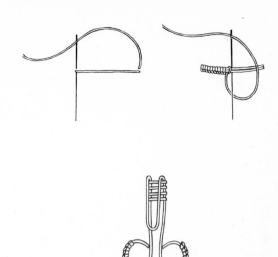

The silk-covered or sunken snap gives a quality finish to more advanced sewing. When a hook and eye are preferred, if the eye is made of matching thread of the garment, it would be less conspicuous and therefore often essential for a quality look.

Sew several strands of thread on underlap of garment where eye is to go. Cover the strands with a blanket stitch. It is made by bringing the needle under the strands and through the loop formed.

The front of this jacket is turned back at A for the photograph, to show the facing, B. Frequently, the top half of a snap, instead of being covered with lining as shown on page 214, *Fashion Sewing by the Bishop Method*, is placed under the facing through which the snap head (C and C) protrudes. This is known as a sunken snap. It is less conspicuous.

When handsewing the top half of snap to the facing (C and C), do not include interfacing or underlining, except on very light fabrics. D half of snap is covered as shown on page 214, *Fashion Sewing by the Bishop Method*.

Triangular buttonholes are easily made and add charm to a garment. Use a bow instead of a button, unless a button is preferred.

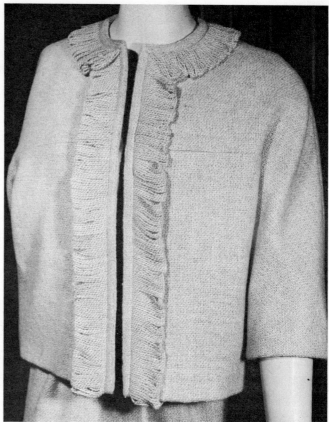

After determining the size of buttonhole and marking garment, make strips for the buttonhole on lengthwise fold. Mark exact size of buttonhole on strip, stitch, and cut, allowing ⅛-inch seam allowance.

Place line of stitching on buttonhole strip to meet marking line for buttonhole; stitch on buttonhole strip through same line of stitching. After stitching on both buttonhole strips, cut from center of triangle to three corners. Turn buttonhole strips to inside and stitch across base of triangle; trim excess fabric from triangle to ⅛-inch seam. Cut through facing to form triangle, turn raw edges, and slip-stitch back of buttonhole.

If the buttonhole strip is one inch wide at the base, then the bow is also made one inch wide. The buttonhole strips represent the ends of the bow. The bow is made of true bias.

Thirteen loops of bias velveteen are handsewn together to make the base of this trim at the lower edge of an overblouse. Eight loops of dull-finish satin are then sewn in place on top of that. A covered button conceals the raw edges.

This detail may be made smaller, and of one fabric, if desired, and may be used at front closing, where two or three would be needed.

Various other suggestions. A folded strip of fringe (see p. 215, *Fashion Sewing by the Bishop Method*) made from self-fabric is used at the front and neckline of this jacket. The raw edges of the fringe were stitched to the jacket before the binding was applied. Fringe is always in fashion.

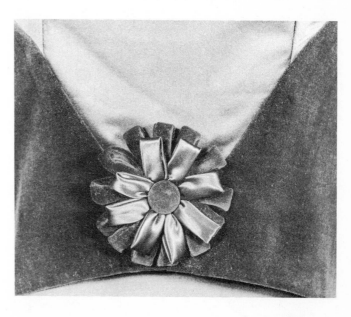

These petals may be made from lighter-weight fabrics by folding a circle in half on the bias. Stitch raw edges together as shown, and draw up thread to form petal.

The petals may also be made by rolling in a square corner of fabric with your finger. Then, stitch across fabric at desired size of petal, draw up thread, and trim away excess fabric.

A scroll of bias (or a button as shown on p. 262) may be used in center of petals.

To reinforce the area where petals are handsewn to garment (or where you may be sewing on other trims or buttons), place a square or strip of pellon on underside before doing hand sewing.

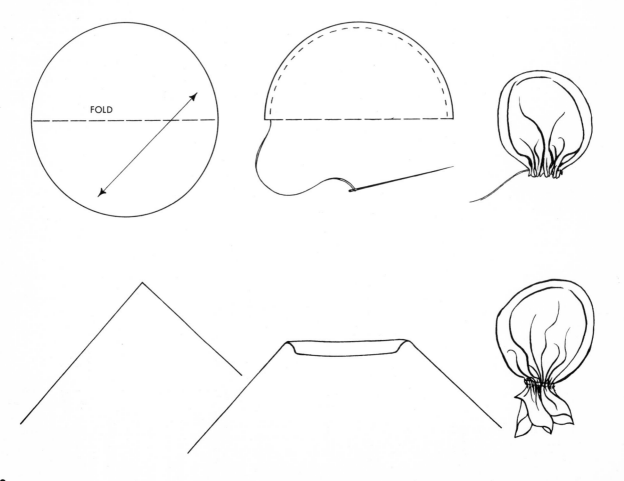

FOLD

Sheet cotton is placed on underside of overblouse where quilting is to be done. Quilting is then done at machine before facings are applied. The fitted facings are cut the depth of the quilting to cover sheet cotton.

These tabs are made from a lengthwise strip of fabric. Make them the size you desire; the dimensions given on the sketch were the size used on this particular jacket. They are also attractive on the bottom of a skirt. They may be used in a seam created several inches from the bottom of a jacket, overblouse, or skirt.

The raw edges of tabs do not require stitching at A when pressed in place.

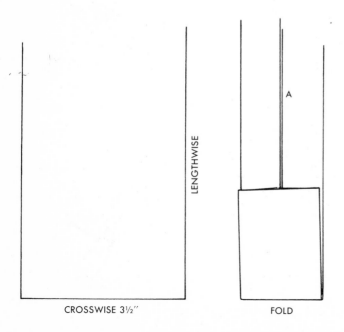

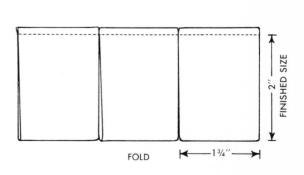

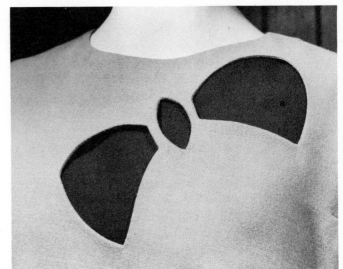

French knots made from heavier floss make an attractive, understated trim at the neckline and down the front of this coat. Sometimes, they are done in a contrasting thread.

The button is the bias scroll (p. 262).

There are many designs you could use for this detail on the front of a dress or overblouse. Another color or a design fabric may be used for the underlay.

Draw design on underside of garment or on underlining. Place facing on dress, right sides together (see A sketch). Stitch around design; cut out center of design, leaving just a narrow seam allowance. Cut up to stitching in corners.

Turn and press facing in place. Place underlay below open design (B).

Lightly sew underlay to dress through facing and seamline (C). In some areas or designs, hand sewing will need to be done only through facing and underlay, and not through the seamline.

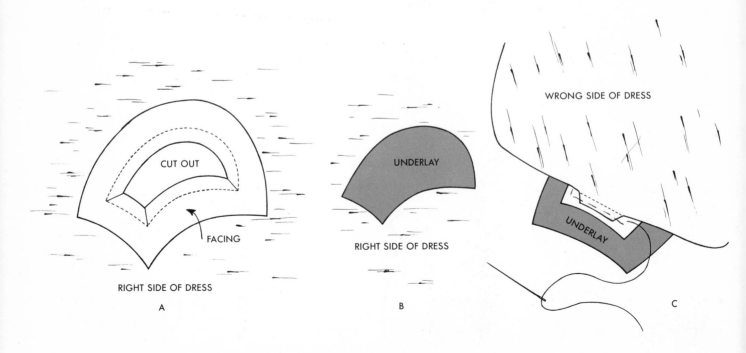

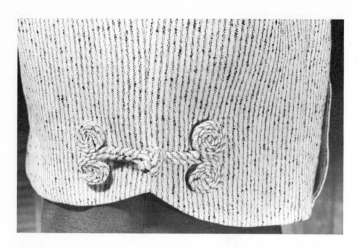

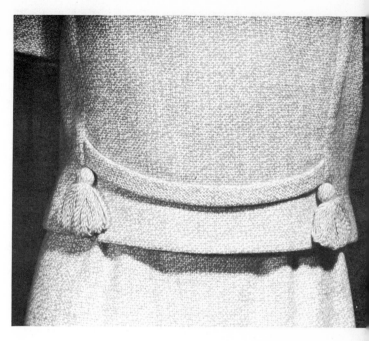

The Chinese knot and scroll are used at the waist-line of the two side seams of this overblouse. They may also be used as a front closing instead of buttons and buttonholes.

Please note another idea for making them on page 263.

This jacket has four flap pockets; two are at the same position on other half of jacket front. The flaps may be worn out as shown at A, or tucked into pocket as shown at B. This could be varied each time you wore the suit, depending upon how many points of interest (p. 258) there would be in the accessories.

The raw edges of the strip of bias are included in seams of overblouse.

To make tassels, cut a piece of cardboard the desired length of tassel. Place one or more threads across top of cardboard; then, wind threads around cardboard to desired fullness. Tie top firmly with thread placed at top of cardboard. Wrap a thread around the top end several times and tie securely to hold strands together.

Lower ends may be cut open or not, as you wish (see one cut on p. 265).

These tassels are made from thread pulled from woven fabric. Yarn or silk threads may also be used.

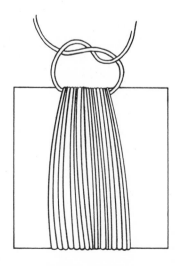

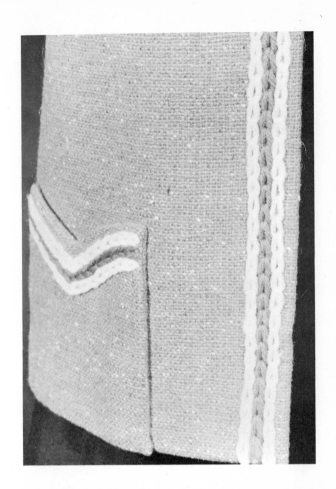

Twenty yards of the banding shown in the lower right corner were purchased and sewn together to make the yardage for this dress. This is an imaginative idea. It can be adapted in many ways.

There are many quality-looking trims you can make yourself. Here are two trims for a Chanel jacket that would be more individual than ready-made braid.

On a blue and white tweed fabric, blue wool yarn and white wool yarn are used in a chain stitch.

On the second jacket, folded fringe is stitched to each side of a strip of velveteen. Velveteen is then handsewn to finished edge of jacket and pocket.

In stitching patch pockets, it is very important to cut ⅛ inch off around entire pocket. Then, key edges of upper and under pocket when sewing together. This will give grace to top pocket.

Slash in center of under pocket piece to turn pocket right side out, then press.

Pocket is handsewn to garment with a punch stitch. From underside of garment, take one stitch at a time, catching underside of pocket and returning to underside of garment. The stitching should be so inconspicuous that it hardly seems to exist.

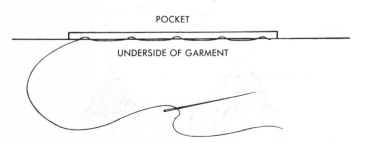

POCKET

UNDERSIDE OF GARMENT

Make this cut-through detail before under collar is applied to top collar. Draw a design on a little square of interfacing, and place on right side of top collar. Stitch around the design with short stitches at the machine. Cut and turn like a fitted facing. When under collar has been applied, cut design through it and finish like the back of a buttonhole.

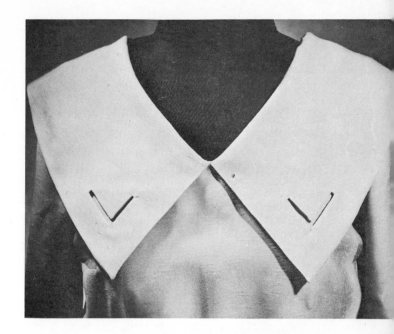

Six-inch pieces of bias are tied into a knot at each end. Raw edges of bias are pushed into center of it with point of scissors, and ends are handsewn. Pieces of bias are then handsewn to bottom of over-blouse.

An arrowhead is often used as a trim at the points of darts, at inside edges of buttonholes, at top of pleats and slits, and in many other ways. It can be seen on garments every season of every year. Make it according to the following directions:

Figure 1. Draw or baste-stitch a triangle on fabric. An average size is ⅝ inch, but it can be made larger or smaller as needed. Insert the needle from underneath, near the center of the triangle, and take a few running stitches, bringing the needle out at corner A. Bring needle up to point B and take one tiny stitch from right to left.

Figure 2. Bring needle down to point C and take a long stitch. Needle should emerge just to the right of point A.

Figure 3. Bring needle up to B again, inserting it on marking line as closely as possible below the first stitch. It should emerge at the corresponding point on marked line at left.

Figure 4. Return the needle to point C and take the next stitch just at the left of the first one. The needle should emerge just to the right of the stitches at A.

Figures 5 and 6. Following this same procedure and taking each stitch close to the previous stitch, continue until the triangle is filled. Be sure to anchor thread well on underside.

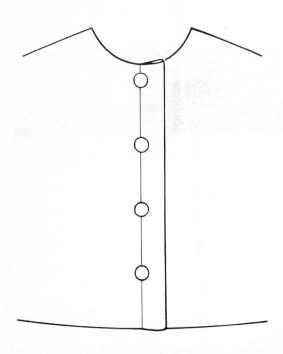

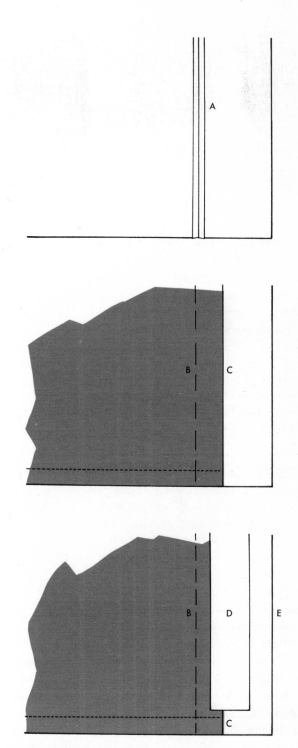

This strip of fabric may be either lengthwise or bias, and is a very popular fashion detail. Not only is it attractive, but it is a substitute for buttonholes in very heavy or problem fabrics. The strip may finish any desired width.

Stitch the strip to garment (A). In width, garment is cut to center front line plus seam allowance. Press open seam.

Then, stitch underlining to garment, and handsew underlining to seamline to hold in place at center front (B). Underlining is cut to extend to fold line of strip (C).

Press bias strip of instant armo (D) to give firmness to roll of strip. E edge is cut desired width for facing to extend when folded back into position (C).

At A, strip is not sewn to garment where strip acts as a buttonhole. Facing must be finished on underside to complete buttonhole.

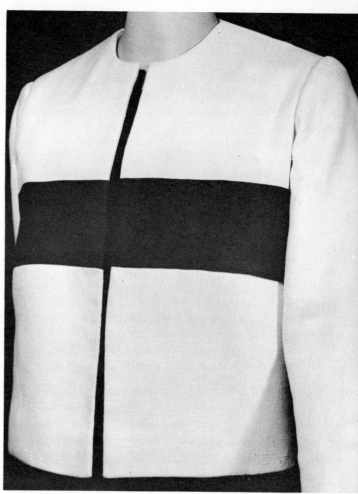

Changing a basic dress. A basic dress will give you a lot of mileage in wardrobe planning. This one is sleeveless, and has a scoop neckline.

In this first photograph, the basic dress is shown with a separate cape. The cape has four buttons and buttonholes in the back.

Here, it is worn with a white linen jacket. A black band has been applied across the front and the back which can be removed, and a different detail applied, if or when desired.

A third way this basic dress is worn is with the overblouse of white cotton lace. The overblouse is underlined throughout with a black cotton underlining. Many other ways could have been shown.

In making a suit, you may prefer to make two tops for the one skirt. In wardrobe planning, this will give you more mileage from the one skirt.

Possibly, as your own designer, you may never use any of the suggested details shown in this chapter. They may serve, however, as suggestions, or as challenges to your own ingenuity.

Let each fabric, each design, each new project inspire you as you work toward developing sewing as the very fine art it is today.

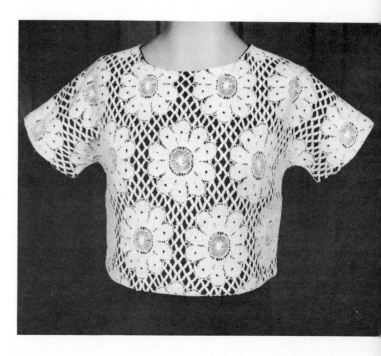

anchor-stitch: stitching about ½ inch long at a given area for reinforcement. Use a short zigzag stitch at machine. If you do not have a zigzag machine, stitch back and forth several times for about ½ inch.

baste-stitch: the longest machine stitch, 6 to 8 per inch. With contrasting thread, it is used for basting and for marking location lines for buttonholes, pockets, and center fronts. With matching thread, it is used for control of ease on sleeve caps.

beveling edges: trimming away the seam allowance inside faced edges by using a slanted angle with the scissors to alleviate bulk in heavy fabric.

bias: a diagonal slant in a fabric that does not follow the lengthwise or crosswise grain. True bias makes a 45° angle across the lengthwise and crosswise grain, and has greater stretch and give and less raveling than any other cut edge.

binding: enclosing both sides of an edge with a strip of fabric.

bodice: the upper part of a dress.

bonded fabric: a fabric with a tricot backing or an underlining fastened or sealed to its underside.

catch-stitch: a hand stitch, taken from right to left at a lower boundary and then at an upper boundary, which forms a triangular design.

clean-finishing: turning a raw edge to the inside for ⅛ or ¼ inch on a line of staystitching, and then stitching on the edge. Clean-finishing is used to finish the raw edges of some facings and hems.

cutting-to-fit: cutting a garment to fit individual measurements.

dart: a fold of fabric stitched to give shape to a garment, wide at one end and tapering to a point at the other end.

directional staystitching: a line of regulation machine stitching with matching thread, usually through a single piece of fabric and placed just outside the seamline unless otherwise stated. It holds the grain threads in position, prevents fabric from stretching, and maintains the pattern line.

directional stitching: stitching seams in the correct direction of the grain to hold the grain threads in position, to prevent the fabric from stretching, and to maintain the pattern line.

drum: lining for a skirt. It is made with a firm fabric and gives support to the skirt. It is not sewn into the seams.

ease: working in extra fabric when stitching to a shorter piece of fabric without having gathers or small tucks.

edge stitching: topstitching close to the edge of a part of a garment, such as waistbands, collars, belts, and cuffs.

facing: a piece of fabric cut on grain identical to the garment's, which is used to finish edges, such as necklines and sleeves. Facing may be finished to either the right side or the wrong side of the garment.

favor: ease fabric slightly on front facings above markings for top button and buttonhole, or at other areas in sewing.

grain: fabric is woven with the threads interlaced lengthwise and crosswise. The crosswise threads from selvage to selvage form the crosswise grain; the lengthwise threads running parallel with the selvage form the lengthwise grain. When the lengthwise and crosswise threads lie at perfect right angles, the fabric is grain perfect.

gusset: various-shaped pieces of fabric inserted underarm to give greater width at the bustline, to add ease to sleeve when arm is raised, and to provide further shaping to garment.

hand-picking: an application of the back-stitch used for applying zippers by hand for a custom finish on a garment.

identical grain: the grain of two pieces of fabric in which the lengthwise and crosswise threads are in exactly the same position.

interfacing: the fabric that is placed between the inside and the outside of the garment sections, such as in collars and cuffs. Interfacing gives body and better form to the appearance of the finished garment.

interlining: an extra lining that is inserted for warmth with the regular lining in a suit or coat.

knit fabric: fabric made from yarns looped together rather than interwoven.

lining: a suitable piece of fabric constructed in the shape of a garment to cover and finish the inside of the entire garment or a section of it.

lockstitching: knotting the machine thread at the beginning and at the end of a line of stitching by releasing pressure on the presser foot, and stitching several times in the same stitch. Lockstitching eliminates the time and nuisance of tying threads, and the time and motion of using a reverse stitch.

miter: the angle formed when the excess fabric has been removed from a corner by a diagonal seam.

nap: the short fibers on the surface of the fabric that have been drawn out from the yarns of the fabric and brushed in one direction.

notches: V-shaped markings on the edge of a pattern that indicate where corresponding pattern pieces are to be joined.

off grain: not with the grain of the fabric.

overcast: long, slanting, loose stitches over the raw edges of a seam to prevent raveling.

overstitching: stitching over a previously stitched seam for greater strength.

pickup stitch: a running stitch for hemming that is done from the underside of the hem. It picks up the hem in one stitch and picks up the garment in the next stitch.

preshrink: to relax or contract fabric before cutting, so the size of the garment will not be altered after laundering or dry cleaning.

regulation or permanent stitch: the permanent stitch that is placed in a garment, 12 to 15 per inch, with matching thread. The number of stitches will vary with the type of fabric; a firm, fine fabric will take a shorter stitch than will a thick, heavy fabric.

running stitch: a hand stitch made by placing the needle in and out of the fabric in an even, straightforward manner.

seam allowance: the portion of a garment allowed for the seam, usually ⅝ inch.

seamline: the exact line where a seam is stitched.

selvage: the two lengthwise finished edges (parallel with the warp threads) on all woven fabric.

shank: the space between button and fabric, on all garments, to give room for the buttonhole side of the garment. It is made with thread unless the button has a metal shank.

short stitch: a shorter machine stitch, 18 to 20 per inch, used for reinforcement on comparatively limited areas, such as points of collars, points of gussets, underarm curves that must be clipped, and tailored buttonholes.

slip-basting: invisible hand-basting, put in from the right side.

slipstitch: a concealed hand stitch that can be used only on an area with a folded edge. The needle is run along the fold of the hem for about ¼ inch; with a downward movement the garment is pricked; the needle is then brought out at the side of the fold. To continue slipstitching, the needle is placed back into the fold of the hem at about the same place, and the same procedure is repeated.

staystitching: see **directional staystitching**

staystitching plus or ease plus: manipulating the fabric with the machine stitch to force together the grain threads. It is an easy method for gaining control of ease.

stretch fabric: fabric which may be stretched lengthwise, crosswise, or both ways and will recover its original size and shape.

termination point: the marking line across the end of a dart or tuck to assure that the two layers of fabric will be stitched the same length.

topstitching: stitching a seam or edge on the right side of a garment with one or more rows of stitching.

trapunto: a trimming detail made by stitching together two pieces of fabric into a design and filling the design to raise it.

tuck: a fold of fabric stitched to give shape to a garment.

underlining: a second piece of fabric, cut from the same pattern pieces and on the same grain as the garment, staystitched to the outside fabric, and treated as one piece with the outside fabric for further construction. It gives a sculptured and quality look to a garment. When a dress is underlined, interfacings are usually not necessary.

understitching: a row of stitching placed close to the edge of any facing, which catches the two trimmed seams to the facing. It keeps the facing to the underside, and sharpens the seam edge.

unit construction: assembling the sections of a garment that make a unit, and completing all stitching and pressing before each unit is joined to another. This process involves less handling, improves organization of work, guarantees better quality-looking clothes, and enables shorter periods of time to be used to advantage.

well of seamline: the line of stitching in a seam.

NEW LEARNINGS

In addition to the new learnings listed below chapter by chapter, most chapters (particularly chapters 6, 7, 10, 11, 12, and 13) include many repeat learnings about the importance of the grain of the fabric, preparing the fabric for cutting, the importance of cutting and marking to perfection, unit construction, the correct use of a commercial pattern, the importance of directional stitching of seams, zipper application, clean-finishing, understitching, and many other techniques for making a quality garment.

Chapter 1

Sewing equipment and use of the sewing machine

1. Essential sewing equipment and standards for it
2. Essential pressing equipment and standards for it
3. Sewing notions used frequently
4. Techniques on use of the sewing machine
5. Various lengths of machine stitching used

Chapter 2

Torn projects

1. Proper selection of fabric
2. Importance of grain of fabric
3. Working with grain of fabric
4. Use of the sewing machine
5. Staystitching
6. Stitching seams
7. First hems
8. First pressing techniques
9. Understitching
10. Clean-finishing
11. Applying a facing, *garment side up*

Chapter 3

Buying patterns correctly

1. How to determine your figure type
2. How to measure to determine correct size pattern to purchase
3. Use of measurement chart
4. How patterns vary in size

Chapter 4

Preparing fabrics for cutting

1. Ascertaining what is grain of fabric
2. How to work with ends of fabric to determine grain perfection
3. How to straighten grain of fabric, when necessary
4. How to shrink cotton and linen fabrics, when necessary
5. How to process woolen fabrics, when necessary
6. Restoring grain to torn edges

Chapter 5

Cutting and marking

1. Working with nap fabrics
2. One way design fabrics
3. Off-grain design fabrics
4. Using a commercial pattern
5. Cutting out a garment
6. Marking pieces of garment
7. Placing garment in units of work
8. Unit method of clothing construction

Chapter 6

Making two skirts

1. Using a commercial pattern
2. Directional staystitching
3. Directional stitching of seams
4. Applying zipper in a skirt
5. Waistband with self-interfacing
6. Applying straight waistband to garment

Chapter 7

Making two blouses and a jerkin

1. Stitching darts
2. Completing neckline facing with zipper in center back seam
3. Applying neckline and armhole facing cut in one
4. Finish for facings besides clean-finishing
5. Reinforcing seams
6. Understitching by hand
7. First steps of sleeve or armhole facings or hems completed with area open

INDEX